The Life o

With Many Choice

this great man never before published by any of his

biographers

M. L. Weems

Alpha Editions

This edition published in 2022

ISBN : 9789356904668

Design and Setting By
Alpha Editions
www.alphaedis.com
Email - info@alphaedis.com

Contents

CHAPTER I.

DR. BENJAMIN FRANKLIN, PRESIDENT OF THE AMERICAN PHILOSOPHICAL SOCIETY; FELLOW OF THE ROYAL SOCIETY OF EDINBURGH, LONDON AND PARIS; GOVERNOR OF THE STATE OF PENNSYLVANIA; AND MINISTER PLENIPOTENTIARY FROM THE UNITED STATES TO THE COURT OF FRANCE, was the son of an obscure tallow-chandler and soap-boiler, of Boston, where he was born on the 17th day of January, 1706.

Some men carry letters of recommendation in their looks, and some in their names. 'Tis the lot but of few to inherit both of these advantages. The hero of this work was one of that favoured number. As to his physiognomy, there was in it such an air of wisdom and philanthropy, and consequently such an expression of majesty and sweetness, as charms, even in the commonest pictures of him. And for his name, every one acquainted with the old English history, must know, that Franklin stands for what we now mean by "Gentleman," or "CLEVER FELLOW."

In the days of AULD LANG SYNE, their neighbours from the continent made a descent "*on the fast anchored isle*," and compelled the hardy, red-ochred natives to buckle to their yoke. Among the victors were some regiments of Franks, who distinguished themselves by their valor, and still more by their politeness to the vanquished, and especially to the females. By this amiable gallantry the Franks acquired such glory among the brave islanders, that whenever any of their own people achieved any thing uncommonly handsome, he was called, by way of compliment, FRANKLIN, *i.e.* a little Frank. As the living flame does not more naturally tend upwards than does every virtue to exalt its possessors, these little Franks were soon promoted to be great men, such as justices of the peace, knights of the shire, and other such names of high renown. Hence those pretty lines of the old poet Chaucer—

"This worthy Franklin wore a purse of silk

Fix'd to his girdle, pure as morning milk;

Knight of the shire; first justice of th' assize,

To help the poor, the doubtful to advise.

In all employments, gen'rous just he prov'd;

Renown'd for courtesy; by all belov'd."

But though, according to Dr. Franklin's own account of his family, whose pedigree he looked into with great diligence while he was in England, it appears that they were all of the "*well born*," or gentlemen in the best sense of the word; yet they did not deem it beneath them to continue the same useful courses which had at first conferred their titles. On the contrary, the doctor owns, and indeed glories in it, that for three hundred years the eldest son, or heir apparent in this family of old British gentlemen, was invariably brought up a blacksmith. Moreover, it appears from the same indubitable authority, that the blacksmith succession was most religiously continued in the family down to the days of the doctor's father. How it has gone on since that time I have never heard; but considering the salutary effects of such a fashion on the prosperity of a young republic, it were most devoutly to be wished that it is kept up: and that the family of one of the greatest men who ever lived in this or any other country, still display in their coat of arms, not the barren *gules* and *garters* of European folly, but those better ensigns of American wisdom—the SLEDGE-HAMMER and ANVIL.

CHAPTER II.

"Were I so tall to reach the pole,

And grasp the ocean in my span,

I must be measur'd by my soul;

For 'tis the MIND that makes the man."

From the best accounts which I have been able to pick up, it would appear that a passion for learning had a long run in the family of the Franklins. Of the doctor's three uncles, the elder, whose name was Thomas, though conscientiously brought up a blacksmith, and subsisting his family by the din and sweat of his anvil, was still a great reader. Instead of wasting his leisure hours, as too many of the trade do, in tippling and tobacco, he acquired enough of the law to render himself a very useful and leading man among the people of Northampton, where his forefathers had lived in great comfort for three hundred years, on thirty acres of land.

His uncle Benjamin, too, another old *English gentleman* of the right stamp, though a very hard-working man at the silk-dying trade, was equally devoted to the pleasures of the mind. He made it a rule whenever he lighted on a copy of verses that pleased him, to transcribe them into a large blank book which he kept for the purpose. In this way he collected two quarto volumes of poems, written in short hand of his own inventing. And, being a man of great piety, and fond of attending the best preachers, whose sermons he always took down, he collected in the course of his life, *eight* volumes of sermons in *folio*, besides near *thirty* in quarto and octavo, and all in the aforesaid short hand! Astonishing proof, what a banquet of elegant pleasures even a poor mechanic may enjoy, who begins early to read and think! 'Tis true, he was a long time about it. His piety afforded him a constant cheerfulness. And deriving from the same source a regular temperance, he attained to a great age. In his seventy-third year, still fresh and strong, he left his native country, and came over to America, to see his younger brother Josias, between whom and himself there had always subsisted a more than ordinary friendship. On his arrival in Boston, he was received with unbounded joy by Josias, who pressed him to spend the residue of his days in his family. To this proposition the old gentleman readily consented; and the more so as he was then a widower, and his children, all married off, had left him. He had the honor to give his name, and to stand godfather to our little hero, for whom, on account of his vivacity and fondness for learning, he conceived an extraordinary affection.

And Ben always took a great delight in talking of this uncle. Nor was it to be wondered at; for he was an old man who wore his religion very much to win young people—a pleasant countenance—a sweet speech—and a fund of anecdotes always entertaining, and generally carrying some good moral in the tail of them. His grandfather before him must have been a man of rare humour, as appears from a world of droll stories which uncle Benjamin used to tell after him, and which his New England descendants to this day are wont to repeat with great glee. I must let the reader hear one or two of them. They will amuse him, by showing what strange things were done in days of yore by kings and priests in the land of our venerable forefathers.

It was his grandfather's fortune to live in the reign of Queen Mary, whom her *friends* called *holy* Mary, but her enemies *bloody* Mary. In the grand struggle for power between those humble followers of the cross, the catholics and the protestants, the former gained the victory, for which 'Te Deums' in abundance were sung throughout the land. And having been sadly rib-roasted by the protestants when in power, they determined, like good christians, now that the tables were turned, to try on them the virtues of fire and faggot. The Franklin family having ever been sturdy protestants, began now to be in great tribulation. "What shall we do to save our Bible?" was the question. After serious consultation in a family caucus, it was resolved to hide it in the close-stool; which was accordingly done, by fastening it, open, on the under side of the lid by twine threads drawn strongly across the leaves. When the grandfather read to the family, he turned up the aforesaid lid on his knees, passing the leaves of his Bible, as he read, from one side to the other. One of the children was carefully stationed at the door, to give notice if he saw the priest, or any of his frowning tribe, draw near. In that event, the lid with the Bible lashed beneath it, was instantly clapped down again on its old place.

These things may appear strange to us, who live under a wise republic, which will not suffer the black gowns of one church to persecute those of another. But they were common in those dark and dismal days, when the clergy thought more of creeds than of Christ, and of learning Latin than of learning love. Queen Mary was one of this gnostic generation, (who place their religion in the *head*, though Christ places it in the HEART,) and finding it much easier to her *unloving* spirit, to burn human beings called heretics, than to mortify her own lust of popularity, she suffered her catholic to fly upon and worry her protestant subjects at a shameful rate. Good old uncle Benjamin used to divert his friends with another story, which happened in the family of his own aunt, who kept an inn at Eaton, Northamptonshire.

A most violent priest, of the name of Asquith, who thought, like Saul, that he should be doing "*God service*" by killing the heretics, had obtained letters patent from queen Mary against those people in the county of Warwick.

On his way he called to dine at Eaton, where he was quickly waited on by the mayor, a strong catholic, to ask how the *good work went on.* Asquith, leaping to his saddle-bags, drew forth a little box, that contained his commission, which he flourished before the mayor, exclaiming with high glee, "*Aye! there's that that will scorch the rogues!*" Old Mrs. Franklin, under the rose a sturdy protestant, overhearing this, was exceedingly troubled; and watching her opportunity when the priest had stepped out with the mayor, slipped the commission out of the box, and put in its place a pack of cards, wrapped in the same paper. The priest returning in haste, and suspecting no trick, huddled up his box, and posted off for Coventry. A grand council of the saints was speedily convoked to meet him. He arose, and having with great vehemence delivered a set speech against the heretics, threw his commission on the table for the secretary to read aloud. With the eyes of the whole council on him, the eager secretary opened the package, when in place of the flaming commission, behold a pack of cards with the knave of clubs turned uppermost! A sudden stupefaction seized the spectators. In silence they stared at the priest and stared at one another. Some looking as though they suspected treachery: others as dreading a judgment in the case. Soon as the dumb-founded priest could recover speech, he swore by the HOLY MARY, that he once had a commission; that he had received it from the queen's own hand. And he also swore that he would get another commission. Accordingly he hurried back to London, and having procured another, set off again for Coventry. But alas! before he got down, poor queen Mary had turned the corner, and the protestants under Elizabeth got the rule again. Having nothing now to dread, our quizzing old hostess, Mrs. Franklin, came out with the knavish trick she had played the priest, which so pleased the protestants of Coventry that they presented her a piece of plate, that cost fifty pounds sterling, equal, as money now goes, to a thousand dollars.

From an affair which soon after this took place there, it appears that Coventry, however famous for saints, had no great cause to brag of her poets.—When queen Elizabeth, to gratify her subjects, made the tour of her island, she passed through Coventry. The mayor, aldermen, and company hearing of her approach, went out in great state to meet her. The queen being notified that they wished to address her, made a full stop right opposite to a stage erected for the purpose, and covered with embroidered cloth, from which a ready orator, after much bowing and arms full extended, made this wondrous speech—"We men of Coventry are glad to see your royal highness—Lord how *fair* you be!"

To this the maiden queen, equal famed for fat and fun, rising in her carriage, and waving her lily white hand, made this prompt reply—"Our royal highness is glad to see you men of Coventry—Lord what FOOLS you be!"

CHAPTER III.

Our hero, little Ben, coming on the carpet—Put to school very young—Learns prodigiously—Taken home and set to candle-making— Curious capers, all proclaiming "the Achilles in petticoats."

Dr. Franklin's father married early in his own country, and would probably have lived and died there, but for the persecutions against his friends the Presbyterians, which so disgusted him, that he came over to New England, and settled in Boston about the year 1682. He brought with him his English wifc and three children. By the same wife he had four children more in America; and ten others afterwards by an American wife. The doctor speaks with pleasure of having seen thirteen sitting together very lovingly at his father's table, and all married. Our little hero, who was the fifteenth child, and last of the sons, was born at Boston the 17th day of January, 1706, old style.

That famous Italian proverb, "*The Devil tempts every man, but the Idler tempts the Devil,*" was a favourite canto with wise old Josias; for which reason, soon as their little lips could well lisp letters and syllables, he had them all to school.

Nor was this the only instance with regard to them, wherein good Josias "*sham'd the Devil;*" for as soon as their education was finished, they were put to useful trades. Thus no leisure was allowed for bad company and habits. Little Ben, neatly clad and comb'd, was pack'd off to school with the rest; and as would seem, at a very early age, for he says himself that, "*he could not recollect any time in his life when he did not know how to read,*" whence we may infer that he hardly ever knew any thing more of childhood than its innocency and playfulness. At the age of eight he was sent to a grammar school, where he made such a figure in learning, that his good old father set him down at once for the church, and used constantly to call him his "*little chaplain.*" He was confirmed in this design, not only by the extraordinary readiness with which he learned, but also by the praises of his friends, who all agreed that he would certainly one day or other become a mighty scholar. His uncle Benjamin too, greatly approved the idea of making a preacher of him; and by way of encouragement, promised to him all his volumes of sermons, written, as before said, in his own short hand.

This his rapid progress in learning he ascribed very much to an amiable teacher who used gentle means only, to encourage his scholars, and make them fond of their books.

But in the midst of this gay career in his learning, when in the course of the first year only, he had risen from the middle of his class to the head of it; thence to the class immediately above it; and was rapidly overtaking the third class, he was taken from school! His father, having a large family, with but a small income, and thinking himself unable consistently with what he owed the rest of his children, to give him a collegiate education, took Ben home to assist him in his own humble occupation, which was that of a SOAP-BOILER and TALLOW-CHANDLER; a trade he had taken up of his own head after settling in Boston; his original one of a DYER being in too little request to maintain his family.

I have never heard how Ben took this sudden reverse in his prospects. No doubt it put his little stock of philosophy to the stretch. To have seen himself, one day, on the high road to literary fame, flying from class to class, the admiration and envy of a numerous school; and the next day, to have found himself in a filthy soap-shop; clad in a greasy apron, twisting cotton wicks!—and in place of snuffing the sacred lamps of the Muses, to be bending over pots of fetid tallow, dipping and moulding candles for the dirty cook wenches! Oh, it must have seem'd a sad falling off! Indeed, it appears from his own account that he was so disgusted with it that he had serious thoughts of going to sea. But his father objecting to it, and Ben having virtue enough to be dutiful, the notion was given up for that time. But the ambition which had made him the first at his school, and which now would have hurried him to sea, was not to be extinguished. Though diverted from its favourite course, it still burned for distinction, and rendered him the leader of the juvenile band in every enterprize where danger was to be confronted, or glory to be won. In the neighbouring mill-pond, he was the foremost to lead the boys to plunge and swim; thus teaching them an early mastery over that dangerous element. And when the ticklish mill-boat was launching from the shore laden with his timid playmates, the paddle that served as rudder, was always put into his hands, as the fittest to steer her course over the dark waters of the pond. This ascendancy which nature had given him over the companions of his youth, was not always so well used as it might have been. He honestly confesses that, once at least, he made such an unlucky use of it as drew them into a scrape that cost them dear. Their favourite fishing shore on that pond was, it seems, very miry. To remedy so great an inconvenience he proposed to the boys to make a wharf. Their assent was quickly obtained: but what shall we make it of? was the question. Ben pointed their attention to a heap of stones, hard by, of which certain honest masons were building a house. The proposition was hailed by the boys, as a grand discovery; and soon as night had spread her dark curtains around them, they fell to work with the activity of young beavers, and by midnight had completed their wharf. The next morning the masons came to work, but, behold! not a stone was to be found! The young rogues, however, detected by the track of their feet in the mud, were quickly summoned before their parents, who not being so partial to Ben as they had been, chastised their folly with a severe flogging. Good old Josias pursued a different course with his son. To deter him from such an act in future, he endeavoured to reason him into a sense of its immorality. Ben, on the other hand, just fresh and confident from his school, took the field of argument against his father, and smartly attempted to defend what he had done, on the principle of its *utility*. But the old gentleman, who was a great adept in moral philosophy, calmly observed to him, that if one boy were to make use of this plea to take away his fellow's goods, another might; and thus contests would arise, filling the world with blood and murder without end. Convinced, in this simple way, of the fatal consequences of "*doing evil that good may come*," Ben let drop the weapons of his rebellion, and candidly agreed with his father that what was not *strictly honest* could never be *truly useful*. This discovery he made at the tender age of *nine*. Some never make it in the course of their lives. The grand angler, Satan, throws out his bait of *immediate gain*; and they, like silly Jacks, snap at it at once; and in the moment of running off, fancy they have got a delicious morsel. But alas! the fatal hook soon convinces them of their mistake, though sometimes too late. And then the lamentation of the prophet serves as the epilogue of their tragedy—"*'Twas honey in the mouth, but gall in the bowels.*"

CHAPTER IV.

Picture of a wise father—To which is added a famous receipt for health and long life.

The reader must already have discovered that Ben was uncommonly blest in a father. Indeed from the portrait of him drawn by this grateful son, full fifty years afterwards, he must have been an enviable old man.

As to his person, though that is but of minor consideration in a rational creature—I say, as to his person, it was of the right standard, *i.e.* medium size and finely formed—his complexion fair and ruddy—black, intelligent eyes—and an air uncommonly graceful and spirited. In respect of *mind*, which is the true jewel of our nature, he was a man of the purest piety and morals, and consequently cheerful and amiable in a high degree. Added to this, he possessed a considerable taste for the fine arts, particularly drawing and music; and having a voice remarkably sonorous and sweet, whenever he sung a hymn accompanied with his violin, which he usually did at the close of his day's labours, it was delightful to hear him. He possessed also an extraordinary sagacity in things relating both to public and private life, insomuch that not only individuals were constantly consulting him about their affairs, and calling him in as an arbiter in their disputes; but even the leading men of Boston would often come and ask his advice in their most important concerns, as well of the town as of the church.

For his slender means he was a man of extraordinary hospitality, which caused his friends to wonder how he made out to entertain so many. But whenever this was mentioned to him, he used to laugh and say, that the world was good natured and gave him credit for much more than he deserved; for that, in fact, others entertained ten times as many as he did. By this, 'tis thought he alluded to the ostentatious practice common with some, of pointing their hungry visitant to their grand buildings, and boasting how many thousands this or that bauble cost; as if their ridiculous vanity would pass with them for a good dinner. For his part, he said, he preferred setting before his visitors a plenty of wholesome fare, with a hearty welcome. Though to do this he was fain to work hard, and content himself with a small house and plain furniture. But it was always his opinion that a little laid out in this way, went farther both with God and man too, than great treasures lavished on pride and ostentation.

But though he delighted in hospitality as a great virtue, yet he always made choice of such friends at his table as were fond of rational conversation. And he took great care to introduce such topics as would, in a pleasant manner, lead to ideas useful to his family, both in temporal and eternal things. As to the dishes that were served up, he never talked of them; never discussed whether they were well or ill dressed; of a good or bad flavour, high seasoned or otherwise.

For this manly kind of education at his table, Dr. Franklin always spoke as under great obligations to his father's judgment and taste. Thus accustomed, from infancy, to a generous inattention to the palate, he became so perfectly indifferent about what was set before him, that he hardly ever remembered, ten minutes after dinner, what he had dined on. In travelling, particularly, he found his account in this. For while those who had been more nice in their diet could enjoy nothing they met with; this one growling over the daintiest breakfast of new laid eggs and toast floated in butter, because his *coffee was not half strong enough!*—that wondering what people can mean by serving up a round of beef when they have *no mustard!*—and a third cursing like a trooper, though the finest rock-fish or sheep's-head be smoking on the table—because there is no *walnut pickle or ketchup!* He for his part, happily engaged in a pleasant train of thinking or conversation, never attended to such trifles, but dined heartily on whatever was set before him. In short, there is no greater kindness that a young man can do himself than to learn the art of feasting on fish, flesh, or fowl as they come, without ever troubling his head about any other sauce than what the rich hand of nature has given; let him but bring to these dishes that good appetite which always springs from exercise and cheerfulness, and he will be an epicure indeed.

He would often repeat in the company of young people, the following anecdote which he had picked up some where or other in his extensive reading. "A wealthy citizen of Athens, who had nearly ruined his constitution by gluttony and sloth, was advised by Hippocrates to visit a certain medicinal spring in Sparta; not that Hippocrates believed that spring to be better than some nearer home; but exercise was the object—" "*Visit the springs of Sparta*," said the great physician. As the young debauchee, pale and bloated, travelled among the simple and hardy Spartans, he called one day at the house of a countryman on the road to get something to eat. A young woman was just serving up dinner—a nice barn-door fowl boiled with a piece of fat bacon. "You have got rather a plain dinner there madam," growled the Athenian. "*Yes, sir*," replied the young woman blushing, "*but my husband will be here directly, and he always brings the sauce with him.*" Presently the young husband stepped in, and after welcoming his guest, invited him to dinner. "I can't dream of dining, sir, *without sauce*," said the Athenian, "and your wife promised you would bring it." "*O, sir, my wife is a wit*," cried the Spartan; "*she only meant the good appetite which I always bring with me from the barn, where I have been threshing.*"

And here I beg leave to wind up this chapter with the following beautiful lines from Dryden, which I trust my young reader will commit to memory. They may save him many a sick stomach and headache, besides many a good dollar in doctor's fees.

"The first physicians by debauch were made;

Excess began and sloth sustains the trade.

By chace, our long liv'd fathers earn'd their bread;

Toil strung their nerves and purified their blood:

But we, their sons, a pamper'd race of men,

Are dwindled down to threescore years and ten.

Better hunt in fields for health unbought,

Than fee the doctor for a nauseous draught.

The wise for health on exercise depend;

God never made his works for man to mend."

CHAPTER V.

Ben continued with his father, assisting him in his humble toils, till his twelfth year; and had he possessed a mind less active might have remained a candle-maker all the days of his life. But born to diffuse a light beyond that of tallow or spermaceti, he could never reconcile himself to this inferior employment, and in spite of his wishes to conceal it from his father, discontent would still lower on his brow, and the half-suppressed sigh steal in secret from his bosom.

With equal grief his father beheld the deep-seated disquietude of his son. He loved all his children; but he loved this young one above all the rest. Ben was the child of his old age. The smile that dimpled his tender cheeks reminded him of his mother when he first saw her, lovely in the rosy freshness of youth. And then his intellect was so far beyond his years; his questions so shrewd; so strong in reasoning; so witty in remark, that his father would often forget his violin of nights for the higher pleasure of holding an argument with him. This was a great trial to his sisters, who would often intreat their mother to make Ben hold his tongue, that their father might take down his fiddle, and play and sing hymns with them: for they took after him in his passion for music, and sung divinely. No wonder that such a child should be dear to such a father. Indeed old Josias' affection for Ben was so intimately interwoven with every fibre of his heart, that he could not bear the idea of separation from him; and various were the stratagems which he employed to keep this dear child at home. One while, to frighten his youthful fancy from the sea, for that was the old man's dread, he would paint the horrors of the watery world, where the maddening billows, lashed into mountains by the storm, would lift the trembling ship to the skies; then hurl her down, headlong plunging into the yawning gulphs, never to rise again. At another time he would describe the wearisomeness of beating the gloomy wave for joyless months, pent up in a small ship, with no prospects but barren sea and skies—no smells but tar and bilge water—no society but men of uncultivated minds, and their constant conversation nothing but ribaldry and oaths. And then again he would take him to visit the masons, coopers, joiners, and other mechanics, at work: in hopes that his genius might be caught, and a stop put to his passion for wandering. But greatly to his sorrow, none of these things held out the attractions that his son seemed to want. His visits among these tradesmen were not, however, without their advantage. He caught from them, as he somewhere says, such an insight into mechanic arts and the use of tools, as enabled him afterwards when there was no artist at hand, to make for himself suitable machines for the illustration of his philosophical experiments.

But it was not long before this obstinate dislike of Ben's to all ordinary pursuits was found out; it was found out by his mother. "Bless me," said she one night to her husband, as he lay sleepless and sighing on his son's account, "why do we make ourselves so unhappy about Ben for fear he should go to *sea!* let him but go to *school*, and I'll engage we hear no more about his running to sea. Don't you see the child is never happy but when he has a book in his hand? Other boys when they get a little money never think of any thing better to lay it out on than their backs or their bellies; but he, poor fellow, the moment that he gets a shilling, runs and gives it for a book; and then, you know, there is no getting him to his meals until he has read it through, and told us all about it."

Good old Josias listened very devoutly to his wife, while she uttered this oration on his youngest son. Then with looks as of a heart suddenly relieved from a heavy burden, and his eyes lifted to heaven, he fervently exclaimed—"O that my son, even my little son Benjamin, may live before God, and that the days of his usefulness and glory may be many!"

How far the effectual fervent prayer of this righteous father found acceptance in heaven, the reader will find perhaps by the time he has gone through our little book.

CHAPTER VI.

Ben taken from school, turns his own teacher—History of the books which he first read —Is bound to the printing trade.

At a learned table in Paris, where Dr. Franklin happened to dine, it was asked by the abbé Raynal, *What description of men most deserves pity?*

Some mentioned one character, and some another. When it came to Franklin's turn, he replied, *A lonesome man in a rainy day, who does not know how to read.*

As every thing is interesting that relates to one who made such a figure in the world, it may gratify our readers to be told what were the books that first regaled the youthful appetite of the great Dr. Franklin. The state of literature in Boston at that time, being like himself, only in its infancy, it is not to be supposed that Ben had any very great choice of books. Books, however, there always were in Boston. [1] Among these was Bunyan's Voyages, which appears to have been the first he ever read, and of which he speaks with great pleasure. But there is reason to fear that Bunyan did no good: for, as it was the reading of the life of Alexander the Great that first set Charles the Twelfth in such a fever to be running over the world killing every body he met; so, in all probability, it was Bunyan's Voyages that fired Ben's fancy with that passion for travelling, which gave his father so much uneasiness. Having read over old Bunyan so often as to have him almost by heart, Ben added a little boot, and made a *swap* of him for *Burton's Historical Miscellanies*. This, consisting of forty or fifty volumes, held him a good long tug: for he had no time to read but on Sundays, and early in the morning or late at night. After this he fell upon his father's library. This being made up principally of old puritanical divinity, would to most boys have appeared like the pillars of Hercules to travellers of old—a bound not to be passed. But so keen was Ben's appetite for any thing in the shape of a book, that he fell upon it with his usual voracity, and soon devoured every thing in it, especially of the lighter sort. Seeing a little bundle of something crammed away very snugly upon an upper shelf, his curiosity led him to take it down: and lo! what should it be but "*Plutarch's Lives.*" Ben was a stranger to the work; but the title alone was enough for him; he instantly gave it one reading; and then a second, and a third, and so on until he had almost committed it to memory; and to his dying day he never mentioned the name of Plutarch without acknowledging how much pleasure and profit he had derived from that divine old writer. And there was another book, by

Defoe, a small affair, entitled "*An Essay on Projects*," to which he pays the very high compliment of saying, that "*from it he received impressions which influenced some of the principal events of his life.*"

Happy now to find that books had the charm to keep his darling boy at home, and thinking that if he were put into a printing office he would be sure to get books enough, his father determined to make a printer of him, though he already had a son in that business. Exactly to his wishes, that son, whose name was James, had just returned from London with a new press and types. Accordingly, without loss of time, Ben, now in his twelfth year, was bound apprentice to him. By the indentures Ben was to serve his brother till twenty-one, *i.e. nine* full years, without receiving one penny of wages save for the last twelve months! How a man pretending to religion could reconcile it to himself to make so hard a bargain with a younger brother, is strange. But perhaps it was permitted of God, that Ben should learn his ideas of oppression, not from reading but from suffering. The deliverers of mankind have all been made perfect through suffering. And to the galling sense of this villanous oppression, which never ceased to rankle on the mind of Franklin, the American people owe much of that spirited resistance to British injustice, which eventuated in their liberties. But Master James had no great cause to boast of this selfish treatment of his younger brother Benjamin; for the old adage "foul play never thrives," was hardly ever more remarkably illustrated than in this affair, as the reader will in due season be brought to understand.

CHAPTER VII.

Ben in clover—Turns a Rhymer—Makes a prodigious noise in Boston—Bit by the Poetic Tarantula—Luckily cured by his father.

Ben is now happy. He is placed by the side of the press, the very mint and coining place of his beloved *books*; and animated by that delight which he takes in his business, he makes a proficiency equally surprising and profitable to his brother. The field of his reading too is now greatly enlarged. From the booksellers' boys he makes shift, every now and then, to borrow a book, which he *never fails to return* at the promised time: though to accomplish this he was often obliged to sit up till midnight, reading by his bed side, that he might be as good as his word.

Such an extraordinary passion for learning soon commended him to the notice of his neighbours, among whom was an ingenious young man, a tradesman, named Matthew Adams, who invited him to his house, showed him all his books, and offered to lend him any that he wished to read.

About this time, which was somewhere in his thirteenth year, Ben took it into his head that he could write poetry: and actually composed several little pieces. These, after some hesitation, he showed to his brother, who pronounced them *excellent*; and thinking that money might be made by Ben's poetry, pressed him to cultivate his *wonderful talent*, as he called it; and even gave him a couple of subjects to write on. The one, which was to be called the LIGHT-HOUSE TRAGEDY, was to narrate the late shipwreck of a sea captain and his two daughters: and the other was to be a sailor's song on the noted pirate Blackbeard, who had been recently killed on the coast of North Carolina, by Captain Maynard, of a British sloop of war.

Ben accordingly fell to work, and after burning out several candles, for his brother could not afford to let him write poetry by daylight, he produced his two poems. His brother extolled them to the skies, and in all haste had them put to the type and struck off; to expedite matters, fast as the sheets could be snatched from the press, all hands were set to work, folding and stitching them ready for market; while nothing was to be heard throughout the office but constant calls on the boys at press—"*more sheets ho! more Light-house tragedy! more Blackbeard!*" But who can tell what Ben felt when he saw his brother and all his journeymen in such a bustle on his account—and when he saw, wherever he cast his eyes, the splendid trophies of his genius scattered on the floor and tables; some in common paper for the multitude; and others in snow-white foolscap, for presents to the GREAT PEOPLE, such as "HIS EXCELLENCY THE GOVERNOR."—"The HON. THE SECRETARY OF STATE."—"The WORSHIPFUL THE MAYOR."—"The ALDERMEN, and GENTLEMEN OF THE COUNCIL."—"The reverend the *clergy*, &c." Ben could never tire of gazing at them; and as he gazed, his heart would leap for joy—"*O you precious little verses*," he would say to himself, "*Ye first warblings of my youthful harp! I'll soon have you abroad, delighting every company, and filling all mouths with my name!*" Accordingly, his *two poems* being ready, Ben, who had been both poet and printer, with a basket full of each on his arm, set out in high spirits to sell them through the town, which he did by singing out as he went, after, the manner of the London cries—

"Choice Poetry! Choice Po-e-try!

Come BUY my choice Po-e-try!"

The people of Boston having never heard any such cry as that before, were prodigiously at a loss to know what he was selling. But still Ben went on singing out as before,

"Choice Poetry! Choice Poetry!

Come, buy my choice Poetry!"

I wonder now, said one with a stare, if it is not *poultry* that that little boy is singing out so stoutly yonder.

O no, I guess not, said a second.

Well then, cried a third, I vow but it must be *pastry*.

At length Ben was called up and interrogated.

"*Pray, my little man, and what's that that you are crying there so bravely?*"

Ben told them it was poetry.

"*O!—aye! poetry!*" said they; "*poetry! that's a sort of something or other in metre—like the old version, isn't it?*"

"*O yes, to be sure*," said they all, "*it must be like the old version, if it is poetry*;" and thereupon they stared at him, marvelling hugely that a "*little curly headed boy like him should be selling such a wonderful thing*!" This made Ben hug himself still more on account of his poetry.

I have never been able to get a sight of the ballad of the Light-house Tragedy, which must no doubt have been a great curiosity: but the sailor's song on Blackbeard runs thus—

"Come all you jolly Sailors,

You all so stout and brave;

Come hearken and I'll tell you

What happen'd on the wave.

Oh! 'tis of that bloody Blackbeard

I'm going now for to tell;

And as how by gallant Maynard

He soon was sent to hell—

With a down, down, down derry down."

The reader will, I suppose, agree with Ben in his criticism, many years afterwards, on this poetry, that it was "wretched stuff; mere blind men's ditties." But fortunately for Ben, the poor people of Boston were at that time no judges of poetry. The silver-tongued Watts had not, as yet, snatched the harp of Zion, and poured his divine songs over New-England. And having never been accustomed to any thing better than an old version of David's Psalms, running in this way—

"Ye monsters of the bubbling deep,

Your Maker's praises spout!

Up from your sands ye codlings peep,

And wag your tails about."—

The people of Boston pronounced Ben's poetry *mighty fine*, and bought them up at a prodigious rate; especially the LIGHT-HOUSE TRAGEDY.

A flood of success so sudden and unexpected, would in all probability have turned Ben's brain and run him stark mad with vanity, had not his wise old father timely stepped in and checked the rising fever. But highly as Ben honoured his father, and respected his judgment, he could hardly brook to hear him attack his beloved poetry, as he did, calling it "*mere Grub-street.*" And he even held a stiff argument in defence of it. But on reading a volume of Pope, which his father, who well knew the force of contrast, put into his hand for that purpose, he never again opened his mouth in behalf of his "*blind men's ditties.*" He used to laugh and say, that after reading Pope, he was so mortified with his *Light-house Tragedy, and Sailor's Song*, which he had once thought so fine, that he could not bear the sight of them, but constantly threw into the fire every copy that fell in his way. Thus was he timely saved, as he ingenuously confesses, from the very great misfortune of being, perhaps, a miserable jingler for life.

But I cannot let fall the curtain on this curious chapter, without once more feasting my eyes on Ben, as, with a little basket on his arm, he trudged along the streets of Boston crying his poetry.

Who that saw the youthful David coming up fresh from his father's sheep cots, with his locks wet with the dews of the morning, and his cheeks ruddy as the opening rose-buds, would have dreamed that this was he who should one day, single handed, meet the giant Goliah, in the war-darkened valley of Elah, and wipe off reproach from Israel. In like manner, who that saw this "*curly headed child*," at the tender age of thirteen, selling his "*blind men's ditties*," among the wonder-struck Jonathans and Jemimas of Boston, would have thought that this was he, who, single handed, was to meet the British ministry at the bar of their own house of Commons, and by the solar blaze of his wisdom, utterly disperse all their dark designs against their countrymen, thus gaining for himself a name lasting as time, and dear to liberty as the name of Washington.

O you time-wasting, brain-starving young men, who can never be at ease unless you have a cigar or a plug of tobacco in your mouths, go on with your puffing and champing—go on with your filthy smoking, and your still more filthy spitting, keeping the cleanly house-wives in constant terror for their nicely waxed floors, and their shining carpets—go on I say; but remember it was not in this way that our little Ben became the GREAT DR. FRANKLIN.

CHAPTER VIII.

'Tis the character of a great mind never to despair. Though glory may not be gained in one way, it may in another. As a river, if it meet a mountain in its course, does not halt and poison all the country by stagnation, but rolls its gathering forces around the obstacle, urging its precious tides and treasures through distant lands. So it was with the restless genius of young Franklin. Finding that nature had never cut him out for a poet, he determined to take revenge on her by making himself a good prose writer. As it is in this way that his pen has conferred great obligations on the world, it must be gratifying to learn by what means, humbly circumstanced as he was, he acquired that perspicuity and ease so remarkable in his writings. This information must be peculiarly acceptable to such youth as are apt to despair of becoming good writers, because they have never been taught the languages. Ben's example will soon convince them that Latin and Greek are not necessary to make English scholars. Let them but commence with *his* passion for knowledge; with *his* firm persuasion, that wisdom is the glory and happiness of man, and the work is more than half done.

Honest Ben never courted a young man because he was rich, or the son of the rich—No. His favourites were of the youth fond of reading and of rational conversation, no matter how poor they were. "*Birds of a feather do not more naturally flock together*," than do young men of this high character. This was what first attracted to him that ingenious young carpenter, Matthew Adams: as also John Collins, the tanner's boy. These three spirited youth, after finding each other out, became as fond as brothers. And often as possible, when the labours of the day were ended, they would meet at a little school-house in the neighbourhood, and argue on some given subject till midnight. The advantages of this as a grand mean of exercising memory, strengthening the reasoning faculty, disciplining the thoughts, and improving a correct and graceful elocution, became daily more obvious and important in their view, and consequently increased their mutual attachment. But from his own observation of what passed in this curious little society, Ben cautions young men against that *war of words*, which the vain are too apt to fall into, and which tends not only to make them insupportably disagreeable through a disputatious spirit, but is apt also to betray into a fondness for *quizzing*, *i.e.* for asserting and supporting opinions which they do not themselves believe. He gives the following as a case in point.

One night, Adams being absent, and only himself and Collins together in the old school-house, Ben observed that he thought it a great pity that the young ladies were not more attended to, as to the improvement of their minds by education. He said, that with their advantages of sweet voices and beautiful faces, they could give tenfold charms to wit and sensible conversation, making heavenly truths to appear, as he had somewhere read in his father's old Bible, "like apples of gold set in pictures of silver."

Collins blowed upon the idea. He said, it was all *stuff,* and no pity at all, that the girls were so neglected in their education, as they were naturally incapable of it. And here he repeated, laughing, that infamous slur on the ladies,

"Substance too soft a lasting mind to bear,

And best distinguish'd by black, brown, or fair."

At this, Ben, who was already getting to be a great admirer of the ladies, reddened up against Collins; and to it they fell, at once, in a stiff argument on the education of women—as whether they were capable of studying the sciences or not. Collins, as we have seen, led off against the ladies. Being much of an infidel, he took the Turkish ground altogether, and argued like one just soured and sullen from the seraglio. *Women study the sciences indeed!* said he, with a sneer; *a pretty story truly! no sir, they have nothing to do with the sciences. They were not born for any such thing.*

Ben wanted to know what they *were* born for?

Born for! retorted Collins, why to *dress* and *dance*; to *sing* and *play*; and, like pretty triflers, to divert the lords of the creation, after their toils and studies. This is all they were born for, or ever intended of nature, who has given them capacities for nothing higher. Sometimes, indeed, they look grave, and fall into such brown studies as would lead one to suppose they meant to go deep; but it is all *fudge.* They are only trying in this new character to play themselves off to a better effect on their lovers. And if you could but penetrate the bosoms of these fair Penserosoes; you would find that under all this affectation of study they were only fatiguing their childish brains about what dress they should wear to the next ball: or what coloured ribands would best suit their new lutestrings.

To this Ben replied with warmth, that it was extremely unphilosophical in Mr. Collins to argue in that way against the FAIR SEX—that in fixing their destination he had by no means given them that high ground to which they were entitled. You say, sir, continued Ben, that the ladies were created to amuse the men by the charm of their vivacity and accomplishments. This to be sure was saying something. But you might, I think, have said a great deal more; at least the Bible says a great deal more for them. The Bible, sir, tells us that God created woman to be the helpmate of man. Now if man were devoid of reason he might be well enough matched by such a monkey-like helpmate as you have described woman. But, sir, since man is a noble God-like creature, endued with the sublime capacities of *reason*, how could woman ever make a helpmate to him, unless she were rational like himself, and thus capable of being the companion of his thoughts and conversation through all the pleasant fields of knowledge?

Here Collins interrupted him, asking very sarcastically, if in this fine flourish in favour of the ladies he was really *in earnest.*

Never more so in all my life, replied Ben, rather nettled.

What, that the women are as capable of studying the sciences as the men?

Yes, that the women are as capable of studying the sciences as the men.

And pray, sir, continued Collins, tauntingly, do you know of any *young woman* of your acquaintance that would make a Newton?

And pray, sir, answered Ben, do you know any young man of your acquaintance that would? But these are no arguments, sir,—because it is not every young man or woman that can carry the science of astronomy so high as Newton, it does not follow that they are incapable of the science altogether. God sees fit in every age to appoint certain persons to kindle new lights among men.—And Newton was appointed greatly to enlarge our views of celestial objects. But we are not thence to infer that he was in all respects superior to other men, for we are told that in some instances he was far inferior to other men. Collins denied that Newton had ever shown himself, in any point of wit inferior to other men.

No, indeed, replied Ben; well what do you think of that anecdote of him, lately published in the New England Courant from a London paper?

And pray what is the anecdote? asked Collins.

Why it is to this effect, said Ben.—Newton, mounted on the wings of astronomy, and gazing at the mighty orbs of fire above, had entirely forgotten the poor little fire that slumbered on his own hearth below, which presently forgot him, that is in plain English, went out. The frost piercing his nerves, called his thoughts home, when lo! in place of the spacious skies, the gorgeous antichamber of the Almighty, he found himself in his own little nut-shell apartment, cold and dark, comparatively, as the dwelling of the winter screech-owl. He rung the bell for his servant, who after making a rousing fire, went out again. But scarcely had the servant recovered his warm corner in the kitchen, before the vile bell, with a most furious ring, summoned him the second time. The servant flew into his master's presence. *Monster!* cried Newton with a face inflamed as if it had been toasting at the tail of one of his comets, *did you mean to burn me alive?*

push back the fire! for God's sake push back the fire, or I shall be a cinder in an instant!

Push back the fire! replied the servant with a growl, zounds, sir, I thought you might have had sense enough to push back your chair!

Collins swore that it was only a libel against Sir Isaac.

Ben contended that he had seen it in so many different publications, that he had no sort of doubt of its truth; especially as Sir Hans Sloan had backed it with another anecdote of Newton, in the same style; and to which he avers he was both eye and ear witness.

And pray what has that butterfly philosopher to say against the immortal Newton? asked Collins, quite angrily.

Why, replied Ben, it is this: Sloan, stepping in one day, to see Sir Isaac, was told by his servant that he was up in his study, but would be down immediately; *for there, sir, you see is his dinner, which I have just set on the table.*—It was a pheasant so neatly browned in the roasting, and withal so plump and inviting to the eye, that Sloan could not resist the temptation; but venturing on his great intimacy with the knight, sat down and picked the delicious bird to the bone; having desired the cook in all haste to clap another to the spit. Presently down came Sir Isaac—was very glad to see his friend Sloan—how had he been all this time? and how did he leave his good lady and family? you have not dined?

No.

Very glad of it indeed; very glad. Well then, come dine with me.—Turning to the table, he sees the dish empty, and his plate strewed with the bones of his favourite pheasant.—*Lord bless me!* he exclaimed, clasping his forehead, and looking betwixt laughing and blushing, at Sloan—*what am I good for? I have dined, as you see, my dear friend, and yet I had entirely forgot it!*

I don't believe a syllable of it, said Collins; not one syllable of it, sir.

No, replied Ben; nor one syllable, I suppose, of his famous courtship, when sitting by an elegant young lady, whom his friends wished him to make love to, he seized her lily white hand. But instead of pressing it with rapture to his bosom, he thrust it into the bowl of his pipe that he was smoking; thus making a tobacco stopper of one of the loveliest fingers in England; to the inexpressible mortification of the company, and to the most dismal scolding and screaming of the dear creature!

'Tis all a lie, sir, said Collins, getting quite mad, all a confounded lie. The immortal Newton, sir, was never capable of acting so much like a blockhead. But supposing all this slang to be true, what would you infer from it, against that prince of philosophy?—Why I would infer from it, replied Ben, that though a great man, he was but a man. And I would also infer from it in favour of my fair clients, that though they did not make Sir Isaac's discoveries in astronomy, they are yet very capable of comprehending them. And besides, I am astonished, Mr. Collins, how any gentleman that loves himself, as I know you do, can thus traduce the ladies. Don't you consider, sir, that in proportion as you lessen the dignity of the ladies, you lessen the dignity of your affections for them, and consequently, your own happiness in them, which must for ever keep pace with your ideas of their excellence.—This was certainly a home thrust; and most readers would suppose, that Ben was in a fair way to crow over his antagonist; but, Collins was a young man of too much pride and talents to give up so easily. A spirited retort, of course, was made; a rejoinder followed, and thus the controversy was kept up until the watchman bawling twelve o'clock, reminded our stripling orators that it was time for them to quit the old school-house; which with great reluctance they did, but without being any nearer the end of their argument than when they began.

CHAPTER IX.

The shades of midnight had parted our young combatants, and silent and alone, Ben had trotted home to his printing-office; but still in his restless thoughts the combat raged in all its fury: still burning for victory, where truth and the ladies were at stake, he fell to mustering his arguments again, which now at the drum-beat of recollection came crowding on him so thick and strong that he felt equally ashamed and astonished that he had not utterly crushed his antagonist at once. He could see no reason on earth why Collins had made a drawn battle of it, but by his vastly superior eloquence. To deprive him of this advantage, Ben determined to attack him with his pen. And to this he felt the greater inclination, as they were not to meet again for several nights. So, committing his thoughts to paper, and taking a fair copy, he sent it to him. Collins, who, "was not born in the woods to be scared by an owl," quickly answered, and Ben rejoined. In this way several vollies had passed on both sides, when good old Josias chanced to light upon them all; both the copies of Ben's letters to Collins, and the answers. He read them with a deep interest, and that very night sent for Ben that he might talk with him on their contents. "*So Ben!*" said he to him as he pressed his beloved hand, "*you have got into a paper war already, have you?*"

Ben blushed.

I don't mean to blame you, my son, continued the old gentleman. I don't blame you; on the contrary I am delighted to see you taking such pains to improve your mind. Go on, my dear boy, go on; for your mind is the only part that is worth your care: and the more you accustom yourself to find your happiness in *that*, the better. The body, as I have a thousand times told you, is but nicely organized earth, that in spite of the daintiest meats and clothes, will soon grow old and withered, and then die and rot back to earth again. But the MIND, Ben, is the HEAVENLY part, the IMMORTAL inhabitant, who, if early nursed with proper thoughts and affections, is capable of a feast that will endure for ever.

This your little controversy with your friend Collins is praiseworthy, because it has a bearing on that grand point, the improvement of your mind.

But let me suggest a hint or two, my son, for your better conduct of it. You have greatly the advantage of Mr. Collins in correctness of spelling and pointing; which you owe entirely to your profession as a printer; but then he is as far superior to you in other respects. He certainly has not so good a cause as you have, but, he manages it better. He clothes his ideas with such elegance of expression, and arranges his arguments with so much perspicuity and art, as will captivate all readers in his favour, and snatch the victory from you, notwithstanding your better cause. In confirmation of these remarks, the old gentleman drew from his pocket the letters of their correspondence, and read to him several passages, as strong cases in point.

Ben sensibly felt the justice of these criticisms, and after thanking his father for his goodness in making them, assured him, that as he delighted above all things in reading books of a beautiful style, so he was resolved to spare no pains to acquire so divine an art.

The next day, going into a fresh part of the town, with a paper to a new subscriber, he saw, on the side of the street, a little table spread out and covered with a parcel of toys, among which lay an odd volume, with a neat old woman sitting by. As he approached the table to look at the book, the old lady lifting on him a most pleasant countenance, said, "*well my little man do you ever dream dreams?*"

Ben rather startled at so strange a salutation, replied, that he had *dream't* in his time.—*Well*, continued the old woman, *and what do you think of dreams; do you put any faith in 'em?*

Why, no, madam, answered Ben; as I have seldom had dreams except after taking too hearty a supper, I have always looked on 'em as a mere matter of indigestion, and so have never troubled my head much about 'em.

Well now, replied the old lady, laughing, *there's just the difference between you and me. I, for my part, always takes great notice of dreams, they generally turn out so true.* And now can you tell what a droll dream I had last night?

Ben answered that he was no Daniel to interpret dreams.

Well, said the old lady, I dreamed last night, that a little man just like you, came along here and bought that old book of me.

Aye! why that's a droll dream sure enough, replied Ben; and pray, Madam, what do you ask for your old book?

Only four pence halfpenny, said the old lady.

Well, Madam, continued Ben, as your dreaming has generally, as you say, turned out true, it shall not be otherwise now; *there's your money*—so now as you have another reason for putting faith in dreams, you can dream again.

As Ben took up his book to go away, the old lady said, stop a minute, my son, stop a minute. I have not told you the whole of my dream yet. Then looking very gravely at him, she said, But though my dream showed that the book was to be bought by a *little* man, it did not say he was always to be little. No; for I saw, in my dream, that he grew up to be a GREAT man; the lightnings of heaven played around his head, and the shape of a kingly crown was beneath his feet. I heard his name as a pleasant sound from distant lands, and I saw it through clouds of smoke and flame, among the tall victor ships that strove in the last battle for the freedom of the seas. She uttered this with a raised voice and glowing cheek, as though the years to come, with all their mighty deeds, were passing before her.

Ben was too young yet to suspect who this old woman was, though he felt as he had read the youthful Telemachus did, when the fire-eyed Minerva, in the shape of Mentor, roused his soul to virtue.

Farewell, Madam, said Ben with a deep sigh, as he went away; you might have spared that part of your dream, for I am sure there is very little chance of its ever coming to pass.

But though Ben went away to attend to his brother's business, yet the old woman's looks made such an impression on his mind, that he could not help going the next day to see her again; but she was not there any more.

On leaving the old woman, he opened his book, when, behold, what should it be but an odd volume of the Spectator, a book which he had not seen before. The number which he chanced to open was the vision of Mirzah; which so caught his attention that he could not take it off until he had got through. What the people thought of him for reading in that manner as he walked along the street, he knew not; nor did he once think, he was so taken up with his book. He felt as though he would give the world to write in so enchanting a style; and to that end he carried his old volume constantly in his pocket, that by committing, as it were, to memory, those sweetly flowing lines, he might stand a chance to fall into the imitation of them. He took another curious method to catch Addison's charming style; he would select some favourite chapter out of the Spectator, make short summaries of the sense of each period, and put them for a few days aside; then without looking at the book, he would endeavour to restore the chapter to its first form, by expressing each thought at full length.

These exercises soon convinced him that he greatly lacked a fund of words, and a facility of employing them; both of which he thought would have been abundantly supplied, had he but continued his old trade of *making verses*. The continual need of words of the same *meaning*, but of different *lengths*, for the *measure*; or of different sounds, for the *rhyme*, would have obliged him to seek a variety of *synonymes*. From this belief he took some of the papers and turned them into verse; and after he had sufficiently forgotten them, he again converted them into prose.

On comparing *his* Spectator with the original, he discovered many faults; but panting, as he did, for perfection in this noble art, nothing could discourage him. He bravely persevered in his experiments, and though he lamented that in most instances he still fell short of the charming original, yet in some he thought he had clearly improved the order and style. And when this happened, it gave him unspeakable satisfaction, as it sprung the dear hope that in time he should succeed in writing the English language in the same enchanting manner.

CHAPTER X.

About this time, which was somewhere in his sixteenth year, Ben lighted on a very curious work, by one *Tryon*, recommending vegetable diet altogether, and condemning "*animal food as a great crime.*" He read it with all the avidity of a young and honest mind that wished to renounce error and embrace truth. "*From start to pole,*" as the racers say, his conscience was under the lash, pointing at him as the dreadful SARCOPHAGIST, or MEAT-EATER alluded to by this severe writer. He could not, without horror reflect, that, young as he was, his stomach had yet been the grave of hundreds of lambs, pigs, birds, and other little animals, "*who had never injured him.*" And when he extended the dismal idea over the vast surface of the globe, and saw the whole human race pursuing and butchering the poor brute creation, filling the sea and land with cries and blood and slaughter, he felt a depression of spirits with an anguish of mind that strongly tempted him, not only to detest man, but even to charge God himself with cruelty. But this distress did not continue long. Impatient of such wretchedness, he set all the powers of his mind to work, to discover designs in all this, worthy of the Creator. To his unspeakable satisfaction he soon made these important discoveries. 'Tis true, said he, man is constantly butchering the inferior creatures. And it is also true that they are constantly devouring one another. But after all, shocking as this may seem, it is but *dying*: it is but giving up life, or returning a something which was not their own; which for the honour of his goodness in their enjoyment, was only lent them for a season; and which, therefore, they ought not to think hard to return.

Now certainly, continued Ben, all this is very clear and easy to be understood. Well then, since all life, whether of man or beast, or vegetables, is a kind loan of God, and to be taken back again, the question is whether the way in which we see it is taken back is not the *best way*. It is true, life being the season of enjoyment, is so dear to us that there is no way of giving it up which is not shocking. And this horror which we feel at the thought of having our own lives taken from us we extend to the brutes. We cannot help feeling shocked at the butcher killing a lamb, or one animal killing another. Nay, tell even a child who is looking with smiles on a good old family horse that has just brought a bag of flour from the mill, or a load of wood from the forest, that this his beloved horse will by and by be eaten up of the buzzards, and instantly his looks will manifest extreme distress. And if his mother, to whom he turns for contradiction of this horrid prophecy, should confirm it, he is struck dumb with horror, or bursts into strong cries as if his little heart would break at thought of the dismal end to which his horse is coming. These, though very amiable, are yet the amiable weaknesses of the child, which, it is the duty of man to overcome. This animal was created of his God for the double purpose of doing service to man, and of enjoying comfort himself. And when these are accomplished, and that life which was only lent him is recalled, is it not better that nature's scavengers, the buzzards, should take up his flesh and keep the elements sweet, than that it should lie on the fields to shock the sight and smell of all who pass by? The fact is, continued Ben, I see that all creatures that live, whether men or beasts, or vegetables, are doomed to die. Now were it not a greater happiness that this universal calamity, as it appears, should be converted into an universal blessing, and this *dying* of all be made the *living* of all? Well, through the admirable wisdom and goodness of the Creator, this is exactly the case. The vegetables all die to sustain animals; and animals, whether birds, beasts, or fishes, all die to sustain man, or one another. Now, is it not far better for them that they should be thus continually changing into each other's substance, and existing in the wholesome shapes of life and vigour, than to be scattered about dying and dead, shocking all eyes with their ghastly forms, and poisoning both sea and air with the stench of their corruption?

This scrutiny into the economy of nature in this matter, gave him such an exalted sense of nature's Great Author, that in a letter to his father, to whom he made a point of writing every week for the benefit of his corrections, he says, though I was at first greatly angered with Tryon, yet afterwards I felt myself much obliged to him for giving me such a hard nut to crack, for I have picked out of it one of the sweetest kernels I ever tasted. In truth, father, continues he, although I do not make much noise or show about religion, yet I entertain a most adoring sense of the GREAT FIRST CAUSE; insomuch that I had rather cease to exist than cease to believe him ALL WISE AND BENEVOLENT.

In the midst, however, of these pleasing speculations, another disquieting idea was suggested.—Is it not cruel, after giving life to take it away again so soon? The tender grass has hardly risen above the earth, in all its spring-tide green and sweetness, before its beauty is all cropped by the lamb; and the playful lamb, full dressed in his snow-white fleece, has scarcely tasted the sweets of existence, before he is caught up by the cruel wolf or more cruel man. And so with every bird and fish: this has scarcely learned to sing his song to the listening grove, or that to leap with transport from the limpid wave, before he is called to resign his life to man or some larger animal.

This was a horrid thought, which, like a cloud, spread a deep gloom over Ben's mind. But his reflections, like the sunbeams, quickly pierced and dispersed them.

These cavillers, said he, in another letter, are entirely wrong. They wish, it seems, *long life* to the creatures; the Creator wishes them a *pleasant* one. They would have but a few to exist in a *long* time; *he* a great many in a *short* time. Now as youth is the season of gaiety and enjoyment, and all after is comparatively insipid, is it not better, before that pleasant state is ended in sorrow, the creature should pass away by a quick and generally easy fate, and appear again in some other shape? Surely if the grass could reason, it would prefer, while fresh and beautiful, to be cropped by the lamb and converted into his substance, than, by staying a little longer, to disfigure the fields with its faded foliage. And the lamb too, if he could but think and choose, would ask for *a short life and a merry one*, rather than, by staying a little longer, degenerate into a ragged old sheep, snorting with the rattles, and dying of the rot, or murrain.

But though Ben, at the tender age of sixteen, and with no other aid than his own strong mind, could so easily quell this host of atheistical doubts, which Tryon had conjured up; yet he hesitated not to become his disciple in another tenet. Tryon asserted of animal food, that though it gave great strength to the body, yet it contributed sadly to grossness of blood and heaviness of mind; and hence he reasoned, that all who wish for cool heads and clear thoughts should make their diet principally of vegetables. Ben was struck with this as the perfection of reason, and entered so heartily into it as a rare help for acquiring knowledge, that he instantly resolved, fond as he was of flesh and fish, to give both up from that day, and never taste them again as long as he lived. This steady refusal of his to eat meat, was looked on as a very inconvenient singularity by his brother, who scolded him for it, and insisted he should give it up. Ben made no words with his brother on this account.—Knowing that avarice was his ruling passion, he threw out a bait to James which instantly caught, and without any disturbance produced the accommodation he wished. "Brother," said he to him one day as he scolded; "you give three shillings and six pence a week for my diet at this boarding-house; give me but *half* that money and I'll diet myself without any farther trouble or expense to you." James immediately took him at his word and gave him in hand his week's ration, one shilling and nine pence, which after the Boston exchange, six shillings to the dollar, makes exactly thirty-seven and a half cents. Those who often give one dollar for a single dinner, and five dollars for a fourth of July dinner, would look very blue at an allowance of thirty-seven and a half cents for a whole week. But Ben so husbanded this little sum, that after defraying all the expenses of his table, he found himself at the end of the week, near twenty cents in pocket—thus expending not quite three cents a day! This was a joyful discovery to Ben—twenty cents a week, said he, and fifty-two weeks in the year; why, that is upwards of ten dollars in the twelve months! what a noble fund for books! Nor was this the only benefit he derived from it; for, while his brother and the journeymen were gone to the boarding-house to devour their pork and beef, which, with lounging and picking their teeth, generally took them an hour, he stayed at the printing-office; and after dispatching his frugal meal, of boiled potatoe, or rice; or a slice of bread with an apple; or bunch of raisins and a glass of water, he had the rest of the time for study. The pure fluids and bright spirits secreted from such simple diet, proved exceedingly favourable to that clearness and vigour of mind, and rapid growth in knowledge which his youthful soul delighted in.

I cannot conclude this chapter without making a remark which the reader has perhaps anticipated—that it was by this simple regimen, vegetables and water, that the Jewish seer, the holy Daniel, while a youth, was of PROVIDENCE made fit for all the learning of the East; hence arose his bright visions into futurity, and his clear pointings to the far distant days of the Messiah, when the four great brass and iron monarchies of Media, Persia, Grecia, and Rome, being overthrown, Christ should set up his last golden monarchy of LOVE, which, though faint in the beginning as the first beam of the uncertain dawn, shall yet at length brighten all the skies, and chase the accursed clouds of sin and suffering from the abodes of man and beast.

In like manner, it was on the simple regimen of vegetables and water, the easy purchase of three cents a day, that the same PROVIDENCE raised up our young countryman to guard the last spark of perfect liberty in the British colonies of North America. Yes, it was on three cents' worth of daily bread and water, that young Ben Franklin commenced his collection of that blaze of light, which early as 1754, showed the infant and unsuspecting colonies their RIGHTS and their DANGERS—and which afterwards, in 1764, blasted the treasonable stamp act—and finally, in '73 and '74, served as the famed star of the East, to guide Washington and his wise men of the revolution, to the cradle of liberty, struggling in the gripe of the British Herod, lord North. There rose the battle of God for an injured people; there spread the star-spangled banner of freedom; and there poured the blood of the brave, fighting for the rights of man under the last republic. O that God may long preserve this precious vine of his own right hand planting, for his own glory and the happiness of unborn millions!

But the reader must not conclude that Ben, through life, tied himself up to a vegetable diet. No. Nature will have her way. And having designed man partly carnivorous, as his canine teeth, his lengthened bowels, and his flesh-pot appetites all evince, she will bring him back to the healthy mixture of animal food with vegetable, or punish his obstinacy with diarrhœa and debility. But she had no great difficulty in bringing Ben back to the use of animal food. According to his own account, no nosegay was ever more fragrant to his olfactories than was the smell of fresh fish in the frying pan.

And as to his objection to such a savory diet on account of its stupifying effects on the brain, he easily got the better of that, when he reflected that the witty queen Elizabeth breakfasted on beef-stake; that sir Isaac Newton dined on pheasants; that Horace supped on fat bacon; and that Pope both breakfasted, dined, and supped on shrimps and oysters. And for the objection taken from the cruelty of killing innocent animals, for their flesh, he got over that by the following curious accident:—On his first voyage to New-York, the vessel halting on the coast for lack of breeze, the sailors all fell to fishing for cod, of which they presently took great numbers and very fine. Instead of being delighted at this sight, Ben appeared much hurt, and began to preach to the crew on their "injustice," as he called it, in thus taking away the lives of those poor little fish, who, "*had never injured them, nor ever could.*" The sailors were utterly dum-founded at such queer logic as this. Taking their silence for conviction, Ben rose in his argument, and began to play the orator quite outrageously on the main deck. At length an old wag of a boatswain, who had at first been struck somewhat aback by the strangeness of this attack, took courage, and luffing up again, with a fine breeze of humour in his weather-beaten sail, called out to Ben, "*Well, but my young Master preacher, may not we deal by these same cod here, as they deal by their neighbours.*"

"To be sure," said Ben.

"Well then, sir, see here," replied the boatswain, holding up a stout fish, "see here what a whaler I took just now out o' the belly of that cod!" Ben looking as if he had his doubts, the boatswain went on, "O sir, if you come to that, you shall have *proof*;" whereupon he laid hold of a large big-bellied cod that was just then flouncing on the deck, and ripping him open, in the presence of Ben and the crew, turned out several young cod from his maw.

Here, Ben, well pleased with this discovery, cried out, Oho! villains! is that the game you play with one another under the water! Unnatural wretches! What! eat one another! Well then, if a cod can eat his own brother, I see no reason in nature why man may not eat him. With that he seized a stout young fish just fresh from his native brine, and frying him in all haste, made a very hearty meal. Ben never after this, made any more scruples about animal food, but ate fish, flesh, or fowl, as they came in his way, without asking any questions for conscience sake.

CHAPTER XI.

Except the ADMIRABLE CRICHTON, I have never heard of a genius that was fitted to shine in every art and science. Even Newton was dull in languages; and Pope used to say of himself, that "he had as leave hear the squeal of pigs in a gate, as hear the organ of Handel!" Neither was our Ben the "*omnis homo*" or "*Jack of all trades*." He never could bear the mathematics! and even arithmetic presented to him no attractions at all. Not that he was not capable of it; for, happening about this time, still in his sixteenth year, to be laughed at for his ignorance in the art of calculation, he went and got himself a copy of old Cocker's Arithmetic, one of the toughest in those days, and went through it by himself with great ease. The truth is, his mind was at this time entirely absorbed in the ambition to be a finished writer of the English language; such a one, if possible, as the SPECTATOR, whom he admired above all others.

While labouring, as we have seen, to improve his style, he laid his hands on all the English Grammars he could hear of. Among the number was a treatise of that sort, an old shabby looking thing, which the owner, marking his curiosity in those matters, made him a present of. Ben hardly returned him a thankee, as doubting at first whether it was worth carrying home. But how great was his surprise, when coming towards the close of it, he found, crammed into a small chapter, a treatise on the art of disputation, after the manner of SOCRATES. The treatise was very short, but it was enough for Ben; it gave an outline, and that was all he wanted. As the little whortleberry boy, on the sands of Cape May, grabbling for his breakfast in a turtle's nest, if he but reaches with his little hand but one egg, instantly laughs with joy, as well knowing that all the rest will follow, like beads on a string. So it was with the eager mind of Ben, when he first struck on this plan of Socratic disputation. In an instant his thoughts ran through all the threads and meshes of the wondrous net; and he could not help laughing in his sleeve, to think what a fine puzzling cap he should soon weave for the frightened heads of Collins, Adams, and all others who should pretend to dispute with him. But the use which he principally had in view to make of it, and which tickled his fancy most, was how completely he should now confound those ignorant and hypocritical ones in Boston, who were continually boring him about religion. Not that Ben ever took pleasure in confounding those who were honestly desirous of *showing their religion by their good works*; for such were always his ESTEEM and DELIGHT. But he could never away with those who neglected JUSTICE, MERCY, and TRUTH, and yet affected great familiarities with the Deity, from certain conceited wonders that Christ had wrought *in* them. As no youth ever more heartily desired the happiness of man and beast than Ben did, so none ever more seriously resented that the religion of love and good works tending to this, should be usurped by a *harsh, barren puritanism, with her disfigured faces, whine and cant.* This appeared to him like Dagon overturning the Ark of God with a vengeance. Burning with zeal against such detestable phariseeism he rejoiced in his Socratic logic as a new kind of weapon, which he hoped to employ with good effect against it. He studied his Socrates day and night, and particularly his admirable argumentations given by Xenophon, in his book, entitled "MEMORABLE THINGS OF SOCRATES;" and in a little time came to wield his new artillery with great dexterity and success.

But in all his rencontres with the *false* christians, he adhered strictly to the spirit of Socrates, as being perfectly congenial to his own. Instead of blunt contradictions and positive assertions, he would put modest questions; and after obtaining of them concessions of which they did not foresee the *consequences*, he would involve them in difficulties and embarrassments, from which they could never extricate themselves. Had he possessed a vanity capable of being satisfied with the triumph of wit over dulness, he might long have crowed the master cock of this Socratic pit. But finding that his victories seldom produced any practical good; that they were acquired at a considerable expense of time, neglect of business, and injury of his temper, which was never formed for altercation with bigots, he abandoned it by degrees, retaining only the habit of expressing himself with a modest diffidence. And not only at that time, but ever afterwards through life, it was remarked of him, that in argument he rarely used the words *certainly*, *undoubtedly*, or any others that might convey the idea of being obstinately conceited of his own opinion. His ordinary phrases were—*I imagine—I suppose*--or, *it appears to me, that such a thing is so and so*—or, *it is so, if I am not mistaken.* By such soothing arts he gradually conciliated the good will of his opponents, and almost always succeeded in bringing them over to his wishes. Hence he used to say, it was great pity that sensible and well-meaning persons should lessen their own usefulness by a positive and presumptuous way of talking, which only serves to provoke opposition from the passionate, and shyness from the prudent, who rather than get into a dispute with such self-conceited characters, will hold their peace, and let them go on in their errors. In short, if you wish to answer one of the noblest ends for which tongues were given to rational beings, which is to *inform* or to be *informed*, to *please* and to *persuade* them, for heaven's sake, treat their opinions, even though erroneous, with great politeness.

"Men must be taught as though you taught them not,"
And things unknown propos'd as things forgot,"

says Mr. Pope; and again

"To speak, though sure, with seeming diffidence;
For want of modesty is want of sense."

CHAPTER XII.

So late as 1720, there was but one newspaper in all North America, and even this by some was thought one too many so little reading was there among the people in those days. But believing that the reading appetite, weak as it was, ran more on newspapers than any thing else, James Franklin took it into his head to *start* another paper. His friends all *vowed* it would be the ruin of him; but James persevered, and a second newspaper, entitled "THE NEW ENGLAND COURANT," was published. What was the number of subscribers, after so long a lapse of time, is now unknown; but it was Ben's humble lot to furnish their papers after having assisted to compose and work them off.

Among his friends, James had a number of literary characters, who, by way of amusement, used to write for his paper. These gentlemen frequently visited him at his office, merely for a little chat, and to tell how highly the public thought of their pieces Ben attended closely to their conversation, and happening to think they were no great wits, he determined to cut in and try his hand among them. But how to get his little adventures into the paper was the question, and a serious one too; for he knew very well that his brother, looking on him as hardly more than a child, would not dream of printing any thing that he knew had come from his pen. Stratagem of course must be resorted to. He took his time, and having written his piece pretty much to his mind, he copied it in a disguised hand, and when they were all gone to bed, slyly shoved it under the door of the office; where it was found next morning. In the course of the day, his friends dropping in as usual, James showed them the stranger paper; a caucus was held, and with aching heart Ben heard his piece read for their criticism. It was highly applauded: and to his greater joy still, among their various conjectures as to the author, not one was mentioned who did not hold a distinguished reputation for talents! Encouraged by such good success of this his first adventure, he wrote on, and sent to the press, in the same sly way, several other pieces, which were equally approved, keeping the secret till his slender stock of information was pretty completely exhausted, when he came out with the real author.

His brother, on this discovery, began to entertain a little more respect for him, but still looked on and treated him as a common apprentice. Ben, on the other hand, thought that, as a brother, he had a right to greater indulgence, and sometimes complained of James as rather too rigorous. This difference in opinion rose to disputes, which were often brought before their father, who either from partiality to Ben, or his *better* cause, generally gave it in his favour. James could not bear these awards of his father in favour of a younger brother, but would fly into a passion and treat him with abuse even to blows. Ben took this tyrannical behaviour of his brother in extremely ill part; and he somewhere says that it imprinted on his mind that deep-rooted aversion to arbitrary power, which he never lost, and which rendered him through life such a firm and unconquerable enemy of oppression. His apprenticeship became insupportable, and he sighed continually for an opportunity of shortening it, which at length unexpectedly offered.

An article in his paper, on some political subject, giving great offence to the assembly, James was taken up; and because he would not discover the author, was ordered into confinement for a month. Ben also was had up and examined before the council, who, after reprimanding, dismissed him, probably because deeming him bound, as an apprentice, to keep his master's secrets.

Notwithstanding their private quarrels, this imprisonment of his brother excited Ben's indignation against the assembly; and having now, during James' confinement, the sole direction of the paper, he boldly came out every week with some severe pasquinade against "*The little tyrants of Boston.*" But though this served to gratify his own angry feelings, and to tickle James, as also to gain himself the character of a wonderful young man for satire; yet it answered no good end, but far contrariwise, proved a fatal blow to their newspaper; for at the expiration of the month, James's enlargement was accompanied with an order from the assembly, that "JAMES FRANKLIN SHOULD NO LONGER PRINT THE NEWSPAPER ENTITLED THE NEW ENGLAND COURANT."

This was a terrible thunder-clap on poor James and his whole scribbling squad; and Ben could find no lightning rod to parry the bolt. A caucus, however, of all the friends was convoked at the printing-office, to devise ways and means of redress. One proposed this measure and another that; but the measure proposed by James himself was at length adopted. This was to carry on the newspaper under Ben's name. *But*, said some, *will not the assembly haul you over the coals for thus attempting to whip the d——l round the stump?*

No, replied James.

Aye, how will you prevent it?

Why, I'll give up Ben's indentures.

So then you'll let Ben run free?

No, nor that neither; for he shall sign a new contract.

This was to be sure a very shallow arrangement. It was however carried into immediate execution, and the paper continued in consequence to make its appearance for some months in Ben's name. At length a new difference arising between the brothers, and Ben knowing that James would not dare to talk of his new *contract*, boldly asserted his freedom!

His numerous admirers will here blush for poor Ben, and hide their reddening cheeks. But let them redden as they may, they will hardly ever equal that honest crimson which glows in the following lines from his *own pen*:

"It was, no doubt, very dishonourable to avail myself of this advantage, and I reckon this as the *first* error of my life. But, I was little capable of seeing it in its true light, embittered as my mind had been by the blows I had received. Exclusively of his passionate *treatment* of me, my brother was by no means an ill tempered man. And even here, perhaps, my *manners* had too much of impertinence not to afford it a very natural pretext."

Go thy way, honest Ben. Such a confession of error will plead thy excuse with all who know their own infirmities, and remember what the greatest saints have done. Yes, when we remember what young Jacob did to his brother Esau, and how he came over him with his mess of pottage, robbing him of his birthright; and also what David did to Uriah, whom he robbed not only of his wife, but of his life also, we surely shall pity not only Ben, but every man his brother for their follies, and heartily rejoice that there is mercy with Christ to forgive *all*, on their repentance and amendment.

CHAPTER XIII.

Finding that to live with James in the pleasant relations of a brother and a freeman was a lost hope, Ben made up his mind to quit him and go on journey-work with some of the Boston printers. But James suspecting Ben's intentions, went around town to the printers, and made such a report of him, that not a man of them all would have any thing to say to him. The door of employment thus shut against him, and all New England furnishing no other printing office, Ben determined, in quest of one, to push off to New-York. He was farther confirmed in this resolution by a consciousness that his newspaper squibs in behalf of his brother, had made the governing party his mortal enemies. And he was also afraid that his bold and indiscreet argumentation against the gloomy puritans, had led those crabbed people to look on him as no better than a young atheist, whom it would be doing God service to worry as they would a wild cat. He felt indeed that it was high time to be off.

To keep his intended flight from the knowledge of his father, his friend Collins engaged his passage with the captain of a New-York sloop, to whom he represented Ben as an amorous young blade, who wished to get away privately in consequence of an intrigue with a worthless hussy, whom her relations wanted to force upon him. Ben had no money. But he had money's worth. Having, for four years past, been carefully turning into books every penny he could spare, he had by this time made up a pretty little library. It went prodigiously against him to break in upon his books. But there was no help for it. So turning a parcel of them back again into money, he slipped privately on board of a sloop, which on the third day landed him safely in New-York, three hundred miles from home, only seventeen years old, without a single friend in the place, and but little money in his pocket.

He immediately offered his services to a Mr. Bradford, the only printer in New-York. The old gentleman expressed his regret that he could give him no employment; but in a very encouraging manner advised him to go on to Philadelphia, where he had a son, a printer, who would probably do something for him. Philadelphia was a good hundred miles farther off; but Ben, nothing disheartened by that, instantly ran down to the wharf, and took his passage in an open boat for Amboy, leaving his trunk to follow him by sea. In crossing the bay, they were overtaken by a dreadful squall, during which a drunken Dutchman, a passenger, fell headlong into the raging waves. Being hissing hot and swollen with rum, he popped up like a dead catfish; but just as he was going down the second time, never to rise again, by a miracle of mercy, Ben caught him by the fore-top, and lugged him in, where he lay tumbled over on the bottom of the boat, fast asleep, and senseless as a corpse of the frightful storm which threatened every moment to bury them all in a watery grave. The violence of the wind presently drove them on the rocky coasts of Long Island; where, to prevent being dashed to pieces among the furious breakers, they cast anchor, and there during the rest of the day, and all night long, lay riding out the gale. Their little boat pitching bows under at every surge, while the water constantly flying over them in drenching showers, kept them as wet as drowned rats; and not only unable to get a wink of sleep, but also obliged to stir their stumps, baling the boat to keep her from sinking.

The wind falling the next day, they reached Amboy about dark, after having passed thirty hours without a morsel of victuals, and with no other drink than a bottle of bad rum; the water upon which they had rowed, being as salt as brine. Ben went to bed with a high fever. Having somewhere read that cold water, plentifully drank, was good in such cases; he followed the prescription, which threw him into a profuse sweat, and the fever left him. The next day, feeble and alone, he set out, with fifty wearisome miles to walk before he could reach Burlington, whence he was told that a passage boat would take him to Philadelphia. To increase his depression, soon as he left the tavern, it set in to rain hard. But though wet to the skin, he pressed on by himself through the gloomy woods till noon, when feeling much fatigued, and the rain still pouring down, he stopped at a paltry tavern, where he passed the rest of the day and night. In this gloomy situation he began seriously to repent that he had ever left home; and the more, as from the wretched figure he made, every body was casting a suspicious eye upon him as a runaway servant. Indeed, from the many insulting questions put to him, he felt himself every moment in danger of being taken up as such, and then what would his father think on hearing that he was in jail as a runaway servant, four hundred miles from home! And what a triumph to his brother. After a very uneasy night, however, he rose and continued his journey till the evening, when he stopped about ten miles from Burlington, at a little tavern, kept by one Dr. Brown. While he was taking some refreshment, Brown came in, and being of a facetious turn, put a number of droll questions to him; to which Ben retorted in a style so superior to his youthful looks and shabby dress, that the Doctor became quite enamoured of him. He kept him up conversing until midnight; and next morning would not touch a penny of his money. This was a very seasonable liberality to poor Ben, for he had now very little more than a dollar in his pocket.

On reaching Burlington, and buying some gingerbread for his passage, he hastened to the wharf. But alas! the boat had just sailed! This was on

Saturday; and there would be no other boat until Tuesday. Having been much struck with the looks of the old woman, of whom he had just bought his cargo of gingerbread, he went back and asked her advice. Her behaviour proved that he had some skill in physiognomy. For the moment he told her of his sad disappointment and his doubts how he should act, she gave him the tender look of a mother, and told him he must stay with her till the next boat sailed. Pshaw! Don't mind these little disappointments, child, said she, seeing him uneasy; they are not worth your being troubled about. When I was young, I used to be troubled about them too. But now I see that it is all but vanity. So stay with me till the boat goes again; and rest yourself, for I am sure you must be mighty tired after such a terrible walk. The good old lady was very right; for what with his late loss of sleep, as also his fever and long walk in the rains, he was tired indeed; so he gladly consented to stay with her and rest himself. Having shown him a small room with a bed in it, for him to take a *nap, for she saw clear enough*, she said, that *he was a dying for sleep*, she turned with a mother's alacrity to get him something to eat. By and by she came again, and from a short but refreshing doze, waked him up to a dinner of hot beef-steaks, of which she pressed him to eat *heartily*, telling him that *gingerbread was fit only for children.* While he was eating, she chatted with him in the affectionate spirit of an aged relative; she asked him a world of questions, such as *how old* he was—and what was his *name*—and whether his mother was alive—and how far he lived from Burlington? Ben told her every thing she asked him. He told her his name and age. He also told her that his mother was alive, and that he had left her only seven days ago in Boston, where she lived. The old lady could hardly believe him that he ever came from Boston. She lifted up her hands, and stared at him as though he had told her he had just dropped from the North Star. From BOSTON! said she with a scream, *now only to think of that! O dear, only to think of that!* And then, O how she pitied his mother. *Poor dear soul!* She, all the way yonder in Boston, and such a sweet looking, innocent child, wandering here at such a distance by himself: how could she stand it?

Ben told her that it was a great affliction to be sure; but could not be helped. That his mother was a poor woman, with sixteen children, and that he the youngest boy of all, was obliged to leave her to seek his livelihood, which he hoped he should find in Philadelphia, at his trade, which was that of a printer.

On hearing that he was a printer, she was quite delighted and pressed him to come and set up in Burlington, for that she would be *bound* for it he would do mighty well there. Ben told her that it was a costly thing to set up printing; that it would take two hundred pounds, and he had not two hundred pence.

Well then, said she, now that you have got no money, it will give me more pleasure to have you stay with me till you can get a good opportunity to go to Philadelphia. I feel for your poor mother, and I know it would give her such a pleasure if she knew you were here with me.

Soon as Ben had enjoyed his beef-steaks, which he did in high style, having the double sauce of his own good appetite and her motherly welcome, he drew out his last dollar to pay the good old lady. But she told him to *put it up, put it up, for she would not take a penny of it.* Ben told her that he was young and able to work, and hoped to do well when he got into business, and therefore could not bear that she who was getting old and weak should entertain him for nothing.

Well, said she, *never mind that, child, never mind that. I shall never miss what little I lay out in entertaining you while you stay with me. So put up your money.* However, while she was busied in putting away the dishes, he slipped out and got a pint of ale for her: and it was all that he could prevail on her to accept.

From the pleasure with which Ben ever afterwards spoke of this good old woman, and her kindness to him, a poor strange boy, I am persuaded as indeed I have always been, that there is nothing on which men reflect with so much complacency as on doing or receiving offices of love from one another.

Ben has not left us the name of this good old woman, nor the sect of christians to which she belonged. But it is probable she was a Quaker. Most of the people about Burlington in those days were Quakers. And besides such kindness as her's seems to be more after the spirit of that wise people, who instead of wrangling about *faith,* which even devils possess, give their chief care to that which is the *end* of all faith, and which the poor devils know nothing about, viz, "*love* and *good works.*"

CHAPTER XIV.

Ben now sat himself down to stay with this good old woman till the following Tuesday; but still Philadelphia was constantly before him, and happening, in the impatience of his mind, to take a stroll along the river side, he saw a boat approaching with a number of passengers in it. *Where are you bound?* said he.

To PHILADELPHIA, was the reply.

His heart leaped for joy. Can't you take a passenger aboard? I'll help you to row. O yes, answered they, and bore up to receive him. With all his heart he would have run back to his good old hostess to bid her farewell, and to thank her for her kindness to him, but the boat could not wait; and carrying, tortoise-like, his all upon his back, in he stepped and went on with them to Philadelphia, where, after a whole night of hard rowing, they arrived about eight o'clock next morning, which happened to be Sunday.

Soon as the boat struck the place of landing, which was Market-street wharf, Ben put his hand into his pocket, and asked, what was the damage. The boatmen shook their heads, and said, *oh no; he had nothing to pay. They could never take pay from a young fellow of his spirit, who had so cheerfully assisted them to row all the way.* As his own stock now consisted of but one Dutch dollar, and about a shilling's worth in coppers, he would have been well content to accept his passage on their own friendly terms; but seeing one of their crew who appeared to be old, and rather poorly dressed, he hauled out his coppers and gave them all to him. Having shaken hands with these honest-hearted fellows, he leaped ashore and walked up Market-street in search of something to appease his appetite, which was now abundantly keen from twenty miles' rowing and a cold night's air. He had gone but a short distance before he met a child bearing in his arms that most welcome of all sights to a hungry man, a fine loaf of bread. Ben eagerly asked him where he had got it. The child, turning around, lifted his little arm and pointing up the street, with great simplicity and sweetness said, *don't you see that little house—that little white house, way up yonder?*

Ben said, yes.

Well then, continued the child, *that's the baker's house; there's where my mammy sends me every morning to get bread for all we children.*

Ben blessed his sweet lips of innocence, and hastening to the house, boldly called for *three pence* worth of bread. The baker threw him down three large rolls.

What, all this for three pence! asked Ben with surprise.

Yes, all that for three pence, replied the baker with a fine yankee snap of the eye, all that for *only* three pence! Then measuring Ben from head to foot, he said with a sly quizzing sort of air, and pray now my little man where may you have come from?

Here Ben felt his old panic, on the runaway servant score, returning strong upon him again. However, putting on a bold face, he promptly answered that he was from Boston.

Plague on it replied the man of dough, and why did'nt you tell me that at first; I might so easily have cabbaged you out of one whole penny; for you know you could not have got all that bread in YANKEE-TOWN for less than a good four-pence? Very cheap, said Ben, three large rolls for three-pence: *quite dog cheap!* So taking them up, began to stow them away in his pockets; but soon found it impossible for lack of room—so placing a roll under each arm, and breaking the third, he began to eat as he walked along up Market-street. On the way he passed the house of that beautiful girl, Miss Deborah Read, who happening to be at the door, was so diverted at the droll figure he made, that she could not help laughing outright. And indeed no wonder. A stout fleshy boy, in his dirty working dress, and pockets all puckered out, with foul linen and stockings, and a loaf of bread under each arm, eating and gazing around him as he walked—no wonder she could not help laughing aloud at him as one of the greatest gawkies she had ever seen. Very little idea had she at that time that she was presently to be up to her eyes in love with this young gawky; and after many a deep sigh and heart-ache, was to marry him and to be made a great woman by him. And yet all this actually came to pass, as we shall presently see, and we hope greatly to the comfort of all virtuous young men, who though they may sometimes be laughed at for their oddities; yet if, like Franklin, they will but stick to the *main chance*, *i.e.* BUSINESS and EDUCATION, they will assuredly, like him, overcome at the last, and render themselves the admiration of those who once despised them.

But our youthful hero is in too interesting a part of the play for us to lose a moment's sight of him; so after this short moral we turn our eyes on him again, as there, loaded with his bundles and his bread, and eating and gazing and turning the corners of the streets, he goes on without indeed knowing where he is going. At length, however, just as he had finished his first roll, his reverie was broken up by finding himself on Market-street wharf, and close to the very boat in which he had come from Burlington. The sight of the silver stream, as it whirled in dimpling eddies around the wharf, awakened his thirst; so stepping into the boat he took a hearty draught, which, to his unvitiated palate, tasted sweeter than ever did mint-sling to any young drunkard. Close by him in the boat sat a poor woman with a little ragged girl leaning on her lap. He asked her if she had breakfasted. With a sallow smile of hunger hoping relief, she replied *no*, for that she had nothing to eat. Upon this he gave her both his other loaves. At sight of this welcome supply of food, the poor woman and her child gave him a look which he never afterwards forgot.

Having given, as we have seen, a tythe of his money in gratitude to the poor boatman, and two thirds of his bread in charity to this poor woman and her child, Ben skipped again upon the wharf, and with a heart light and gay with conscious duty, a second time took up Market-street, which was now getting to be full of well-dressed people all going the same way. He cut in, and following the line of march, was thus insensibly led to a large Quaker meeting-house. Sans ceremonie, he pushed in and sat down with the rest, and looking around him soon felt the *motions*, if not of a devout, yet of a pleasantly thoughtful spirit. It came to his recollection to have heard that people must go abroad to see strange things. And here it seemed to be verified. *What, no pulpit! Whoever saw a meeting-house before without a pulpit?* He could not for his life conceive where the preacher was to stand. But his attention was quickly turned from the meeting-house to the congregation, whose appearance, particularly that of the young females, delighted him exceedingly. Such simplicity of dress with such an air of purity and neatness! He had never seen any thing like it before, and yet all admirably suited to the gentle harmony of their looks. And then their eyes! for meekness and sweetness of expression, they looked like dove's eyes. With a deep sigh he wished that his brother James and many others in Boston were but gentle and good as these people appeared to be. Young as he was, he thought the world would be a great deal the happier for it. As leaning back he indulged these soothing sentiments, without any sound of singing or preaching to disturb him, and tired nature's soft languors stealing over him too, he sunk insensibly into sleep. We are not informed that he was visited during his slumber, by any of those benevolent spirits who once descended in the dreams of the youthful patriarch, as he slept in the pleasant plains of Bethel. But he tells us himself, that he was visited by one of that benevolent sect in whose place of worship he had been overtaken by sleep. Waked by some hand on his shoulder that gently shook him, he opened his eyes, and lo! a female countenance about middle age and of enchanting sweetness, was smiling on him. Roused to a recollection of the impropriety he had been guilty of, he was too much confused to speak; but his reddened cheeks told her what he felt. But he had nothing to fear. Gently shaking her head, though without a frown, and with a voice of music, she said to him "*My son, thee ought not to sleep in meeting.*" Then giving him the look of a mother as she went out, she bade him farewell. He followed her as well as he could, and left the meeting-house much mortified at having been caught asleep in it; but deriving at the same time great pleasure from this circumstance, because it had furnished opportunity to the good Quaker lady to give him that *motherly look*. He felt it sweetly melting along his soul as he walked. O *how different, thought he, that look from the looks which my brother and the council men of Boston gave me, though I was younger then and more an object of sympathy!*

As he walked along the street, looking attentively in the face of every one he met, he saw a young Quaker with a fine countenance, whom he begged to tell him where a stranger might find a lodging. With a look and voice of great sweetness, the young Quaker said, they receive travellers *here*, but it is not a house that bears a good character; if thee will go with me, I will show thee a better one.

This was the *Crooked Billet*, in Water-street. Directly after dinner, his drowsiness returning, he went to bed and slept, without waking till next morning.

Having put himself in as decent a trim as he could, he waited on Mr. Bradford, the printer, who received him with great civility, and invited him to breakfast, but told him he was sorry he had no occasion for a journeyman. There is, however, continued he in a cheering manner, there is another printer here, of the name of Keimer, to whom if you wish it, I will introduce you. Perhaps he may want your services.

Ben gratefully accepting the offer, away they went to Mr Keimer's. But alas, poor man! both he and his office put together, made no more than a miserable burlesque on printing. Only one press, and that old and damaged! only one font of types, and that nearly worn out! and only one set of letter cases, and that occupied by himself! and consequently no room for a journeyman.

Here was a sad prospect for poor Ben—four hundred miles from home—not a dollar in his pocket—and no appearance of any employment to get one.—But having, from his childhood, been accustomed to grapple with difficulties and to overcome them, Ben saw nothing here but another trial of his courage, and another opportunity for victory and triumph.

As to Keimer, suspecting from his youthful appearance, that Ben could hardly understand any thing of the printing art, he slyly put a COMPOSING STICK into his hand. Ben saw his drift, and stepping to the letter cases, filled the stick with such celerity and taste as struck Keimer with surprise, not without shame, that one so inferior in years should be so far his superior in professional skill. To complete this favourable impression, Ben modestly proposed to repair his old press.—This offer being accepted, Ben instantly fell to work, and presently accomplished his undertaking in such a workman-like style, that Keimer could no longer restrain his feelings, but relaxing his rigid features into a smile of admiration, paid him several flattering compliments, and concluded with promising him, that though, for the present, he had no work on hand, yet he expected an abundance shortly, and then would *be sure* to send for him.

In a few days Keimer was as good as his word; for having procured another set of letter cases, with a small pamphlet to print, he sent in all haste for Ben, and set him to work.

CHAPTER XV.

As Keimer is to make a considerable figure in the early part of Ben's life, it may gratify the reader to be made acquainted with him. From the account given of him by Ben, who had the best opportunity to know, it appears that he possessed but little either of the amiable or estimable in his composition. A man he was of but slender talents—quite ignorant of the world—a wretched workman—and worse than all yet, utterly destitute of religion, and therefore very uneven and unhappy in his temper, and abundantly capable of playing the knave whenever he thought it for his interest. Among other evidences of his folly, he miserably envied his brother printer, Bradford, as if the Almighty was not rich enough to maintain them both. He could not endure, that while working with him, Ben should stay at Bradford's; so he took him away, and having no house of his own, he put him to board with Mr. Read, father of the young lady who of late had laughed so heartily at him for eating his rolls along the street. But Miss Deborah did not long continue in this wind. For on seeing the favourable change in his dress, and marking also the wittiness of his conversation, and above all, his close application to business, and the great respect paid him on that account by her father, she felt a wonderful change in his favour, and in place of her former sneers, conceived those tender sentiments for him, which, as we shall see hereafter, accompanied her through life.

Ben now began to contract acquaintance with all such young persons in Philadelphia as were fond of reading, and spent his evenings with them very agreeably: at the same time he picked up money by his industry, and being quite frugal, lived so happy, that except for his parents, he seldom ever thought of Boston nor felt any wish to see it. An affair, however, turned up, which sent him home much sooner than he expected.

His brother-in-law, a captain Holmes, of a trading sloop from Boston to Delaware, happening at Newcastle to hear that Ben was in Philadelphia, wrote to him that his father was all but distracted on account of his sudden elopement from home, and assured him that if he would but return, which he earnestly pressed him to do, every thing should be settled to his satisfaction. Ben immediately answered his letter, thanked him for his advice, and stated his reasons for quitting Boston, with a force and clearness that so highly delighted captain Holmes, that he showed it to all his acquaintance at Newcastle, and among the rest to sir William Keith, governor of the province, with whom he happened to dine. The governor read it, and appeared surprised when he learnt his age. "*Why, this must be a young man of extraordinary talents, captain Holmes*," said the governor, "*very extraordinary talents indeed, and ought to be encouraged; we have no printer in Philadelphia now worth a fig, and if this young man will but set up, there is no doubt of his success. For my part, I will give him all the public business, and render him every other service in my power.*"

One day as Keimer and Ben were at work near the window, they saw the governor and colonel French cross the street, and make directly for the printing-office. Keimer not doubting it was a visit to himself, hurried down stairs to meet them. The Governor taking no notice of Keimer, but eagerly inquiring for young Mr. FRANKLIN, came up stairs, and with a condescension to which Ben had not been accustomed, introduced himself to him—desired to become acquainted with him—and after obligingly reproaching him for not having made himself known when he first came to town, invited him to the tavern where he and colonel French were going to break a bottle of old Madeira.

If Ben was surprised, old Keimer was thunderstruck. Ben went, however, with the governor and the colonel to the tavern, where, while the Madeira was circulating in cheerful bumpers, the governor proposed to him to set up a printing-office, stating at the same time the great chances of success, and promising that both himself and colonel French would use their influence in procuring for him the public printing of both governments. As Ben appeared to doubt whether his father would assist him in this enterprize, sir William said that he would give the old gentleman a letter, in which he would represent the advantages of the scheme in a light that would, he'd be bound, determine him in his favour. It was thus concluded that Ben should return to Boston by the first vessel, with the governor's letter to good old Josias: in the mean time Ben was to continue with Keimer, from whom this project was to be kept a secret.

The governor sent every now and then to invite Ben to dine with him, which he considered as a very great honour, especially as his excellency always received and conversed with him in the most familiar manner.

In April, 1724, Ben embarked for Boston, where, after a fortnight passage, he arrived in safety. Having been absent seven months from his relatives, who had never heard a syllable of him all that time, his sudden appearance threw the family into a scream of joy, and excepting his sour-faced brother James, the whole squad gave him a most hearty welcome. After much embracing and kissing, and some tears shed on both sides, as is usual at such meetings, Ben kindly inquired after his *brother James*, and went to see him at his printing-office, not without hopes of making a favourable impression on him by his dress, which was handsome far beyond what he had ever worn in his brother's service; a complete suit of broad cloth, branding new—an elegant silver watch and chain—and his purse crammed with nearly five pound sterling—all in silver dollars. But it would not all do to win over James. Nor indeed is it to be wondered at; for in losing Ben he had lost a most cheerful, obliging lad, whose rare genius and industry in writing, printing, and selling his pamphlets and papers, had brought a noble grist to his mill.

Ben's parade therefore of his fine clothes, and watch, and silver dollars, only made things worse with James, serving but to make him the more sensible of his loss; so after eyeing him from head to foot with a dark side-long look, he turned again to his work without saying a syllable to him. The behaviour of his own journeymen contributed still the more to anger poor James: for instead of taking part with him in his prejudices against Ben, they all appeared quite delighted with him; and breaking off from their work and gathering around him, with looks full of curiosity, they asked him a world of questions.

PHILADELPHIA! said they, O dear! have you been all the way there to Philadelphia!

Ben said, yes.

Why Philadelphia must be a *tarnal nation way off*!

Four hundred miles, said Ben.

At this they stared on him in silent wonder, for having been four hundred miles from Boston!

And so they have got a printing-office in Philadelphia!

Two or three of them, said Ben.

O la! why that will starve us all here in Boston.

Not at all, said Ben: their advertising "*lost pocket books*"—"*runaway servants*" and "*stray cows*" in Philadelphia, can no more starve you here in Boston, than the catfish of Delaware, by picking up a few soft-crabs there, can starve our catfish here in Boston harbour. The world's big enough for us all.

Well, I wonder now if they have any such thing as *money* in Philadelphia?

Ben thrust his hand into his pocket, and brought up a whole fist full of dollars!

The dazzling silver struck them all speechless—gaping and gazing at him and each other. Poor fellows, they had never, at once, seen so much of that precious metal in Boston, the money there being nothing but a poor paper proc.

To keep up their stare, Ben drew his silver watch, which soon had to take the rounds among them, every one insisting to have *a look at it.* Then, to crown all, he gave them a shilling to drink his health; and after telling them what great things lay before them if they would but continue *industrious* and *prudent*, and make themselves *masters of their trade*, he went back to the house.

This visit to the office stung poor James to the quick; for when his mother spoke to him of a reconciliation with Ben, and said how happy she should be to see them like brothers again before she died, he flew into a passion and told her such a thing would never be, for that Ben had so insulted him before his men that he would never forgive nor forget it as long as he lived. But Ben had the satisfaction to live to see that James was no prophet. For when James, many years after this, fell behind hand and got quite low in the world, Ben lent him money, and was a steady friend to him and his family all the days of his life.

CHAPTER XVI.

But we have said nothing yet about the main object of Ben's sudden return to Boston, *i.e.* governor Keith's letter to his father, on the grand project of setting him up as a printer in Philadelphia. The reader has been told that all the family, his brother James excepted, were greatly rejoiced to see Ben again. But among them all there was none whose heart felt half such joy as did that of his father. He had always doted on this young son, as one whose rare genius and unconquerable industry, if but conducted by prudence, would assuredly, one day, lead him to greatness. His sudden elopement, as we have seen, had greatly distressed the old man, especially as he was under the impression that he was gone to sea. And when he remembered how few that go out at his young and inexperienced age, ever return better than blackguards and vagabonds, his heart sickened within him, and he was almost ready to wish he had never lived to feel the pangs of such bitter disappointment in a child so beloved. He counted the days of Ben's absence; by night his sleep departed from his eyes for thinking of his son; and all day long whenever he heard a rapping at the door, his heart would leap with expectation: "who knows," he would say to himself, "but this may be my child?" And although he would feel disappointed when he saw it was not Ben who rapped, yet he was afraid, at times, to see him lest he should see him covered with the marks of dishonour. Who can tell what this anxious father felt when he saw his son return as he did? Not in the mean apparel and sneaking looks of a drunkard, but in a dress far more genteel than he himself had ever been able to put on him; while his beloved cheeks were fresh with temperance, and his eyes bright with innocence and conscious well doing. Imagination dwells with pleasure on the tender scene that marked that meeting, where the withered cheeks of seventy and the florid bloom of seventeen met together in the eager embrace of parental affection and filial gratitude:

"*God bless my son!*" the sobbing sire he sigh'd.

"*God bless my sire!*" that pious son replied.

Soon as the happy father could recover his articulation, with great tenderness he said, "but how, my beloved boy could you give me the pain to leave me as you did?"

"Why you know, my dear father," replied Ben, "that I could not live with my brother; nor would he let me live with the other printers; and as I could not bear the thought of living on an aged father now that I was able to work for myself, I determined to leave Boston and seek my fortune abroad.

And knowing that if I but hinted my intentions you would prevent me, I thought I would leave you as I did."

"But why, my son, did you keep me so long unhappy about your fate, and not write to me sooner?"

"I knew, father, what a deep interest you took in my welfare, and therefore I resolved never to write to you until by my own industry and economy I had got myself into such a state, that I could write to you with pleasure. This state I did not attain till lately. And just as I was a going to write to you, a strange affair took place that decided me to come and see you, rather than write to you."

"Strange affair! what can that mean, my son?"

"Why, sir, the governor of Pennsylvania, sir William Keith—I dare say, father, you have often heard of governor Keith?"

"I may have heard of him, child—I'm not positive—but what of governor Keith?"

"Why he has taken a wonderful liking to me, father!"

"Aye! has he so?" said the old man, with joy sparkling in his eyes. "Well I pray God you may be grateful for such favours, my son, and make a good use of them!"

"Yes, father, he has taken a great liking to me sure enough; he says I am the only one in Philadelphia who knows any thing about printing; and he says too, that if I will only come and set up in Philadelphia, he will make my fortune for me in a trice!!"

Old Josias here shook his head; "No, no, Ben!" said he, "that will never do: that will never do: you are too young yet, child, for all that, a great deal too young."

"So I told him, father, that I was too young. And I told him too that I was certain you would never give your consent to it."

"You were right there, Ben; no indeed, I could never give my consent to it, that's certain."

"So I told the governor, father; but still he would have it there was a fine opening in Philadelphia, and that I would fill it so exactly, that nothing could be wanting to insure your approbation but a clear understanding of it. And to that end he has written you a letter."

"A letter, child! a letter from governor Keith to me!"

"Yes, father, here it is."

With great eagerness the old gentleman took it from Ben; and drawing his spectacles, read it over and over again with much eagerness. When he was done he lifted his eyes to heaven, while in the motion of his lips and change of countenance, Ben could clearly see that the soul of his father was breathing an ejaculation of praise to God on his account. Soon as his *Te Deum* was finished, he turned to Ben with a countenance bright with holy joy, and said, "Ben, I've cause to be happy; my son, I've cause to be happy indeed. O how differently have things turned out with you! God's blessed name be praised for it, how differently have they turned out to what I dreaded! I was afraid you were gone a poor vagabond, on the seas; but instead of that you had fixed yourself in one of the finest cities in the country. I was afraid to see you; yes, my dear child, I was afraid to see you, lest I should see you clad in the mean garb of a poor sailor boy; but here I behold you clad in the dress of a gentleman! I trembled lest you had been degrading yourself into the low company of the profane and worthless; and lo! you have been all the time exalting yourself into the high society of great men and governors. And all this in so short a time, and in a way most honourable to yourself, and therefore most delightful to me, I mean by your virtues and your close attention to the duties of a most useful profession. Go on, my son, go on! and may God Almighty, who has given you wisdom to begin so glorious a course, grant you fortitude to persevere in it!"

Ben thanked his father for the continuance of his love and solicitude for him; and he told him moreover, that one principal thing that had stirred him up to act as he had done, was the joy which he knew he should be giving him thereby; as also the great trouble which he knew a contrary conduct would have brought upon him. Here his father tenderly embraced him, and said, "Blessed be God for giving me such a son! I have always, Ben, fed myself with hopes of great things from you. And now I have the joy to say my hopes were not in vain. Yes, glory to God, I trust my precious hopes of you were not in vain." Then, after making a short pause, as from fullness of joy, he went on, "but as to this letter, my son; this same letter here from governor Keith; though nothing was ever more flattering to you, yet depend upon it, Ben, it will never do; at least not yet awhile.—The duties of the place are too numerous, child, and difficult for any but one who has had many more years of experience than you have had."

"Well then, father, what's to be done, for I know that the governor is so very anxious to get me into this place, that he will hardly be said nay?"

"Why, my dear boy, we must still decline it, for all that: not only because from your very unripe age and inexperience, it may involve you in ruin; but also because it actually is not in your power. It is true the governor, from his letter, appears to have the greatest friendship in the world for you; but yet, it is not to be expected that he would advance funds to set you up. O no, my dear boy, that's entirely out of the question. The governor, though perhaps rich, has no doubt too many poor friends and relations hanging on him, for you to expect any thing from that quarter. And as to myself, Ben, with all my love for you, it is not in my power to assist you in such an affair. My family you know, is very large, and the profits of my trade but small, insomuch that at the end of the year there is nothing left. And indeed I never can be sufficiently thankful to God for that health and blessing which enables me to feed and clothe them every year so plentifully."

Seeing Ben look rather serious, the old gentleman, in a livelier tone, resumed his speech, "Yes, Ben, all this is very true; but yet let us not be disheartened. Although we have no funds now, yet a noble supply is at hand."

"Where, father," said Ben, roused up, "where?"

"Why, in your own virtues, Ben, in your own virtues, my boy—There are the noblest funds that God can bestow on a young man. All other funds may easily be drained by our vices and leave us poor indeed. But the virtues are fountains that never fail: they are indeed the true riches and honours, only by other names. Only persevere, my son, in the virtues, as you have already so bravely begun, and the grand object is gained. By the time you reach twenty-one, for every friend that you now have, you will have ten; and for every dollar an hundred; and with these you will make thousands more. Thus, under God, you will have the glory to be the artificer of your own fame and fortune: and that will bring ten thousand times more honour and happiness, to you, Ben, than all the money that governors and fathers could ever give you."

Ben's countenance brightened as his father uttered this; then heaving a deep sigh, as of strong hope that such great things might one day be realized, he said, "Well father, God only knows what I am to come to; but this I know, that I feel in myself a determination to do my best."

"I believe you do, my son, and I thank God most heartily that I have such good reason to believe you do. And when I consider, on the one hand, what a fine field for fame and fortune this new country presents to young men of talents and enterprise: and on the other hand, what wonders you, a poor unknown and unfriended boy have done in Philadelphia, in only six months, I feel transported at the thought of what you may yet attain before my gray hairs descend to the grave. Who knows, Ben, for God is good, my son, who knows but that a fate like that of young Joseph, whom his brethren drove into Egypt, may be in reserve for you? And who knows but that old Jacob's joys may be mine? that like him, after all my anxieties on your account, I may yet hear the name of my youngest son, my beloved

Benjamin, coming up from the South, perfumed with praise for his great virtues and services to his country? Then when I hear the sound of his fame rising from that distant land, like the pleasant thunders of summer before refreshing showers, and remember how he used to stand a little prattling boy by my side, in his rosy cheeks and flaxen locks filling the candle moulds, or twisting the snow white cotton wicks with his tender fingers, O how will such remembrance lighten up the dark evening of my days, and cause my setting sun to go down in joy!"

He spoke this in tones so melting, that Ben, who was sitting by his father's side, fell with his face on his bosom, without saying a word. The fond parent, hearing him sob, tenderly embraced him, and with a voice broken with sighs, went on, "Yes, my son, the measure of my joys will then be full. I shall have nothing to detain me any longer in this vale of troubles, but shall gladly breathe out my life in praise to God for this his last, his crowning act of goodness—for this his blessing me in my son."

After a moment's pause, the feelings of both being too deliciously affected for speech, Ben gently raised his face from his father's bosom, and with his eyes yet red and wet with tears, tenderly looking at him, said, "I would to God, father, you would go and live in Philadelphia."

"Why so, my son?"

"Because, I don't want ever to part with you, father, and I am, you know, obliged to go back to Philadelphia immediately."

"Not immediately, my son, I cannot let you go from me immediately."

"Father, I would never go from you, if I could help it; but I must be doing something to make good your fond hopes of me; and I can't stay here."

"Why not, my son?"

"Father, I can't stay with those who hate me; and you know that brother James hates me very much."

"O! he does not hate you, I hope, my son."

"Yes, he does, father, indeed he does; because I only differed from him in opinion and ventured to reason with him, he kindled into passion and abused me even to *blows*, though I was in the right, as you told him afterwards. And because I told him I did not think he acted the part of a brother by me in wishing to make me a slave so many years, he went about town and set all the printers against me, and thus drove me away from home, and from you, my father, whom I so much love. And just now, when I went to his office to see him, instead of running to meet me and rejoicing to see me returned safe and sound and so well dressed and a plenty of money in my pocket, he would not even speak to me, but looked as dark and angry as though he would have torn me to pieces. And yet he can turn up his eyes, and make long prayers and graces, and talk a great deal about JESUS CHRIST!"

The old man here shook his head with a deep groan, while Ben thus went on, "No, father, I can't stay here; I must be going back to Philadelphia and to my good friend governor Keith; for I long to be realizing all the great hopes that you have been forming of me. And should God but give me a good settlement in Philadelphia, then you will come and live with me. O say, my father, wont you come and live with me?"

Ben spoke this, looking up to his father with that joy of filial love sparkling in his youthful eyes which made him look like all that we fancy of angels.

The old man embraced him and said, "I will, my son, I will; but stay with me a little while, at the least three days, and then you may depart." Ben consenting to this, the old gentleman wrote a polite letter to governor Keith, thanking him very heartily for that he, so great a man, should have paid such attentions to his poor boy: but at the same time begged his pardon for declining to do any thing for him, not only because he had very little in his power to do; but also because he thought him too young to be intrusted with the conduct of an enterprise that required much more experience than he possessed.

CHAPTER XVII.

Of the three days which Ben, as we have seen above, had consented to stay at home, he spent the chiefest part with his father, in his old candle manufactory. 'Tis true, this happy sire, whose *natural* affection for Ben as a *son*, was now exalted into the highest respect for him as a youth of *talents* and *virtues*; and *perhaps* too, looking up to him as a young mountain oak, whose towering arms would soon protect the parent tree, insisted that Ben should not stay in *that dirty place*, as he called it. But knowing that his father could not be spared from his daily labour, Ben insisted to be with him in the old shop, and to assist in his labours, reminding his father how sweetly the time passes away when at work and conversing with those we love. His father at length consented: and those three days, now spent with Ben, were the happiest days he had spent for a long time. His aged bosom was now relieved from his six months' load of fears and anxieties about this beloved child; nor only so, but this beloved child, shining in a light of his own virtues, was now with him, and as a volunteer of filial love was mingling in his toils—eagerly lending his youthful strength to assist him in packing and boxing his candles and soap; while his sensible conversation, heightened all the time by the charm of that voice and those eyes that had ever been so dear to him, touched his heart with a sweetness inexpressible, and made the happy hours fly away as on angels' wings.

On the afternoon of the third day, as they were returning from dinner, walking down the garden, at the foot of which the factory stood, the old gentleman lifting his eyes to the sun, suddenly heaved a deep sigh and put on a melancholy look.

"High, father!" said Ben, "I see no cloud over the sun that we should fear a change of weather."

"No, Ben, there is no cloud over the sun, but still his beams throw a cloud over my spirits. They put me in mind that I shall walk here to-morrow, but with no son by my side!"

The idea was mournful: and more so by the tender look and plaintive tones in which it was conveyed.—It wrung the heart of Ben, who in silence glanced his eyes on his father. It was that tender glance of sorrowing love which quickest reaches the heart and stirs up all its yearnings. The old gentleman felt the meaning of his son's looks. They seemed to say to him, "*O my father, must we part to-morrow?*"

"Yes, Ben, we part to-morrow, and perhaps never to meet again!"

After a short pause, with a sigh, he thus resumed his speech—"Then, O my son, what a wretch were man without religion? Yes, Ben, without the hopes of immortality, how much better he had never been born? Without these, his noblest capacities were but the greater curses. The more delightful his friendships the more dreadful the thought they may be extinguished for ever; and the gayer his prospects the deeper his gloom, that endless darkness may so quickly cover all. We were yesterday feeding fond hopes, my son; we were yesterday painting bright castles in the air: you were to be a great man and I a happy father. But alas! this is the last day, my child, that we may ever see each other again. And the sad reverse of all this may even now be at the door; when I, instead of hearing of my son's glory in Philadelphia, may hear that he is cold in his grave. And when you, returning—after years of virtuous toils, returning laden with riches and honours for your happy father to share in, may see nothing of that father but the tomb that covers his dust."

Seeing the moisture in Ben's eyes, the old gentleman, with a voice rising to exultation, thus went on. "Yes, Ben, this may soon be the case with us, my child; the dark curtain of our separation soon may *drop*, and your cheeks or mine be flooded with sorrows. But thanks be to God, that curtain will rise again, and open to our view those scenes of happiness, one glance at which is sufficient to start the tear of transport into our eyes. Yes, Ben, religion assures us of all this; religion assures us that this life is but the morning of our existence—that there is a glorious eternity beyond—and that to the penitent, death is but the passage to that happy life where they shall soon meet again to part no more, but to congratulate their mutual felicities for ever. Then, O my son, lay hold of religion, and secure an interest in those blessed hopes that contribute so much to the virtues and the joys of life."

"Father," said Ben with a sigh, "I know that many people here in Boston think I never had any religion; or, that if I had I have apostatized from it."

"God forbid! But whence, my son, could these prejudices have arisen?"

"Why, father, I have for some time past discovered that there is no effect without a cause. These prejudices have been the effect of my youthful *errors*. You remember father, the old story of the pork, don't you?"

"No, child; what is it, for I have forgotten it?"

"I thought so, father, I thought you had been so good as to forget it. But I have not, nor ever shall forget it."

"What is it, Ben?"

"Why, father, when our pork, one fall, lay salted and ready for the barrel, I begged you to say grace over it all at once; adding that it would *do as well* and save *a great deal of time*."

"Pshaw, Ben, such a trifle as that, and in a child too, cannot be remembered against you now."

"Yes, father, I am afraid it is. All are not so loving, and so forgetful of my errors as you. It was at the time inserted in the Boston NEWS LETTER, and is now recollected to the discredit of my religion. And they have a prejudice against me on another account. While I lived with you, father, you always took me to meeting with you; but when I left you and went to live with my brother James, I often neglected going to meeting; preferring to stay at home and read my books."

"I am sorry to hear that, Ben; very sorry that you could neglect the preachings of Christ."

"Father, I never neglected them. I look on the preaching of Christ as the finest system of morality in the world; and his parables, such as "The Prodigal Son"—"The Good Samaritan"—"The Lost Sheep," &c. as models of divine goodness. And if I could only hear a preacher take these for his texts, and paint them in those rich colours they are capable of, I would never stay from meeting. But now, father, when I go, instead of those benevolent preachings and parables which Christ so delighted in, I hardly ever hear any thing but lean, chaffy discourses about the TRINITY, and BAPTISMS, and ELECTIONS, and REPROBATIONS, and FINAL PERSEVERANCES, and COVENANTS, and a thousand other such things which do not strike my fancy as religion at all, because not in the least calculated, as I think, to sweeten and ennoble men's natures, and make them love and do good to one another."

"There is too much truth in your remark, Ben; and I have often been sorry that our preachers lay such stress on these things, and do not stick closer to the preachings of Christ."

"Stick closer to them, father! O no, to do them justice, sir, we must not charge them with not *sticking to the text*, for they never take Christ for their text, but some dark passage out of the prophets or apostles, which will better suit their gloomy education. Or if they should, by some lucky hit, honour Christ for a text, they quickly give him the *go-by* and lug in Calvin or some other angry doctor; and then in place of the soft showers of Gospel pity on sinners, we have nothing but the dreadful thunderings of eternal hate, with the unavailing screams of little children in hell not a span long! Now, father, as I do not look on such preaching as this to be any ways pleasing to the Deity or profitable to man, I choose to stay at home and read my books; and this is the reason, I suppose, why my brother James and the council-men here of Boston think that I have no religion."

"Your strictures on some of our ministers, my son, are in rather a strong style: but still there is too much truth in them to be denied. However, as to what your brother James and the council think of you, it is of little consequence, provided you but possess true religion."

"Aye, TRUE RELIGION, father, is another thing; and I should like to possess it. But as to such religion as theirs, I must confess, father, I never had and never wish to have it."

"But what do you mean by *their* religion, my son?"

"Why, I mean, father, a religion of gloomy forms and notions, that have no tendency to make men good and happy, either in themselves or to others."

"So then, my son, you make *man's happiness* the end of religion."

"Certainly I do, father."

"Our catechisms, Ben, make *God's glory* the end of religion."

"That amounts to the same thing, father; as the framers of the catechisms, I suppose, placed God's glory in the happiness of man."

"But why do you suppose that so readily, Ben?"

"Because, father, all wise workmen place their glory in the perfection of their works. The gunsmith glories in his rifle, when she never misses her aim; the clockmaker glories in his clock when she tells the time exactly. They thus glory, because their works answer the ends for which they were made. Now God, who is wiser than all workmen, had, no doubt, his ends in making man. But certainly he could not have made him with a view of getting any thing from him, seeing man has nothing to give. And as God, from his own infinite riches, has a boundless power to give; and from his infinite benevolence, must have an equal delight in giving, I can see no end so likely for his making man as to make him happy. I think, father, all this looks quite reasonable."

"Why, yes, to be sure, Ben, it does look very reasonable indeed."

"Well then, father, since all wise workmen glory in their works when they answer the ends for which they designed them, God must glory in the happiness of man, that being the end for which he made him."

"This seems, indeed, Ben, to be perfectly agreeable to reason."

"Yes, sir, not only to *reason*, but to *nature* too: for even nature, I think, father, in all her operations, clearly teaches that God must take an exceeding glory in our happiness; for what else could have led him to build for us such a noble world as this; adorned with so much beauty; stored with such treasures; peopled with so many fair creatures; and lighted up as it is with such gorgeous luminaries by day and by night?"

"I am glad, my son, I touched on this subject of religion in the way I did; your mode of thinking and reasoning on it pleases me greatly. But now taking all this for granted, what is still your idea of the true religion?"

"Why, father, if God thus places his glory in the happiness of man, does it not follow that the most acceptable thing that man can do for God, or in other words, that the true religion of man consists in his so living, as to attain the highest possible perfection and happiness of his nature, that being the chief end and glory of the Deity in creating him?"

"Well, but how is this to be done?"

"Certainly, father, by imitating the Deity."

"By imitating him, child! but how are we to imitate him?"

"In his goodness, father."

"But why do you pitch on his GOODNESS rather than on any other of his attributes?"

"Because, father, this seems, evidently, the prince of all his other attributes, and greater than all."

"Take care child, that you do not blaspheme. How can one of God's attributes be greater than another, when all are infinite?"

"Why, father, must not that which moves be greater than that which is moved?"

"What am I to understand by that, Ben?"

"I mean, father, that the power and wisdom of the Deity, though both unspeakably great, would probably stand still and do nothing for men, were they not moved to it by his goodness. His goodness then, which comes and puts his power and wisdom into motion, and thus fills heaven and earth with happiness, must be the greatest of all his attributes."

"I don't know what to say to that, Ben; certainly his power and wisdom must be very great too."

"Yes, father, they are very great indeed: but still they seem but subject to his *greater benevolence* which enlists them in its service and constantly gives them its own delightful work to do. For example, father, the wisdom and power of the Deity can do any thing, but his benevolence takes care that they shall do nothing but for good. The power and wisdom of the Deity could have made changes both in the earth and heavens widely different from their present state. They could, for instance, have placed the sun a great deal farther off or a great deal nearer to us. But then in the first case we should have been frozen to icicles, and in the second scorched to cinders. The power of the Deity could have given a tenfold force to the winds, but then no tree could have stood on the land, and no ship could have sailed on the seas. The power of the Deity could also have made changes as great in all other parts of nature; it could have made every fish as monstrous as a whale, every bird dreadful as the condor, every beast as vast as the elephant, and every tree as big as a mountain. But then it must strike every one that these changes would all have been utterly for the worse, rendering these noble parts of nature comparatively useless to us.—I say the power of the Deity could have done all this, and might have so done but for his benevolence, which would not allow such discords, but has, on the contrary, established all things on a scale of the exactest harmony with the convenience and happiness of man. Now, for example, father, the sun, though placed at an enormous distance from us, is placed at the very distance he should be for all the important purposes of light and heat; so that the earth and waters, neither frozen nor burnt, enjoy the temperature fittest for life and vegetation. Now the meadows are covered with grass; the fields with corn; the trees with leaves and fruits; presenting a spectacle of universal beauty and plenty, feasting all senses and gladdening all hearts; while man, the favoured lord of all, looking around him amidst the mingled singing of birds and skipping of beasts and leaping of fishes, is struck with wonder at the beauteous scenery, and gratefully acknowledges that benevolence is the darling attribute of the Deity."

"I thank God, my son, for giving you wisdom to reason in this way. But what is still your inference from all this, as to true religion?"

"Why, my dear father, my inference is still in confirmation of my first answer to your question relative to the true religion, that it consists in our imitating the Deity in his goodness. Every wise parent, wishing to allure his children to any particular virtue, is careful to set them the fairest examples of the same, as knowing that example is more powerful than precept. Now since the Deity, throughout all his works, so invariably employs his great power and wisdom as the ministers of his benevolence to make his creatures happy, what can this be for but an example to us; teaching that if we wish to please him—the true end of all religion—we must imitate him in his moral goodness, which if we would but all do as steadily as he does, we should recall the golden age, and convert this world into Paradise.

"All this looks very fair, Ben; but yet after all what are we to do without FAITH?"

"Why, father, as to Faith, I cannot say; not knowing much about it. But this I can say, that I am afraid of any substitutes to the moral character of the Deity. In short, sir, I don't love the fig-leaf."

"Fig-leaf! I don't understand you, child: what do you mean by the fig-leaf?"

"Why, father, we read in the Bible that soon as Adam had lost that true image of the Deity, his MORAL GOODNESS, instead of striving to recover it again, he went and sewed fig-leaves together to cover himself with."

"Stick to the point, child."

"I am to the point, father. I mean to say that as Adam sought a vain fig-leaf covering, rather than the imitation of the Deity in moral goodness, so his posterity have ever since been fond of running after fig-leaf substitutes."

"Aye! well I should be glad to hear you explain a little on that head, Ben."

"Father, I don't pretend to explain a subject I don't understand, but I find in PLUTARCH'S LIVES and the HEATHEN ANTIQUITIES, which I read in your old divinity library, and which no doubt give a true account of religion among the ancients, that when they were troubled on account of their crimes, they do not seem once to have thought of conciliating the Deity by *reformation*, and by acts of benevolence and goodness to be like him. No, they appear to have been too much enamoured of lust, and pride, and revenge, to relish moral goodness; such lessons were too much against the grain. But still something must be done to appease the Deity. Well then, since they could not sum up courage enough to attempt it by imitating his goodness, they would try it by coaxing his vanity—they would build him grand temples; and make him mighty sacrifices; and rich offerings. This I am told, father, was *their* fig-leaf."

"Why this, I fear, Ben, is a true bill against the poor Heathens."

"Well, I am sure, father, the Jews were equally fond of the fig-leaf; as their own countrymen, the Prophets, are constantly charging them. JUSTICE, MERCY, and TRUTH had, it seems, no charms for them. They must have fig-leaf substitutes, such as tythings of *mint*, *anise*, and *cummmin*, and making '*long prayers in the streets*,' and deep groanings with '*disfigured faces in the synagogues*.' If they but did all this, then surely they must be Abraham's children even though they devoured widows' houses."

Here good old Josias groaned.

"Yes, father," continued Ben, "and it were well if the rage for the fig-leaf stopped with the Jews and Heathens; but the Christians are just as fond of substitutes that may save them the labour of imitating the Deity in his moral goodness. It is true, the old Jewish hobbies, mint, anise, and cummin, are not the hobbies of Christians; but still, father, you are not to suppose that they are to be disheartened for all that. Oh no. They have got a hobby worth all of them put together—they have got FAITH."

Here good old Josias began to darken; and looking at Ben with great solemnity, said, "I am afraid, my son, you do not treat this great article of our holy religion with sufficient reverence."

"My dear father," replied Ben eagerly, "I mean not the least reflection on FAITH, but solely on those hypocrites who abuse it to countenance their vices and crimes."

"O then, if that be your aim, go on, Ben, go on."

"Well, sir, as I was saying, not only the Jews and Heathens, but the Christians also have their fig-leaf substitutes for *Moral Goodness*. Because Christ has said that so great is the DIVINE CLEMENCY, that if even the worst of men will but have faith in it so as to repent and amend their lives by the golden law of '*love and good works*,' they should be saved, many lazy Christians are fond of overlooking those excellent conditions 'LOVE AND GOOD WORKS,' which constitute the moral image of the Deity, and fix upon the word FAITH for their salvation."

"Well, but child, do you make no account of faith?"

"None, father, as a fig-leaf cloak of immorality."

"But is not faith a great virtue in itself, and a qualification for heaven?"

"I think not, sir; I look on faith but as a *mean* to beget that *moral goodness*, which, to me, appears to be the only qualification for Heaven."

"I am astonished, child, to hear you say that faith is not a virtue in itself."

"Why, father, the Bible says for me in a thousand places. The Bible says that *faith without good works is dead*."

"But does not the Bible, in a thousand places, say that without faith no man can please God?"

"Yes, father, and for the best reason in the world; for who can ever hope to please the Deity without his moral image? and who would ever put himself to the trouble to cultivate the virtues which form that image, unless he had a belief that they were indispensible to the perfection and happiness of his nature?"

"So then, you look on faith as no virtue in itself, and good for nothing unless it exalt men to the likeness of God?"

"Yes, sir, as good for nothing unless it exalt us to the likeness of God—nay, as worse; as utterly vile and hypocritical."

"And perhaps you view in the same light the IMPUTED RIGHTEOUSNESS, and the Sacraments of BAPTISM and the LORD'S SUPPER."

"Yes, father, faith, imputed righteousness, sacraments, prayers, sermons; all, all I consider as mere barren fig-leaves which will yield no good unless they ripen into the fruits of BENEVOLENCE and GOOD WORKS."

"Well, Ben, 'tis well that you have taken a turn to the printing business; for I don't think, child, that if you had studied divinity, as your uncle Ben and myself once wished, you would ever have got a *licence* to preach."

"No, father, I know that well enough; I know that many who think themselves mighty good Christians, are for getting to heaven on easier terms than imitating the Deity in his moral goodness. To them, faith and imputed righteousness, and sacraments, and sour looks, are very convenient things. With a good stock of these they can easily manage matters so as to make a little morality go a great way. But I am thinking they will have to *back out* of this error, otherwise they will make as bad a hand of their barren faith, as the poor Virginia negroes do of their boasted freedom."

"God's mercy, child, what do you mean by that?"

"Why, father, I am told that the Virginia negroes, like our faith-mongers, fond of ease and glad of soft substitutes to hard duties, are continually sighing for freedom; '*O if they had but freedom! if they had but freedom! how happy should they be! They should not then be obliged to work any more. Freedom would do every thing for them. Freedom would spread soft beds for them, and heap their tables with roast pigs, squealing out, 'come and eat me.' Freedom would give them fine jackets, and rivers of grog, and mountains of segars and tobacco, without their sweating for it.*' Well, by and by, they get their freedom; perhaps by running away from their masters. And now see what great things has freedom done for them. Why, as it is out of the question to think of *work* now they are *free*, they must give themselves up like gentlemen, to visiting, sleeping, and pastime. In a little time the curses of hunger and nakedness drive them to stealing and house-breaking, for which their backs are ploughed up at whipping-posts, or their necks snapped under the gallows! and all this because they must needs live easier than by honest labour, which would have crowned their days with character and comfort. So, father, it is, most exactly so it is, with too many of our FAITH-MONGERS. They have not courage to practise those exalted virtues that would give them the moral likeness of the Deity. Oh no: they must get to heaven in some easier way. They have heard great things of faith. Faith, they are told, has done wonders for other people; why not for them? Accordingly they fall to work and after many a hard throe of fanaticism, they conceit they have got faith sure enough. And now they are happy. Like the poor Virginia negroes, they are clear of all *moral working now*: thank God they can get to heaven without it; yes, and may take some indulgences, by the way, into the bargain. If, as jovial fellows, they should waste their time and family substance in drinking rum and smoking tobacco, where's the harm, *an't they sound believers*? If they should, as *merchants*, sand their sugar, or water their molasses, what great matter is that? Don't they keep up family prayer? If, as men of HONOUR, they should accept a challenge, and receive a shot in a duel, what of that? They have only to send for a priest, and take the sacrament. Thus, father, as freedom has proved the ruin of many a lazy Virginian negro, so I am afraid that such faith as this has made many an hypocritical christian ten times more a child of the devil than he was before."

Good old Josias, who, while Ben was speaking at this rate, had appeared much agitated, sometimes frowning, sometimes smiling, here replied, with a deep sigh, "Yes, Ben, this is all too true to be denied: and a sad thing it is that mankind should be so ready, as you observe, to go to heaven *in any other way* than by imitating God in his *moral likeness*. But I rejoice in hope of you, my son, that painting this lamentable depravity in such strong colours as you do, you will ever act on wiser and more magnanimous principles."

"Father, I don't affect to be better than other young men, yet I think I can safely say, that if I could get to heaven by playing the hypocrite I would not, while I have it in my choice to go thither by acquiring the virtues that would give me a resemblance to God. For to say nothing of the exceeding honour of acquiring even the *faintest resemblance* of him, nor yet of the immense happiness which it must afford hereafter, I find that even here, and young as I am, the least step towards it, affords a greater pleasure than any thing else; indeed I find that there is so much more pleasure in getting knowledge to resemble the Creator, than in living in ignorance to resemble brutes; so much more pleasure in BENEVOLENCE and DOING GOOD to resemble him, than in *hate* and *doing harm* to resemble demons, that I hope I shall always have wisdom and fortitude sufficient even for my own sake, to spend my life in getting all the useful knowledge, and in doing all the little good I possibly can."

"God Almighty confirm my son in the wise resolutions which his grace has enabled him thus early to form!"

"Yes, father, and besides all this, when I look towards futurity; when I consider the nature of that felicity which exists in heaven; that it is a felicity flowing from the smiles of the Deity on those excellent spirits whom his own admonitions have adorned with the virtues that resemble himself; that the more perfect their virtues, the brighter will be his smiles upon them, with correspondent emanations of bliss that may, for aught we know, be for ever enlarged with their ever enlarging understandings and affections; I say, father, when I have it in my choice to attain to all this in a way so pleasant and honourable as that of imitating the Deity in WISDOM and GOODNESS, should I not be worse than mad to decline it on such terms, and prefer substitutes that would tolerate me in *ignorance* and *vice*?"

"Yes, child, I think you would be mad indeed."

"Yes, father, especially when it is recollected, that if the ignorant and vicious could, with all their pains, find out substitutes that would serve as passports to heaven, they could not rationally expect a hearty welcome there. For as the Deity delights in the wise and good, because they resemble him in those qualities which render him so amiable and happy, and would render all his creatures so too; so he must proportionably abhor the STUPID and VICIOUS, because deformed with qualities diametrically opposite to his own, and tending to make both themselves and others most vile and miserable."

"This is awfully true, Ben; for the Bible tells us, that the *wicked are an abomination to the Lord; but that the righteous are his delight.*"

"Yes, father, and this is the language not only of the BIBLE, which is, perhaps, the grand class book of the Deity, but it is also the language of his first or *horn* book, I mean REASON, which teaches, that if '*there be a God, and that there is all nature cries aloud through all her works, he must delight in virtue,*' because most clearly conducive to the perfection of mankind; which must be the chief aim and glory of the Deity in creating them. And for the same reason he must abhor vice, because tending to the disgrace and destruction of his creatures. Hence, father, I think it follows as clearly as a demonstration in mathematics, that if it were possible for bad men, through *faith*, *imputed righteousness*, or any other leaf-covering, to get to Paradise, so far from meeting with any thing like cordiality from the Deity, they would be struck speechless at sight of their horrible dissimilarity to him. For while he delights above all things in giving life, and the duellist glories in destroying it; while he delights in heaping his creatures with good things, and the gambler triumphs in stripping them; while he delights in seeing love and smiles among brethren, and the slanderer in promoting strifes and hatreds; while he delights in exalting the intellectual and moral faculties to the highest degree of heavenly wisdom and virtue, and the drunkard delights in polluting and degrading both below the brutes; what cordiality can ever subsist between such opposite natures? Can infinite purity and benevolence behold such monsters with complacency, or could they in his presence otherwise than be filled with intolerable pain and anguish, and fly away as weak-eyed owls from the blaze of the meridian sun?"

"Well, Ben, as I said before, I am richly rewarded for having drawn you into this conversation about religion; your language indeed is not always the language of the scriptures; neither do you rest your hopes, as I could have wished, on the *Redeemer*; but still your idea in placing our qualification for heaven in resembling God in *moral goodness*, is truly evangelical, and I hope you *will one day become* a great christian."

"I thank you, father, for your good wishes; but I am afraid I shall never be the christian you wish me to be."

"What, not a christian!"

"No, father, at least not in the *name*; but in the nature I hope to become a christian. And now, father, as we part to-morrow, and there is a strong presentiment on my mind that it may be a long time before we meet again, I beg you to believe of me that I shall never lose sight of my great obligations to an active pursuit of knowledge and usefulness. This, if persevered in, will give me some humble resemblance of the great Author of my being in loving and doing all the good I can to mankind. And then, if I live, I hope, my dear father, I shall give you the joy to see realized some of the fond expectations you have formed of me. And if I should die, I shall die in hope of meeting you in some better world, where you will no more be alarmed for my welfare, nor I grieved to see you conflicting with age and labour and sorrow: but where we may see in each other all that we can conceive of what we call ANGELS, and in scenes of undeserved splendour, dwell with those enlightened and benevolent spirits, whose conversation and perfect virtues, will for ever delight us. And where, to crown all, we shall perhaps, at times, be permitted to see that UNUTTERABLE BEING, whose disinterested goodness was the spring of all these felicities."

Thus ended this curious dialogue, between one of the most amiable parents, and one of the most acute and sagacious youths that our country, or perhaps any other has ever produced.

CHAPTER XVIII.

The three days of Ben's promised stay with his father being expired, the next morning he embraced his parents and embarked a second time for Philadelphia, but with a much lighter heart than before, because he now left home with his parents' blessing, which they gave him the more willingly as from the dark *sanctified* frown on poor James' brow they saw in him no disposition towards reconciliation.

The vessel happening to touch at Newport, Ben gladly took that opportunity to visit his favourite brother John, who received him with great joy. John was always of the mind that Ben would one day or other become a great man; "*he was so vastly fond*," he said, "*of his book*."

And when he saw the elegant size that Ben's person had now attained, and also his fine mind-illuminated face and manly wit, he was so proud of him that he could not rest until he had introduced him to all his friends. Among the rest was a gentleman of the name of Vernon, who was so pleased with Ben during an evening's visit at his brother's, that he gave him an order on a man in Pennsylvania for thirty pounds, which he begged he would collect for him. Ben readily accepted the order, not without being secretly pleased that nature had given him a face which this stranger had so readily credited with thirty pounds.

Caressed by his brother John and by his brother John's friends, Ben often thought that if he were called on to point out the time in his whole life that had been spent more pleasantly than the rest, he would, without hesitation, pitch on this his three days' visit to Newport.

But alas! he has soon brought to cry out with the poet,

"The brightest things beneath the sky,

Yield but a glimmering light;

We should *suspect some danger nigh*,

Where we possess *delight*."

His thirty pound order from Vernon, was at first ranked among his dear honied delights enjoyed at Newport; but it soon presented, as we shall see, a roughsting. This however, was but a flea bite in comparison of that mortal wound he was within an ace of receiving from this same Newport trip. The story is this: Among a considerable cargo of live lumber which they took on board for Philadelphia, were three females, a couple of gay young damsels, and a grave old Quaker lady. Following the natural bent of his disposition, Ben paid great attention to the old Quaker. Fortunate was it for him that he did; for in consequence of it she took a motherly interest in his welfare that saved him from a very ugly scrape. Perceiving that he was getting rather too fond of the two young women above, she drew him aside one day, and with the looks and speech of a mother, said, "Young man, I am in pain for thee: thou hast no parent to watch over thy conduct, and thou seemest to be quite ignorant of the world and the snares to which youth is exposed. I pray thee rely upon what I tell thee.—These are women of bad character; I perceive it in all their actions. If thou dost not take care they will lead thee into danger!!"

As he appeared at first not to think so ill of them as she did, the old lady related of them many things she had seen and heard, and which had escaped his attention, but which convinced him she was in the right. He thanked her for such good advice, and promised to follow it.

On their arrival at New-York the girls told him where they lived, and invited him to come and see them. Their eyes kindled such a glow along his youthful veins that he was on the point of melting into consent. But the motherly advice of his old quaker friend happily coming to his aid, revived his wavering virtue, and fixed him in the resolution, though much against the grain, *not to go.* It was a most blessed thing for him that he did not; for the captain missing a silver spoon and some other things from the cabin, and knowing these women to be prostitutes, procured a search warrant, and finding his goods in their possession, had them brought to the whipping-post.

As God would have it, Ben happened to fall in with the constable and crowd who were taking them to whip. He would fain have run off. But there was a drawing of sympathy towards them which he could not resist: so on he went with the rest. He said afterwards that it was well he did: for when he beheld these poor devils tied up to the stake, and also their sweet faces distorted with terror and pain, and heard their piteous screams under the strokes of the cowhide on their bleeding backs, he could not help melting into tears, at the same time saying to himself—"now had I but *yielded to the allurements of these poor creatures, and made myself an accessary to their crimes and sufferings, what would now be my feelings*!"

From the happy escape which he had thus made through the seasonable advice of the good old quaker lady he learned that acts of this sort hold the first place on the list of charities: and entered it as a resolution on his journal that he would imitate it and do all in his power to open the eyes of all, but especially of the young, to a timely sense of the follies and dangers that beset them. How well he kept his promise, will, 'tis likely, gentle reader, be remembered by thousands when you and I are forgotten.

CHAPTER XIX.

On the arrival of the vessel at New-York, Ben went up to a tavern, and lo! who should he first cast his eyes on there, but his old friend Collins, of Boston!

Collins had, it seems, been so charmed with Ben's account of Philadelphia, that he came to the determination to try his fortune there also; and learning that Ben was shortly to return by the way of New-York, he had jumped into the first vessel, and was there before him, waiting his arrival. Great was the joy of Ben at the sight of his friend Collins, for it drew after it a train of the most pleasant recollections.—But who can describe his feelings, when flying to embrace that long esteemed youth, he beheld him now risen from his chair equally eager for the embrace, but alas! only able to make a staggering step or two before down he came sprawling on the floor, drunk as a lord!

To see a young man of his wit—his eloquence—his education—his hitherto unstained character and high promise, thus overwhelmed by a worse than brutal vice, would have been a sad sight to Ben, even though that young man had been an entire stranger. But oh! how tenfold sad to see such marks of ruinous dishonour on one so dear, and from whom he had expected so much.

Ben had just returned from assisting to put poor Collins to bed, when the captain of the vessel which had brought him to New-York, stepped up and in a very respectful manner put a note into his hand.—Ben opened it, not without considerable agitation, and read as follows:—

"G. Burnet's compliments await young Mr. Franklin—and should be glad of half an hour's chat with him over a glass of wine."

"G. Burnet!" said Ben, "who can that be?"

"Why, 'tis the governor," replied the captain with a smile. "I have just been to see him, with some letters I brought for him from Boston. And when I told him what a world of books you have, he expressed a curiosity to see you, and begged I would return with you to his palace."

Ben instantly set off with the captain, but not without a sigh as he cast a look back on the door of poor Collins' bed-room, to think what an honour that wretched young man had lost for the sake of two or three vile gulps of filthy grog.

The governor's looks, at the approach of Ben, showed somewhat of disappointment. He had, it seems, expected considerable entertainment from Ben's conversation. But his fresh and ruddy countenance showed him so much younger than he had counted on, that he gave up all his promised entertainment as a lost hope. He received Ben, however, with great politeness, and after pressing on him a glass of wine, took him into an adjoining room, which was his library, consisting of a large and well-chosen collection.

Seeing the pleasure which sparkled in Ben's eyes as he surveyed so many elegant authors, and thought of the rich stores of knowledge which they contained, the governor, with a smile of complacency, as on a young pupil of science, said to him, "Well, Mr. Franklin, I am told by the captain here, that you have a fine collection too."

"Only a trunk full, sir," said Ben.

"A trunk full!" replied the governor. "Why, what use can you have for so many books? Young people at your age have seldom read beyond the 10th chapter of Nehemiah."

"I can't boast," replied Ben, "of having read any great deal beyond that myself; but still, I should be sorry if I could not get a trunk full of books to read every six months." At this, the governor regarding him with a look of surprise, said, "You must then, though so young, be a scholar; perhaps a teacher of the languages."

"No sir," answered Ben, "I know no language but my own."

"What, not Latin nor Greek!"

"No sir, not a word of either."

"Why, don't you think them necessary?"

"I don't set myself up as a judge. But I should not suppose them necessary."

"Aye! well, I should like to hear your reasons."

"Why, sir, I am not competent to give reasons that may satisfy a gentleman of your learning, but the following are the reasons with which I satisfy myself. I look on languages, sir, merely as arbitrary sounds of characters, whereby men communicate their ideas to each other. Now, if I already possess a language which is capable of conveying more ideas than I shall ever acquire, were it not wiser in me to improve my time in getting *sense* through that one language, than waste it in getting mere *sounds* through fifty languages, even if I could learn as many?"

Here the governor paused a moment, though not without a little red on his cheeks, for having only a minute before put Ben and the 10th chapter of Nehemiah so close together. However, catching a new idea, he took another start. "Well, but, my dear sir, you certainly differ from the learned world, which is, you know, decidedly in favour of the languages."

"I would not wish wantonly to differ from the learned world," said Ben, "especially when they maintain opinions that seem to be founded on truth. But when this is not the case, to differ from them I have ever thought my duty; and especially since I studied Locke."

"Locke!" cried the governor with surprise, "*you studied Locke!*"

"Yes, sir, I studied Locke on the Understanding three years ago, when I was thirteen."

"You amaze me, sir. You studied Locke on the Understanding at thirteen!"

"Yes, sir, I did."

"Well, and pray at what college did you study Locke at thirteen; for at Cambridge college in Old England, where I got my education, they never allowed the senior class to look at Locke till eighteen?"

"Why, sir, it was my misfortune never to be at a college, nor even at a grammar school, except nine months when I was a child."

Here the governor sprung from his seat, and staring at Ben, cried out, "the devil! well, and where—where did you get your education, pray?"

"At home, sir, in a tallow chandler's shop."

"In a tallow chandler's shop!" screamed the governor.

"Yes, sir; my father was a poor old tallow chandler, with sixteen children, and I the youngest of all. At eight he put me to school, but finding he could not spare the money from the rest of the children to keep me there, he took me home into the shop, where I assisted him by twisting the candle wicks and filling the moulds all day, and at night I read by myself. At twelve, my father bound me to my brother, a printer, in Boston, and with him I worked hard all day at the press and cases, and again read by myself at night."

Here the governor, spanking his hands together, put up a loud whistle, while his eye-balls, wild with surprise, rolled about in their sockets as if in a mighty mind to hop out. "Impossible, young man!" he exclaimed: "Impossible! you are only sounding my credulity. I can never believe one half of all this." Then turning to the captain, he said, "captain, you are an intelligent man, and from Boston; pray tell me can this young man here, be aiming at any thing but to quiz me?"

"No, indeed, please your excellency," replied the captain, "Mr. Franklin is not quizzing you. He is saying what is really true, for I am acquainted with his father and family."

The governor then turning to Ben said, more moderately, "Well, my dear wonderful boy, I ask your pardon for doubting your word; and now pray tell me, for I feel a stronger desire than ever to hear your objection to learning the dead languages."

"Why, sir, I object to it principally on account of the shortness of human life. Taking them one with another, men do not live above forty years. Plutarch, indeed, puts it only thirty-three. But say forty. Well, of this full ten years are lost in childhood, before any boy thinks of a Latin grammar. This brings the forty down to thirty. Now of such a moment as this, to spend five or six years in learning the dead languages, especially when all the best books in those languages are translated into ours, and besides, we already have more books on every subject than such short-lived creatures can ever acquire, seems very preposterous."

"Well, but what are you to do with their great poets, Virgil and Homer, for example; I suppose you would not think of translating Homer out of his rich native Greek into our poor homespun English, would you?"

"Why not, sir?"

"Why I should as soon think of transplanting a pine-apple from Jamaica to Boston."

"Well, sir, a skilful gardener, with his hot-house, can give us nearly as fine a pine-apple as any in Jamaica. And so Mr. Pope, with his fine imagination, has given us Homer, in English, with more of his beauties than ordinary scholars would find in him after forty years' study of the Greek. And besides, sir, if Homer was not translated, I am far from thinking it would be worth spending five or six years to learn to read him in his own language."

"You differ from the critics, Mr. Franklin; for the critics all tell us that his beauties are inimitable."

"Yes, sir, and the naturalists tell us that the beauties of the basilisk are inimitable too."

"The basilisk, sir! Homer compared with the basilisk! I really don't understand you, sir."

"Why, I mean, sir, that as the basilisk is the more to be dreaded for the beautiful skin that covers his poison, so Homer for the bright colourings he throws over bad characters and passions. Now, as I don't think the beauties of poetry are comparable to those of philanthropy, nor a thousandth part so important to human happiness, I must confess I dread Homer, especially as the companion of youth. The humane and gentle virtues are certainly the greatest charms and sweeteners of life. And I suppose, sir, you would hardly think of sending your son to Achilles to learn these."

"I agree he has too much revenge in his composition."

"Yes, sir, and when painted in the colours which Homer's glowing fancy lends, what youth but must run the most imminent risk of catching a spark of bad fire from such a blaze as he throws on his pictures?"

"Why this, though an uncommon view of the subject, is, I confess, an ingenious one, Mr. Franklin; but surely 'tis overstrained."

"Not at all, sir; we are told from good authority, that it was the reading of Homer that first put it into the head of Alexander the great to become a HERO: and after him of Charles the 12th. What millions of human beings have been slaughtered by these two great butchers is not known; but still probably not a tythe of what have perished in duels between individuals from the pride and revenge nursed by reading Homer."

"Well, sir," replied the governor, "I never heard the prince of bards treated in this way before. You must certainly be singular in your charges against Homer."

"I ask your pardon, sir, I have the honour to think of Homer exactly as did the greatest philosopher of antiquity; I mean Plato, who strictly forbids the reading of Homer in his republic. And yet Plato was a heathen. I don't boast myself as a christian; and yet I am shocked at the inconsistency of our Latin and Greek teachers (generally christians and DIVINES too,) who can one day put Homer into the hands of their pupils, and in the midst of their recitations can stop them short to point out the *divine beauties* and *sublimities* which the poet gives to his hero, in the bloody work of slaughtering the poor Trojans; and the next day take them to church to hear a discourse from Christ on the blessedness of meekness and forgiveness. No wonder that hot-livered young men thus educated, should despise meekness and forgiveness, as mere cowards' virtues, and deem nothing so glorious as fighting duels, and blowing out brains."

Here the governor came to a pause, like a gamester at his last trump. But perceiving Ben cast his eyes on a splendid copy of Pope's works, he suddenly seized that as a *fine* opportunity to turn the conversation. So stepping up, he placed his hand on his shoulder, and in a very familiar manner said, "Well, Mr. Franklin, there's an author that I am sure you'll not quarrel with; an author that I think you'll pronounce *faultless.*"

"Why, sir," replied Ben, "I entertain a most exalted opinion of Pope; but still, sir, I think he is not without his faults."

"It would puzzle you, I suspect, Mr. Franklin, as keen a critic as you are, to point out *one.*"

"Well, sir," answered Ben, hastily turning to the place, "what do you think of this famous couplet of Mr. Pope's—

"Immodest words admit of no defence,

For want of decency is want of sense."

"I see no fault there."

"No, indeed!" replied Ben, "why now to my mind a man can ask no better excuse for any thing wrong he does, than his *want of sense.*"

"Well, sir," said the governor, sensibly staggered, "and how would you alter it?"

"Why, sir, if I might presume to alter a line in this great Poet, I would do it in this way:—

"Immodest words admit but *this* defence—

That want of decency is want of sense."

Here the governor caught Ben in his arms as a delighted father would his son, calling out at the same time to the captain, "How greatly am I obliged to you, sir, for bringing me to an acquaintance with this charming boy? O! what a delightful thing it would be for us old fellows to converse with sprightful youth if they were but all like him!—But the d——l of it is, most parents are as blind as bats to the true glory and happiness of their children. Most parents never look higher for their sons than to see them delving like muckworms for money; or hopping about like jay-birds, in fine feathers. Hence their conversation is generally no better than froth and nonsense."

After several other handsome compliments on Ben, and the captain expressing a wish to be going, the governor shook hands with Ben, begging at the same time that he would for ever consider him as one of his fastest friends, and also never came to New-York without coming to see him.

CHAPTER XX.

On returning to the tavern, he hastened into his chamber, where he found his drunken comrade, poor Collins, in a fine perspiration, and considerably sobered, owing to the refrigerating effects of a pint of strong sage tea, with a tea-spoonful of saltpetre, which Ben, before he set out to the governor's, had pressed on him as a remedy he had somewhere read, much in vogue among the London topers, to *cool off* after a rum fever. Collins appeared still to have enough of brandy in him for a frolic; but when Ben came to tell him of the amiable governor Burnet, in whose company, at his own palace, he had spent a most delightful evening; and also to remind him of the golden opportunity he had lost, of forming an acquaintance with that noble gentleman, poor Collins wept bitterly.

Ben was exceedingly affected to see him in tears, and endeavoured to comfort him. But he refused comfort. He said, "if this had been the *first time*, he should not himself think much of it; but he candidly confessed, that for a long time he had been guilty of it, though till of late he had always kept it to himself, drinking in his chamber. But now he felt at times," he said, "an awful apprehension that he was a *lost man.* His cravings for liquor were so strong on the one hand, and on the other his powers of resistance so feeble, that it put him fearfully in mind of the dismal state of a poor wretch, within the fatal attraction of a whirlpool, whose resistless suction, in spite of all his feeble efforts, was hurrying him down to sure and speedy destruction."

Collins, who was exceedingly eloquent on every subject, but especially on one so nearly affecting himself, went on deploring his misfortune in strains so tender and pathetic, that Ben, whose eyes were fountains ever ready to flow at the voice of sorrow, could not refrain from weeping, which he did most unfeignedly for a long esteemed friend now going to ruin. He could bear, he said, to see the brightest plumed bird, charmed by the rattle-snake, descending into the horrid sepulchre of the monster's jaws. He could bear to see the richest laden Indiaman, dismasted and rudderless, drifting ashore on the merciless breakers; because made of dust, these things must at any rate return to dust, again. But to see an immortal mind stopped in her first soarings, entangled and limed in the filth of so brutal a vice as drunkenness—that was a sight he could not bear. And as a mother looking on her child that is filleted for the accursed Moloch, cannot otherwise than shed tears, so Ben, when he looked on poor Collins, could not but weep when he saw him the victim of destruction.

However, as a good wit turns every thing to advantage, this sudden and distressing fall of poor Collins, set Ben to thinking: and the result of his thoughts noted down in his journal of that day, deserves the attention of all young men of this day; and even will as long as human nature endures.

"Wit," says he, "in young men, is dangerous, because apt to breed vanity, which, when disappointed, brings them down, and by depriving them of *natural* cheerfulness, drives them to the bottle for that which is *artificial.*— And learning also is dangerous, when it is aimed at as an *end* and not a *mean.* A young man who aspires to be learned merely for *fame*, is in danger; for, familiarity breeding contempt, creates an uneasy void that drives him to the bottle. Hence so many learned men with red noses. But when a man from a benevolent heart, seeks learning for the sublime pleasure of imitating the Deity in *doing good*, he is always made so happy in the spirit and pursuit of this godlike object, that he needs not the stimulus of brandy."

This one hint, if duly reflected on by young men, would render the name of Franklin dear to them for ever.

CHAPTER XXI.

The next day, when they came to settle with the tavern-keeper, and Ben with his usual alacrity had paraded his dollars for payment, poor Collins hung back, pale and dumb-founded, as a truant school-boy at the call to recitation. The truth is, the fumes of his brandy having driven all the wit out of his noddle, had puffed it up with such infinite vanity, that he must needs turn in, red faced and silly as he was, to gamble with the cool-headed water-drinking sharpers of New-York. The reader hardly need be informed, that poor Collins' pistareens, which he had scraped together for this expedition, were to these light-fingered gentlemen as a fry of young herrings to the hungry dog-fish.

Ben was now placed in a most awkward predicament. To pay off Collins' scores at New-York, and also his expenses on the road to Philadelphia, would drain him to the last farthing. But how could he leave in distress a young friend with whom he had passed so many happy days and nights in the elegant pleasure of literature, and for whom he had contracted such an attachment! Ben could not bear the idea, especially as his young friend, if left in this sad condition, might be driven to despair; so drawing his purse he paid off Collins' bill, which, from the quantity of liquor he had drank, was swelled to a serious amount; and taking him by the arm, set out with a heart much heavier than his purse, which indeed was now so empty that had it not been replenished at Bristol by the thirty pounds for which, as we have seen, Vernon gave him an order on a gentleman living there, who readily paid it, would never have carried him and his drunken companion to Philadelphia. On their arrival Collins endeavoured to procure employment as a merchant's clerk, and paraded with great confidence his letters of recommendation. But his breath betrayed him. And the merchants would have nothing to say to him notwithstanding all his letters; he continued, therefore, to lodge and board with Ben at his expense. Nor was this all; for knowing that Ben had Vernon's money, he was continually craving loans of it, promising to pay as soon as he should get into business. By thus imposing on Ben's friendship, getting a little of him at one time, and a little at another, he had at last got so much of it, that when Ben, who had gone on *lending* without taking note, came to count Vernon's money, he could hardly find a dollar to count!

It is not easy to describe the agitation of Ben's mind on making this discovery; nor the alternate chill and fever, that discoloured his cheeks, as he reflected on his own egregious folly in this affair. "What demon," said he to himself, as he bit his lip, "could have put it into my head to tell Collins that I had Vernon's money! Didn't I know that a drunkard has no more reason in him than a hog; and can no better be satisfied, unless like him he is eternally pulling at his filthy swill? And have I indeed been all this time throwing away Vernon's money for brandy to addle the brain of this poor *self-made* brute? Well then, I am served exactly as I deserve, for thus making myself a pander to his vices. But now that the money is all gone, and I without a shilling to replace it, what's to be done? Vernon will, no doubt, soon learn that I have collected his money; and will of course be daily expecting to hear from me. But what can I write? To tell him that I have collected his money, but lent it to a poor, pennyless sot, will sound like a pretty story, to a man of business! And if I don't write to him, what will he think of me, and what will become of that high opinion he had formed of me, on which it appeared he would have trusted me with thousands? So you see, I have got myself into a pretty hobble. And worse than all yet, how shall I ever again lift up my booby face to my affectionate brother John, after having thus basely stabbed him, through his friend, as also through the honour of our family! O my dear, dear old father; now I see your wisdom and my own folly! A thousand times did you tell me I was too young; too inexperienced yet, to undertake by myself.—But no. It would not all do. For the life of you, you could not lead or drive such divine counsel into this conceited noddle of mine. I despised it as the *weakness of old age*, and much too *slow* for me. I wanted to save time, and get three or four years ahead of other young men; and that tempted me to disobedience. Well, I am justly punished for it! My bubble is broke. And now I see I shall be thrown back as long as if I had continued the apprentice of my brother James!!"

O young men! young men! you that with segars in your mouths, and faces flushed with libations of whiskey, can fancy yourselves *clever fellows*, and boast the long list of your *dear friends*, O think of the curses that Ben bestowed on his dear friend Collins, for bringing him in such a scrape; and learn that an idle, drinking rascal has no friends. If you think otherwise, it is only a proof that you don't even yet understand the meaning of the word. FRIENDS indeed! you talk of friends! What, *you*, who instead of nobly pressing on for VIRTUE and KNOWLEDGE and WEALTH, to make yourselves an honour and blessing to your connexions, are constantly, by your drunken and gambling courses, making yourselves a disgrace and curse to them. And when, like that fool in the parable, your all is gone, then, instead of modestly going with him into the fields, to feed the swine, you have the impudence to quarter your rags and red noses on your *dear friends*, spunging and borrowing of them as long as they'll lend. And if at last, they should get wise enough to refuse such unconscionable leechers, as would suck every drop of their blood, instantly you can turn tail and abuse your *dear friends* as though they were pick-pockets.—Witness now master Collins.

Just as Ben was in the midst of his fever and pet, on discovering as aforesaid, the great injury which Collins had done him, who but that promising youth should come in, red faced and blowzy, and with extreme confidence, demand of him a couple of dollars. Ben, rather tartly, replied that he had no more to spare. "Pshaw," answered Collins, "'tis only a brace of dollars I want, just to treat an old Boston acquaintance I fell in with at the tavern, and you know Vernon tipt you 'the shiners' t'other day to the tune of a round hundred." "Yes," replied Ben, "but what with two dollars at one time, and two at another, you have taken nearly the whole." "Well, man, and what of that," rejoined Collins, swaggeringly; "suppose I had taken the *whole*; yes, and twice as much, sha'nt I get into fine business presently, some head clerk's place, or governor's secretary? And then you'll see how I'll tumble you in the *yellow boys* hand over hand, and pay you off these little beggarly items all at a dash."

"*Fair words, Mr. Collins*," answered Ben, "*butter no parsnips*. And you have been so long talking at this rate, and yet doing nothing, that I really am afraid——"

"Afraid, the d——l," interrupted Collins, insultingly, "afraid of what? But see here, Mr. Franklin, I came to you, not to preach to me, but to lend me a couple of dollars. And now all that you have to do is just to tell me, at a word, whether you can lend them or not."

"Well then, at a word, I cannot," said Ben.

"Well then, you are an ungrateful fellow," retorted Collins.

"Ungrateful?" asked Ben, utterly astonished.

"Yes, an ungrateful fellow," replied Collins. "You dare not deny, sir, that it was I who first took you out of the tallow pots and grease of your old father's candle shop in Boston, and made a man of you. And now after all, when I only ask you to lend me a couple of shabby dollars to treat a friend, you can refuse me! Well, keep your dollars to yourself and be d——d for an ungrateful fellow as you are!" then wheeling on his heel he went off, blustering and swollen with passion, as though he had been most outrageously ill-treated. Soon as Ben had recovered himself a little from the stupefaction into which this tornado of Collins had thrown him, he clapped his hands, and rolling up his eyes like one devoutly given, exclaimed, "O Ulysses, well called wise! You, though a heathen, could lash your sailors to the mast to keep them from going ashore to be made hogs of at the *grog shops of Circe*, while I, the son of an old presbyterian christian, the son of his old age, and heir elect of all his wisdom, have been here now for weeks together, lending money to brutalize my own friend! Would to heaven, I had been but half as wise as you, I should not have been so shamefully fleeced, and now so grossly insulted by this young swine, Collins. But what brain of man could have suspected this of him? After taking him out of the stye of a jug tavern in New-York, where he was up to the back in dirt and debt—after paying all his expenses to Philadelphia, and here supporting him cheerfully, out of my hard and scanty earnings;—after submitting, for cheapness sake, to sleep in the same bed with him every night, scorched with his rum-fevered flesh, drenched in his nocturnal sweats, and poisoned with his filthy breath; and still worse, after lending him nearly the whole of Vernon's money, and thereby brought my own silly nose to the grindstone, perhaps for many a doleful year, I should now at last be requited with all this abuse: d—n—d for an *ungrateful fellow*!! Well, I don't know where all this is to end; but I will still hope for the best. I hope it will teach me this important lesson, never to have any thing to do with a *sot* again, as long as I live. But stop, though I refused him money to get drunk with, I still feel a friendship for this wretched young man, this Collins; and will still work to support him, while he stays with me. It is likely that now, that he can get no more money from me, he will take his departure; and then, if my senses remain, I think I will for ever hereafter shun, as I would a beast, the young man who drinks *drams and grog*."

From his going off in such a pet, Ben had supposed at first, that Collins would not return again. But having no money nor friends in Philadelphia, the poor fellow came back at night, to his old roosting place with Ben, by whom he was received with the same good humour as if nothing had happened. But though the injured may forgive, the injurer seldom does. Collins never looked straight at Ben after this. The recollection of the past kept him sore. And to be dependent on one whom, in the pride of former days, he had thought his inferior, rendered his condition so uneasy, that he longed for an opportunity to get out of it. Fortunately an opportunity soon offered. The captain of a trader to the West Indies, falling in with him one day at a tavern, where he was spouting away at a most elegant rate, was so charmed with his vivacity and wit, which most young fools, half shaved, are apt to figure in, that he offered him the place of a private tutor in a rich family in Jamaica. Dame fortune, in her best humour, with all her cogged dice in the bargain, could not, as Collins himself thought, have thrown him a luckier hit. Young black eyed creoles, with fourth proof spirit, in all its delicious modifications, of *slings, bumbo and punch*, dancing before his delighted fancy, in such mazes of pleasurable promise, that 'tis likely he would hardly have exchanged places with the grand Turk. With a countenance glowing with joy, he hastened to Ben to tell him the glorious news, and to take leave. After heartily congratulating him on his good fortune, Ben asked, if he would not want a little money to *fit him out*. Collins thanked him, but said that the captain, who had engaged him, was such a noble-hearted fellow, that he had, of his own accord, advanced him *three half joes* to put him into what he called "*complete sailing trim.*" Though Ben had of late been so scurvily treated by Collins, as to think it very desirable to be quit of him; yet, when the time came, he found it no such easy matter for the heart to dissolve the ties of a long and once pleasant friendship. He had passed with Collins many of his happiest hours, and these too, in the sweetest season of life, and amidst pleasures which best lift the soul from earth, and spring those unutterable hopes she delights in. How then, without tears, could he for the last time, feel the strong pressure of his hand, and catch the parting glance? On the other side, through watery eyes and broken accents, poor Collins sobbed out his last adieu, not without hearty thanks, for the many favors which Ben had done him, and solemn promises of speedily *writing to him, and remitting all his money.* Charity would fain believe, that he fully so intended; but alas! nor money, nor friend did Ben ever hear of afterwards. This elegant victim of rum, was no doubt presented by the captain to the wealthy family in Jamaica. And being introduced, under the genial influence perhaps of a cheerful glass, 'tis likely that with his advantages of education and eloquence, he made such a figure in the eyes of those wealthy and hospitable islanders, that they were in raptures with him, and fondly counted that they had got an elegant young schoolmaster who was to make scholars and wits of the whole family. Perhaps too, their darling hope, a blooming daughter, was seen to heave the tender sigh, as blushing she darted the side-long glance upon him. But alas! the next day sees the elegant young schoolmaster *dead drunk!* and the amiable family all in the dumps again. 'Tis more than probable, that after having been alternately received and dismissed from a dozen wealthy families, he sunk at length, into tattered garments, and a grog-blossomed face; the mournful victim of intemperance. And now perhaps, after all the fair prospects of his youth, and all the fond hopes of his parents, poor Collins, untimely buried in a foreign church-yard, only serves for the pious to point their children to his early tomb and remind them how vain are talents and education without the restraints of religion.

CHAPTER XXII.

Soon as Ben reached Philadelphia, as aforesaid, he waited on the governor, who received him with joy, eagerly calling out, "*Well my dear boy, what success? What success?*" Ben, with a smile, drew his father's letter from his pocket. The governor snatched it, as if all impatient to see its contents, which he ran through with a devouring haste. When he was done, he shook his head and said, "it was to be sure a sensible letter, a vastly sensible letter; *but—but,*—it won't do," continued he to Ben, "no, it won't do; your father is too cautious, entirely too cautious, sir." Hereupon he fell into a brown study, with his eyes nailed to the ground, as in a profound reverie. After a moment's pause, he suddenly looked up, and with a countenance bright as with some happy thought, he cried out, "I've got it, my dear young friend, I've got it exactly. Zounds! what signifies making two bites at a cherry? *In for a penny, in for a pound*, is my way. Since your father will do nothing for you, I'll do it all myself. A printer I want, and a printer I'll have, that's a clear case: and I am sure you are the lad that will suit me to a fraction. So give me a list of the articles you want from England, and I will send for them by the very next ship, and set you up at once: and all I shall expect of you, is that you'll pay me when you are able!!" Seeing the tear swelling in Ben's eye, the governor took him by the hand, and in a softened tone said, "come, nothing of that my dear boy, nothing of that. A lad of your talents and merit, must not languish in the back ground for lack of a little money to bring you forward. So make me out, as I said, a list of such articles as you may want, and I'll send for them at once to London.—But stop! would it not be better for you to go to London, and choose these things yourself? you could then, you know, be sure to have them all of the best quality. And besides, you could form an acquaintance with *some clever fellows* in the book selling and stationary line, whose friendship might be worth a Jew's eye to you, in your business here."

Ben, hardly able now to speak, thanked the governor as well as he could for so generous an offer.—"Well then," continued the governor, "get yourself in readiness to go with the Annis." The reader will please to be informed, that the Annis was, at that time, (1722) the only regular trader between London and Philadelphia; and she made but one voyage in the year! Finding that the Annis was not to sail for several months yet, Ben prudently continued to do journey work for old Keimer; but often haunted with the ghost of Vernon's money which he had lent to Collins, and for fear of what would become of him if Vernon should be strict *to mark his iniquities* in that mad affair. But happily for him, Vernon made no demand.

It appeared afterwards that this worthy man had not forgotten his money. But learning from a variety of quarters, that Ben was a perfect non-descript of industry and frugality, he concluded that as the money was not paid, Ben was probably under the hatches. He therefore, generously, let the matter lie over till a distant day, when Ben, as we shall by and by see, paid him up fully, both principal and interest, and thus recovered the high ground he formerly held in his friendship. Thanks be to God, who has given to inflexible honesty and industry, such power over the "*heart strings*," as well as "*purse strings*," of mankind.

CHAPTER XXIII.

Ben was naturally comic in a high degree, and this pleasant vein, greatly improved by his present golden prospects, betrayed him into many a frolic with Keimer, to whom he had prudently attached himself as a journeyman, until the Annis should sail. The reader will excuse Ben for these frolics when he comes to learn what were their aims; as also what an insufferable old creature this Keimer was. Silly as a BOOBY, yet vain as a JAY, and garrulous as a PIE, he could never rest but when in a stiff argument, and acting the orator, at which he looked on Cicero himself as but a boy to him. Here was a fine target for Ben's SOCRATIC ARTILLERY, which he frequently played off on the old pomposo with great effect. By questions artfully put, he would obtain of him certain points, which Keimer readily granted, as seeing in them no sort of connexion with the matter in debate. But yet these points, when granted, like distant nets slyly hauling round a porpoise or sturgeon, would, by degrees, so completely circumvent the silly fish, that with all his flouncing and fury he could never extricate himself, but rather got more deeply entangled. Often caught in this way, he became at last so afraid of Ben's *questions*, that he would turn as mad when one of them was "*poked at him*," as a bull at sight of a scarlet cloak; and would not answer the simplest question without first asking, "*well, and what would you make of that?*" He came at length to form so exalted an opinion of Ben's talents for refutation, that he seriously proposed to him one day that they should turn out together and preach up a NEW RELIGION! Keimer was to preach and make the converts, and Ben to answer and put to silence the gainsayers. He said a *world of money* might be made by it.

On hearing the outlines of this new religion, Ben found great fault with it. This he did only that he might have another frolic with Keimer; but his frolics were praiseworthy, for they all "leaned to virtue's side." The truth is, he saw that Keimer was prodigiously a hypocrite. At every whip-stitch he could play the knave, and then for a pretence would read his Bible. But it was not the *moral part* of the Bible, the sweet precepts and parables of the Gospel that he read. No verily. Food so angelic was not at all to the tooth of his childish fancy, which delighted in nothing but the *novel* and *curious*. Like too many of the saints now-a-days, he would rather read about the WITCH OF ENDOR, than the GOOD SAMARITAN, and hear a sermon on the *brazen candlesticks* than on the LOVE OF GOD. And then, O dear! who was Melchizedeck? Or where was the land of Nod? Or, was it in the shape of a *serpent or a monkey* that the devil tempted Eve? As he was one day poring over the pentateuch as busy after some nice game of this sort as a terrier on the track of a weazle, he came to that famous text where Moses says, "*thou shall not mar the corners of thy beard.*" Aye! this was the divinity for Keimer. It struck him like a new light from the clouds: then rolling his eyes as from an apparition, he exclaimed, "miserable man that I am! and was I indeed forbidden to mar even the corners of my beard, and have I been all this time shaving myself as smooth as an eunuch! Fire and brimstone, how have you been boiling up for me, and I knew it not! Hell, deepest hell is my portion, that's a clear case, unless I reform. And reform I will if I live. Yes, my poor naked chin, if ever I but get another crop upon thee and I suffer it to be touched by the ungodly steel, then let my right hand forget her cunning."

From that day he became as shy of a razor as ever Samson was. His long black whiskers "*whistled in the wind.*" And then to see how he would stand up before his glass and stroke them down, it would have reminded you of some ancient Druid, adjusting the *sacred Mistletoe.*

Ben could not bear that sight. Such shameless neglect of angel morality, and yet such fidgetting about a goatish beard! "Heavens, sir," said he to Keimer, one day in the midst of a hot argument,

"Who can think, with common sense,

A smooth shaved face gives God offence?

Or that a whisker hath a charm,

Eternal justice to disarm?"

He even proposed to him to get *shaved.* Keimer swore outright that he would never lose his beard. A stiff altercation ensued. But Keimer getting angry, Ben agreed at last to give up the beard. He said that, "as the beard at best was but an external, a mere excrescence, he would not insist on that as so very essential. But certainly sir," continued he, "there is one thing that is."

Keimer wanted to know what that was.

"Why sir," added Ben, "this turning out and preaching up a NEW RELIGION, is, without doubt, a very serious affair, and ought not to be undertaken too hastily. Much time, sir, in my opinion at least, should be spent in making preparation, in which, fasting should certainly have a large share."

Keimer, who was a great glutton, said he could *never fast.*

Ben then insisted that if they were not to fast altogether, they ought, at any rate, to abstain from animal food, and live as the saints of old did, on *vegetables* and *water.*

Keimer shook his head, and said that if he were to live on vegetables and water, he should soon die.

Ben assured him that it was entirely a mistake. He had tried it often, he said, and could testify from his own experience that he was never more healthy and cheerful than when he lived on vegetables alone. "Die from feeding on vegetables, indeed! Why, sir, it contradicts reason; and contradicts all history, ancient and profane. There was Daniel, and his three young friends, Shadrach, Meshach, and Abednego, who fed on a vegetable diet, of choice; did they languish and die of it? or rather did they not display a rouge of health and fire of genius, far beyond those silly youths who crammed on all the luxuries of the royal table? And that amiable Italian nobleman, Lewis Cornaro, who says of bread, that it was such a dainty to his palate, that he was almost afraid, at times, it was too good for him to eat; did he languish and die of this simple fare? On the contrary, did he not out-live three generations of gratified epicures; and after all, go off in his second century, like a bird of Paradise, singing the praises of Temperance and Virtue? And pray, sir," continued Ben, "where's the wonder of all this? Must not the blood that is formed of vegetables be the purest in nature? And then, as the spirits depend on the blood, must not the spirits secreted from such blood be the purest too? And when this is the case with the blood and spirits, which are the very life of the man, must not that man enjoy the best chance for such healthy secretions and circulations as are most conducive to long and happy life?"

While Ben argued at this rate, Keimer regarded him with a look which seemed to say, "Very true, sir; all this is very true; but still I cannot *go it.*"

Ben, still unwilling to give up his point, thought he would make one more push at him. "What a pity it is," said he with a sigh, "that the blessings of so sublime a religion should be all lost to the world, merely for lack of a little fortitude on the part of its propagators."

This was touching him on the right string; for Keimer was a man of such vanity, that a little flattery would put him up to any thing. So after a few *hems* and *ha's*, he said, he believed he would, at any rate, make a trial of this new regimen.

Having thus carried his point, Ben immediately engaged a poor old woman of the neighbourhood to become their cook; and gave her off hand, written receipts for three and forty dishes; not one of which contained a single atom of fish, flesh, or fowl. For their first day's breakfast on the *new regimen,* the old woman treated them with a terrene of oatmeal gruel. Keimer was particularly fond of his breakfast, at which a nice beef-stake with onion sauce was a standing dish. It was as good as a farce to Ben, to see with what an eye Keimer regarded the terrene, when entering the room, in place of his stake, hot, smoking, and savory, he beheld this pale, meagre-looking slop.

"What have you got there?" said he, with a visage grum, and scowling eye.

"A dish of hasty pudding," replied Ben, with the smile of an innocent youth who had a keen appetite, with something good to satisfy it—"a dish of nice hasty pudding, sir, made of oats."

"Of OATS!" retorted Keimer, with a voice raised to a scream.

"Yes, sir, *oats*," rejoined Ben,—"*oats*, that precious grain which gives such elegance and fire to our noblest of quadrupeds, the horse."

Keimer growled out, that he was no horse to eat oats.

"No matter for that," replied Ben, "'tis equally good for men."

Keimer denied that any human being ever eat oats.

"Aye!" said Ben, "and pray what's become of the Scotch? Don't they live on oats; and yet, where will you find a people so 'bonny, blythe, and gay;' a nation of such wits and warriors."

As there was no answering this, Keimer sat down to the terrene, and swallowed a few spoonfuls, but not without making as many wry faces as if it had been so much jalap; while Ben, all smile and chat, breakfasted most deliciously.

At dinner, by Ben's order, the old woman paraded a trencher piled up with potatoes. Keimer's grumbling fit came on him again. "He saw clear enough," he said, "that he was to be poisoned."

"Poh, cheer up, man," replied Ben; "this is your right preacher's bread."

"Bread the d——l!" replied Keimer, snarling.

"Yes, bread, sir," continued Ben, pleasantly; "the bread of *life*, sir; for where do you find such health and spirits, such bloom and beauty, as among the honest-hearted IRISH, and yet for their breakfast, dinner, and supper, the potato is their tetotum; the *first*, *second*, and *third* course." In this way, Ben and his old woman went on with Keimer; daily ringing the changes on oat-meal gruel, roasted potatoes, boiled rice, and so on, through the whole family of roots and grains in all their various genders, moods, and tenses.

Sometimes, like a restive mule, Keimer would kick up and show strong symptoms of flying the way. But then Ben would prick him up again with a touch of his ruling passion, vanity; "only think, Mr. Keimer," he would say, "only think what has been done by the founders of *new religions*: how they have enlightened the ignorant, polished the rude, civilized the savage, and made heroes of those who were little better than brutes. Think, sir, what Moses did among the stiff-necked Jews; what Mahomet did among the wild Arabs—and what you may do among these gentle drab-coated Pennsylvanians." This, like a spur in the flank of a jaded horse, gave Keimer a new start, and pushed him on afresh to his gruel breakfasts and potato dinners. Ben strove hard to keep him up to this gait. Often at table, and especially when he saw that Keimer was in good humour and fed kindly, he would give a loose to fancy, and paint the advantages of their new regimen in the most glowing colours. "Aye, sir," he would say, letting drop at the same time his spoon, as in an ecstasy of his subject, while his pudding on the platter cooled—"aye, sir, now we are beginning to live like men going a preaching indeed. Let your epicures gormandize their fowl, fish, and flesh, with draughts of intoxicating liquors. Such gross, inflammatory food may suit the brutal votaries of Mars and Venus. But our views, sir, are different altogether; we are going to teach wisdom and benevolence to mankind. This is a heavenly work, sir, and our minds ought to be heavenly. Now, as the mind depends greatly on the body, and the body on the food, we should certainly select that which is of the most pure and refining quality. And this, sir, is exactly the food to our purpose. This mild potato, or this gentle pudding, is the thing to insure the light stomach, the cool liver, the clear head, and, above all, those celestial passions which become a preacher that would moralize the world. And these celestial passions, sir, let me add, though I don't pretend to be a prophet, these celestial passions, sir, were you but to stick to this diet, would soon shine out in your countenance with such apostolic majesty and grace, as would strike all beholders with reverence, and enable you to carry the world before you."

Such was the style of Ben's rhetoric with old Keimer. But it could not all do. For though these harangues would sometimes make him fancy himself as big as Zoroaster or Confucius, and talk as if he should soon have the whole country running after him, and worshipping him for the GREAT LAMA of the west; yet this divinity fit was too much against the grain to last long. Unfortunately for poor Keimer, the kitchen lay between him and his bishobprick: and both nature and habit had so wedded him to that swinish idol, that nothing could divorce him. So after having been led by Ben a "*very d——l of a life*," as he called it, "*for three months*," his flesh-pot appetites prevailed, and he swore, "*by his whiskers, he would suffer it no longer.*" Accordingly he ordered a nice roast pig for dinner, and desired Ben to invite a young friend to dine with them. Ben did so: but neither himself nor his young friend were any thing the better for the pig. For before they could arrive, the pig being done, and his appetite beyond all restraint, Keimer had fallen on it and devoured the whole. And there he sat panting and torpid as an ANACONDA who had just swallowed a young buffaloe. But still his looks gave sign that the "*Ministers of Grace*" had not entirely deserted him, for at sight of Ben and his young friend, he blushed up to the eye lids, and in a glow of scarlet, which showed that he paid dear for his *whistle*, (gluttony) he apologized for disappointing them of their dinner. "Indeed, the smell of the pig," he said, "was so sweet, and the nicely browned skin so inviting, especially to him who had been *long starved*, that for the soul of him he could not resist the temptation to *taste it*—and then, O! if Lucifer himself had been at the door, he must have gone on, let what would have been the consequences." He said too, "that for his part he was glad it was a *pig* and not a *hog*, for that he verily believed he should have bursted himself."—Then leaning back in his chair and pressing his swollen abdomen with his paws, he exclaimed with an awkward laugh, "*Well*, I don't believe I was ever cut out for a bishop!"—Here ended the farce: for Keimer never after this uttered another word about his NEW RELIGION.

Ben used, laughing, to say that he drew Keimer into this scrape that he might enjoy the satisfaction of *starving him out of his gluttony*. And he did it also that he might save the more *for books and candles:* their vegetable regimen costing him, in all, rather less than three cents a day! To those who can spend twenty times this sum on tobacco and whiskey alone, *three* cents per day must appear a scurvy allowance, and of course poor Ben must be sadly pitied. But such philosophers should remember that all depends on our loves, whose property it is to make bitter things sweet, and heavy things light.

For example: to lie out in the darksome swamp with no other canopy but the sky, and no bed but the cold ground, and his only music the midnight owl or screaming alligator, seems terrible to servile minds; but it was joy to Marion, whose "*whole soul*," as general Lee well observes, "*was devoted to liberty and country.*"

So, to shut himself up in a dirty printing-office, with no dinner but a bit of bread, no supper but an apple, must appear to every epicure as it did to Keimer, "*a mere d——l of a life*;" but it was joy to Ben, whose whole soul was on his *books*, as the sacred lamps that were to guide him to usefulness and glory.

Happy he who early strikes into the path of *wisdom*, and bravely walks therein till habit sprinkles it with roses. He shall be led as a lamb among the green pastures along the water courses of pleasure, nor shall he ever experience the pang of those

"Who see the right, and approve it too;

Condemn the wrong—and yet the wrong pursue."

CHAPTER XXIV.

Ben, as we have seen, was never without a knot of choice spirits, like satellites, constantly revolving around him, and both receiving and reflecting light. By these satellites I mean young men of fine minds, and fond of books. He had at this time a *trio* of such. The first was of the name of Osborne, the second Watson, and the third Ralph. As the two first were a good deal of the nature of wandering stars, which, though bright, soon disappear again, I shall let them pass away in silence. But the last, that's to say, Ralph, shone so long in the same sphere with Ben, both in America and Europe, that it will never do to let him go without giving the reader somewhat at least of a telescopic squint at him. James Ralph, then, was a young man of the first rate talents, ingenious at argument, of flowery fancy, most fascinating in his manners, and uncommonly eloquent. In short, he appears to have been built and equipped to run the voyage of life with as splendid success as any. But alas! as the seamen say of their ships, "*he took the wrong sheer.*" Hence, while many a DULL GENIUS, with only a few plain-sailing virtues on board, such as honest industry, good humour, and prudence, have made fine weather through life, and come into port at last laden *up to the bends* with riches and honours, this gallant PROA, this stately GONDOLA, the moment he was put to sea, was caught up in a Euroclydon of furious passions and appetites that shivered his character and peace, and made a wreck of him at the very outset.

According to his own account, it appears that Ben was often haunted with fears that he himself had some hand in Ralph's disasters. Dr. Franklin was certainly one of the wisest of mankind. But with all his wisdom he was still but a man, and therefore liable to err. Solomon, we know, was fallible; what wonder then young Franklin?

But here lies the difference between these two wise men, as to their errors. Solomon, according to scripture, was sometimes overcome of Satan, even in the bone and sinew of his strength; but the devil was too hard for Franklin only while he was in the *gristle* of his youth. The case was thus: among the myriads of books which came to his eager tooth, there was a most unlucky one on deism, written, 'tis said, by Shaftesbury, a man admirably calculated to pervert the truth; or, as Milton says of one of his fallen spirits, to make "*the worse appear the better reason.*" Mark now this imposing writer—he does not utter you a word against religion; not he indeed: no, not for the world. Why, sirs, he's the best friend of religion. He praises it up to the skies, as the sole glory of man, the strong pillar of his virtues, and the inexhaustible fountain of all his hopes. But then he cannot away with that false religion, that detestable superstition called christianity. And here, to set his readers against it, he gives them a most horrible catalogue of the cruelties and bloody persecutions it has always occasioned in the world; nay, he goes so far as to assert that christians are the *natural enemies of mankind*; "vainly conceiting themselves," says he, "to be the favourites of heaven, they look on the rest of the world but as 'heathen dogs' whom it is 'doing God service to kill,' and whose goods it is right to seize on, as spoil for the Lord's people! Who," he asks crowingly, "filled Asia with fire and sword in the bloody wars of the Crusades? The christians. Who depopulated the fine negro-coasts of Africa? The christians. Who extirpated many of the once glorious Indian nations of America? The christians; nay," continues he, "so keen are those christians for blood, that when they can't get their 'heathen dogs' to fall on, they fall on one another: witness the papist christians destroying the protestants, and the protestant christians destroying the papists. And still greater shame," says he, "to these sweet followers of the Lamb, these papist and protestant christians, when they can no longer worry each other, will worry those of their own party, as in numberless and shameful cases of the calvinists and arminians; nay, so prone are the christians to hate, that their greatest doctors even in their *pulpits*, instead of exhorting to piety and those godlike virtues, that make men honour and love one another, will fix on the vainest speculations; which, though not understood by one soul among them, yet serve abundantly to set them all by the ears; yes, they can hate one another:

"For believing that there are three persons in the Godhead; or only one person.

"For believing that there are children in hell not a span long; or for not believing it.

"For believing that every body will be saved; or for believing that scarcely any body will be saved.

"For baptizing in mill ponds; or only out of china bowls.

"For taking the sacrament in both elements; or only in the bread.

"For praying in Latin; or for praying only in English.

"For praying with a book; or for praying without a book.

"For praying standing; or for praying kneeling.

"For reading the Bible by themselves; or for reading it only with a priest.

"For wearing long beards; or for shaving their beards.

"For preaching up predestination; or for preaching up free will.

"Now," continues our writer, "barely to *hate* one's neighbours for such notions as these, were enough, one would think, to make any common d——l blush; but these christians, as if to out-d——l Satan himself, can not only hate, but actually murder one another for these contradictory notions! yes; and oh, horrible to think! not only murder, but even glory in it: at every shower of cruel bullets on their flying victims; or at every plunge of the reeking spear into the bodies of shrieking mothers and infants, they can cheer each other to *the glorious spot* with animating huzzas! and even when the infernal tragedy is closed, they can write congratulatory letters, and sing *Te Deums*, giving glory to God that the MONSTERS—the BEASTS—the HERETICS, are rooted out."

Such was the prince of infidels. And it was the very argument to stagger Ben, even the dangerous argument of example, which young as he was, he had learned to consider as a short way of coming at men's real principles.

"Example is a living law, whose sway

Men more than all the living laws obey."

Or as Hudibras has it,

"Men oft prove it by their *practice*:

No argument like matter of *fact* is.

And we are, best of all, led to

Men's principles, by what they do."

'Tis true, that to tax the gospel with these accursed deeds of mad papists and protestants, is just about as good logic as to accuse our excellent civil code with all the crimes of gamblers and horse thieves—the very rascals it aims to hang. Or like charging the sun as the cause of *darkness*, which indeed it was given to dispel.

But Ben was too young yet, to know everything. And besides, led altogether as he was by the strongest feelings of sympathy, it is not much to be wondered at, that this popular argument, "*the barbarities of christians*," should have excited so lasting prejudice against christianity. As some men of delicate natures who have taken an emetic, though in the best madeira, can never afterwards bear the smell of that generous liquor; so christianity, steeped in tears and blood, excited in Ben an aversion that stuck by him a long time. In short, Ben became an unbeliever. And, like Paul of Tarsus, during the reign of his unbelief, "*he thought verily he ought to do many things contrary to the name of Jesus of Nazareth, which things he also did*," arguing powerfully for *natural* religion.

How many converts he made to infidelity, I have never been able exactly to learn. But certain it is, he made two, viz. John Collins and James Ralph. As to Collins, we have seen already, that in converting him to scepticism, he soon *drew down an old house over his head*, his pupil quickly turning out a most impudent drunkard and swindler. And though he expected better luck from Ralph, yet he quickly discovered in him also certain very dismal symptoms of the cloven foot.

Some short time before the sailing of the Annis, Ben, in the warmth of his heart, told Ralph of the immense affair which Sir William Keith had engaged him in, viz. to make him the KING'S PRINTER in Philadelphia. And also that he was about to sail in a few days on that very errand for London. Ralph suddenly turned serious; the next day he came and told Ben that he had made up his mind to go with him. "How can that be," said Ben, "seeing you have a young wife and child?" To this Ralph replied, with an oath, that "that should be no obstacle." "It was true," he said, "he had married the wench, but it was only for her money. But since the old rascal, her father, would not give it to him, he was determined to be revenged on him, by leaving his daughter and grandchild on his hands for life."

Ben, though greatly shocked by this trait in his character, was yet so blindly partial to Ralph that he could not find in his heart to spurn him from his acquaintance. But for this, as he afterwards called it, *great error in his life*, he received a chastisement, which, though pretty severe, was not one stripe more than he richly deserved.

CHAPTER XXV.

The day at length arrives, the long wished day for the sailing of the Annis; and Ben gladly hails it as the fairest he had ever seen.

All in the stream the ship she lies,

Her topsails loosen'd from above,

When Ben to DEBBY fondly flies

To bid farewell to his TRUE LOVE.

But brightly as shone the day, yet in this, as in all the past, he found a canker. If the season served his ambition, it crossed his love. The reader will please be reminded that the *Debby*, immortalized in the lines above, was the beautiful Miss Deborah Read, who had at first so heartily laughed at Ben for munching his roll along the street; but afterwards had fallen very much in love with him. And, on the other hand, living in her father's family, and daily a spectator of her prudence and sweetness of spirit, he had become equally partial to her; and had even asked her in marriage, before he set out for London. The old gentleman, her father, was quite keen for the match, it having always been his opinion, he said, that in choosing a husband for his daughter, it was better to get *a man without money, than money without a man.*

But old Mrs. Read flatly refused her consent; or, at any rate, until his return, when, as she said, it would be full time enough for "*such young people to marry.*" The truth is, the printing trade, then in its infancy in Pennsylvania, was of such little account that the old lady had her fears that her daughter would *starve* if she married Ben.

Having taken leave of his fair sweetheart, with many a vow of love and swift return, Ben, accompanied by Ralph, hastened on board the ship, which fell down the river for Newcastle. Immediately on his arrival at this place, he went on shore to see his dear friend the governor, who was come down to despatch the packet. The governor could not be seen! This was a sad shock to Ben, and would have been much more so, but for the attentions of the governor's secretary, Dr. Bar, who, with the finest smile imaginable, presented the "GOVERNOR'S *compliments to his young friend Mr. Franklin—was extremely sorry indeed he could not see him, owing to a press of business, among which was that of writing some letters for his own special service, which should be sent on board to him—but though his* EXCELLENCY *could not enjoy the pleasure of seeing Mr. Franklin, yet he begged he would accept the assurances of his eternal friendship, with the best wishes for his prosperous voyage and speedy return; and above all, his earnest hopes that he would continue to improve his extraordinary talents.*"

Though this was to Ben somewhat like a sugar-plumb to a child after a dose of wormwood, yet could it not so entirely take off the bitter, but that he was at first prodigiously in a humour to break with the governor. His characteristic prudence, however, came to his aid; and fortunately recollecting that it was not a common man, but a GOVERNOR, he was dealing with, and that such great men have their ways of doing things quite different from little people, he smothered his resentment, and went peaceably on board the ship—not even yet suspecting any fraud on the part of the governor. When we consider how dear to the young and virtuous bosom is the glow of gratitude to benefactors, we cannot but mourn that governor Keith should so cruelly have chilled those joys in the bosom of our young countryman. But, though chilled for a moment, they were not extinct. The heavy heart which he at first felt on being denied the pleasure of seeing the governor, is already much relieved by his gracious message through the secretary, and afterwards so completely cured by the sublime and beautiful scenes around Newcastle, that he went back to the ship in good spirits again. On the return of the last boat, bringing the mail, he modestly asked the captain for the letters which the governor had addressed to his care. To this the rough son of Neptune replied, "*that they were all there*, he supposed, *higglety, pigglety, together in the letter bag, and that as the ship with a fine breeze was getting under weigh, he could not spare the time now to make a search for them, but that before they got to London he might overhaul the bag and take 'em out for himself.*"

Ben was perfectly satisfied with this answer. And charmed at thought of the great things awaiting him in London, he threw off his coat and bravely joined the crew in all their haste and bustle to weigh the anchor, and spread the sails before the freshening gale.

But while the sailors, many of them at least, poor fellows, for lack of education, were straining at the clanking windlass, or creaking halyards, as void of thought as the timber-heads of the ship, the spirits of Ben were in a constant succession of pleasurable reflections on the magnificent scenes around him—the grand floating castle which bore him so high above the foaming billows—the rapid flight of the ship, as flying before the stormy winds she left the lessening shores behind her—the boundless fields of the blue rolling ocean, with all her porpoises gathering round in blackening shoals, bounding and blowing, as if to greet the monster vessel, and by their furious romps, adding to the crash and foam of the tempest.

Though Ben was no poet, nor ever affected to be "*religious overmuch*," yet could he not behold such magnificent scenes without that adoring sense of eternal power and goodness which has been so elegantly expressed by the sweet voice of Zion:—

"Shout to the Lord, ye surging seas,

In your eternal roar;

Let wave to wave resound his praise,

And shore reply to shore.

While monsters sporting on the flood

In scaly silver shine,

Speak terribly their Maker—God,

And lash the foaming brine."

CHAPTER XXVI.

Ben getting into trouble—finds out his old friend governor Keith to be a black sheep—and learns that a good trade and virtuous habits are the best wealth that a father can give his son.

"Who dares think one thing and another tell,

My soul abhors him like the gates of hell."

On the arrival of the ship in the Thames (or London river) the captain, like an honest fellow of his word, ordered the letter-bag on deck, and told Ben he was welcome now to overhaul it and pick out the governor's letters to him. After eagerly turning them all over and over again, not a single letter could he find that had his name on it, either directed to himself, or to his care. He picked out however a few that seemed to have some little squinting that way, one especially, that was directed to a PRINTER, and another to a BOOKSELLER. These he immediately carried to their respective owners. But in place of those smiles and prompt offers of money and merchandize, which his illustrious patron, governor Keith, had promised him, scarcely were his letters opened before they were nearly thrown back into his face, as coming from a couple of scoundrel debtors, who, instead of paying off their old scores, were now impudently asking for new credits.

Here were strong symptoms of treachery on the part of the governor. And in spite of all his credulity, Ben was brought to his doubtings. In this dilemma he went back to a worthy Quaker of the name of Denham, with whom he had contracted a great friendship on ship-board, and told him the whole story from beginning to end. With all his professional gravity, Denham could not help smiling, as Ben related the history of his credulity: but when he came to tell of governor Keith's LETTERS of *Credit*, and the vast supplies of TYPES, and PAPER, and PRESSES, which they were instantly to procure him, he broke into a horse laugh. "He give thee letters of credit, friend Benjamin! Governor Keith give thee letters of credit! Why, man, he has not credit for himself, no not for a brass farthing, from any one who ever heard of him."

Poor Ben was struck "all in a heap"—dumb as a codfish. He stood for all the world like a shipwrecked sailor boy, who, after dreaming of gold and diamond coasts, and black-eyed Polls, and whole seas of grog, and mountains of segars, wakes up all at once, and finds himself, like poor Robinson Crusoe, on a desolate island, with not even a scape-goat of hope before him. In silence he rolled his eyes in woeful cogitation—for three months he had been feasting on the smiles and promises of his illustrious friend, governor Keith—for three months had been anticipating his grand Printing Establishment, in Philadelphia, and his complete triumph over old Keimer and Bradford—for three months he had been drinking in streams of rapture from the love-beaming eyes of the beauteous Miss Read, shortly as his wife to rustle in silks and roll in her carriage—but dearer still than all, for three months he had been looking forward to the time, close at hand, when his infirm parents should come to enjoy with him, in Philadelphia, the welcome repose of their age, in an elegant retreat, purchased for them, by his own virtues. But lo! in a moment the whole goodly structure is dissipated in smoke, leaving him pennyless and friendless, in a strange country, three thousand miles from home, and at a long, long distance from all these dear objects!

Denham saw in Ben's looks what was passing in his heart; but knowing that it is good for virtuous and heroic minds to bear the cross in their youth, he suffered him to go on, undisturbed, with his dismal cogitations.

But a young man early trained in the school of wisdom is not long to be depressed. After relieving his bosom with a deep sigh; he turned to Denham and said, in a plaintive tone, "*but was it not cruel in governor Keith to deceive me so?*"

"Yes, Benjamin," replied Denham, "'twas, to our view, very cruel in the governor of Pennsylvania thus to deceive an inexperienced lad as thou art."

Here Ben turning on him his fine blue eyes, softened by misfortune, said again to Denham, "*well, and what would you advise me?*"

"Advise thee, Benjamin," replied Denham, in a cheerful tone, "why, I would advise thee not to give thyself one moment's uneasiness about this affair. Thee remembers the story of Joseph, does thee not? how he was betrayed by his brethren into Egypt, not only a poor lad like thee, but indeed a slave too? And yet this event, though at the time highly disheartening, proved to him in the end, one of the happiest incidents of his life. So, by good management, Benjamin, this may prove to thee. Thou art young, very young yet, with a plenty of time before thee; and this is a great city for thy business. Now if thou wilt but seek employment with some printer of distinction, thou mayest make thyself more completely master of thy trade, and also gain friends, that may enable thee to settle so much more advantageously in Philadelphia, as to make it good for thee that governor Keith ever betrayed thee here. And this will be a triumph much to thine own honour, as also to the benefit of other youth, who shall ever hear of thy story."

As when a sweet breeze of the ocean suddenly strikes a becalmed ship, that with flapping sails lay tossing on the sluggish flood, instantly the joy-wakened billows roll a brighter foam, and the hearts of the sailors spring forward with transport to their native shores. Thus exhilarating to Ben's soul was the counsel of his friend Denham. Without a moment's loss of time he went, as his friend Denham had advised, and sought business at the offices of two of the most eminent book-printers in London, Palmer and Watts. With the latter he spent most of his time during his stay in England.

This Palmer was an amiable man, and in Ben's countenance, now mellowed more than ordinary, by his late disappointment, he saw a something that interested him greatly in his favour. He asked Ben in what part of London he had learned the art of printing. Ben told him he had never set a type in London. "Aye! where then," said Palmer; "in Paris?" Ben replied, that he was just from Pennsylvania, in North America; and that what little he knew of printing he had picked up there. Palmer, though, in other respects, amiable, was one of those thorough-gone COCKNEYS, who can't believe that any thing can be learned out of the sound of "*Bow-bell.*" He stared at Ben on saying he had learned to print in North America, as would a French petit maitre at one who said he had learned to *dance among the Hottentots.* "I am afraid, sir," said he to Ben, "that I cannot employ you, as I really felt a wish to do; for though I now command fifty workmen, I want a *Gabber, i.e.* a man uncommonly quick, and of a satirical turn. And in neither of these characters, sir, will you, probably, suit me, sir—however, sir, as it is late now, and I have business out, if you will call in the morning, we will see about it." Next morning, before sunrise, Ben waited at Palmer's office, where numbers of his journeymen, having heard of the young North American printer, were assembled to see him work. Palmer was not yet up. An apprentice went to inform him that the young printer from North America, was come. Presently Mr. Palmer made his appearance, looking somewhat confused.

"And so you are a buckskin, sir," said he, rather cavalierly.

"Yes sir," replied Ben, "I am a buckskin."

"Well sir, I am afraid you'll not make your fortune by that here in London," said Palmer.

"No sir," answered Ben, "I find it is thought a misfortune here, to have been born in America. But I hope it was the will of heaven, and therefore must be right."

"Aye!" replied Palmer, a little tauntingly; "and so you have *preaching* there too!! But do the buckskins generally stir so early as this?"

Ben replied, that the Pennsylvanians were getting to find out that it was *cheap burning sun-light.* Here Palmer and his cockneys stared at him, as country buckskins are wont to do at a monkey, or parrot, or any such creature that pretends to mimic man.

"You talk of *sun-light*, sir," said the foreman to Ben: "can you tell the cause of that wide difference between the light of the sun in England and America?"

Ben replied that he had never discovered that difference.

"What! not that the sun shines brighter in London than in America—the sky clearer—the air purer—and the light a thousand times more vivid—and luminous—and cheering—and all that?"

Ben said that he could not understand how that could be, seeing it was the same sun that gave light to both.

"The same sun, sir! the same sun!" replied the cockney, rather nettled, "I am not positive of that sir. But admitting that it is the same sun, it does not follow that it gives the same light in America as in England. Every thing, you know, suffers by going to the *West*, as the great French philosophers have proved; then why not the sun?"

Ben said he wondered the gentleman should talk of the sun going to the west.

"What, the sun not go to the west!" retorted the cockney, quite angry, "a pretty story, indeed. You have eyes, sir; and don't these show you that the sun rises in the east and travels to the west?"

"I thought, sir," replied Ben, modestly, "that your own great countryman, sir Isaac Newton, had satisfied every body that it is the earth that is thus continually travelling, and not the sun, which is stationary, and gives the same light to England and America."

Palmer, who had much of the honest Englishman about him, equally surprised and pleased to see Ben thus chastise the pride and ignorance of his foreman, put a stop to the conversation by placing a composing stick in the hands of Ben, while the journeymen gathering around, marvelled hugely to see the young North American take *a composing stick in his hand*!

Having spent a moment or two in running his eyes over the letter cases, to see if they were fixed as in the printing-offices in America, and glancing at his watch, Ben fell to work, and in less than four minutes finished the following—

"And Nathaniel said, can there any thing good come out of Nazareth?—Philip said, come and see."

Palmer and his workmen were petrified. Near eighty letters set up in less than four minutes, and without a blunder? And then such a delicate stroke at their prejudice and nonsense! Ben was immediately employed.

This was a fine introduction of Ben to the printing office, every person in which seemed to give him a hearty welcome; he wore his rare talents so modestly.

It gave him also a noble opportunity to be useful, which he failed not to improve.

Passing by one of the presses at which a small man, meagre and hollow-eyed, was labouring with unequal force, as appeared by his paleness and big-dropping sweat, Ben touched with pity, offered to give him "*a spell.*" As the pressman and compositor, like the parson and the clerk, or the coffin-maker and the grave-digger are of entirely distinct trades in London, the little pressman was surprised that Ben, who was a compositor, should talk of giving him "*a spell.*" However, Ben insisting, the little pressman gave way, when Ben seized the press, and possessing both a skill and spirit extraordinary, he handled it in such a workman-like style, that the men all declared they should have concluded he had done nothing but *press-work* all his life. Palmer also, coming by at the time, mingled his applauses with the rest, saying that he had never seen a fairer impression; and, on Ben's requesting it, for *exercise* and *health sake*, he permitted him to work some hours every day at press.

On his entrance into Palmer's printing-office, Ben paid the customary *garnish* or treat-money, for the journeymen to drink. This was on the first floor, among the pressmen. Presently Palmer wanted him up stairs, among the compositors. There also the journeymen called on him for *garnish*. Ben refused, looking upon it as altogether an unfair demand, and so Palmer himself, to whom it was referred, decided; insisting that Ben should *not pay* it. But neither justice nor patronage could bear Ben out against the spite of the journeymen. For the moment his back was turned they would play him an endless variety of mischievous tricks, such as mixing his letters, transposing his pages, breaking down his matter, &c. &c. It was in vain he remonstrated against such injustice. They all with one accord excused themselves, laying all the blame on RALPH, for so they called a certain evil spirit who, they pretended, haunted the office and always tormented such as were not *regularly admitted.* Upon this Ben paid his garnish—*being fully convinced of the folly of not keeping up a good understanding with those among whom we are destined to live.*

Ben had been at Palmer's office but a short time before he discovered that all his workmen, to the number of fifty, were terrible drinkers of porter, insomuch that they kept a stout boy all day long on the trot to serve them alone. Every man among them must have, viz.

		d.
1	A pint of porter before breakfast,—cost	1½
1	A pint, with his bread and cheese, for breakfast,	1½
1	A pint betwixt his breakfast and dinner,	1½
1	A pint at his dinner,	1½
1	A pint betwixt his dinner and night,	1½
1	A pint after his day's work was done,	1½
6	Total, three quarts!—equal to *nine pence sterling per day*!	9

A practice so fatal to the health and subsistence of those poor people and their families, pained Ben to the soul, and he instantly set himself to break it up. But they laughed him to scorn, boasting of their beloved porter, that it was "*meat and drink too*," and the only thing to give them *strength* to work. Ben was not to be put out of heart by such an argument as this. He offered to prove to them that the strength they derived from the beer could only be in proportion to the barley dissolved in the water of which the beer was made—that there was a larger portion of flour in a penny loaf; and that if they ate this loaf and drank a pint of water with it, they would get more strength than from a pint of beer. But still they would not hearken to any thing said against their darling beer. Beer, they said, was "*the liquor of life*," and beer they must have, or *farewell strength.*

"Why, gentlemen," replied Ben, "don't you see me with great ease carry up and down stairs, a large form of letters in each hand; while you, with *both* hands, have much ado to carry one? And don't you perceive that these heavy weights which I bear produce no manner of change in my breathing, while you, with only half the weight, cannot mount the stairs without puffing and blowing most distressingly? Now is not this sufficient to prove that water, though apparently the weakest, is yet in reality the strongest liquor in nature, especially for the young and healthy?"

But alas! on most of them, this excellent logic was all thrown away.

"The ruling passion, be it what it will—

The ruling passion governs reason still."

Though they could not deny a syllable of Ben's reasoning, being often heard to say that, "THE AMERICAN AQUATIC (or *water drinker*) as they called him, was much stronger than any of the beer drinkers," still they would drink.

"But suppose," asked some of them, "we were to quit our beer with bread and cheese for breakfast, what substitute should we have?"

"Why, use," said Ben, "the substitute that I do; which is a pint of nice oatmeal gruel brought to me from your beer-house, with a little butter, sugar and nutmeg, and a slice of dry toast. This, which is more palatable and still less costly than a pint of beer, makes a much better breakfast, and keeps the head clearer to boot. At dinner I take a cup of cold water, which is the wholesomest of all beverages, and requires nothing but a little use, to render it as pleasant. In this way, gentlemen, I save *nine* pence sterling every day, making in the year nearly *three thousand pence*! an enormous sum, let me tell you, my friends, to a small family; and which would not only save parents the disgrace of being dunned for trifling debts, but also procure a thousand comforts for the children."

Ben did not entirely lose his reward, several of his hearers affording him the unspeakable satisfaction of following his counsel. But the major part, "*poor devils*," as he emphatically styled them, "*went on to drink—thus continuing all their lives in a state of voluntary poverty and wretchedness!!*"

Many of them, for lack of punctuality to pay the publican, would often have their porter stopped.—They would then apply to Ben to become security for them, *their light*, as they called it, *being out*. I never heard that he upbraided them with their folly; but readily gave his word to the publican, though it cost him the trouble of attending at the pay-table, every *Saturday night*, to take up the sums he had made himself accountable for.

Thus, by virtue of the right education, *i.e.* a good trade, and early fondness for labour and books, did Ben rise, like a young swan of heaven, above the dark billows of adversity; and cover himself with glory in the eyes of these young Englishmen, who had at first been so prejudiced against him. And, better still, when night came, instead of sauntering with them to the filthy yet costly ale-houses and porter cellars, he hastened to his little chamber at his *frugal* boarding-house, (only 1s. 6d. per week) there to enjoy the divine society of his books, which he obtained on *hire* from a neighbouring book-store. And commanding, as he always did, through his steadiness and rapidity at work, all the *quick off-hand jobs*, generally the best paid, he might have made money and enjoyed great peace; but alas! there was a moth in his purse which kept him constantly poor; a canker in his peace which filled his life with vexation. That canker and that moth was his young friend Ralph, whom, as we have seen, he had made an infidel of in Philadelphia; and for which good office, Ralph, as we shall presently see, requited him as might have been expected.

CHAPTER XXVII.

"Who reasons wisely, is not therefore *wise*;

His pride in reasoning, not in acting, lies."

Some years ago a certain empiric whispered in the ear of a noble lord, in the British parliament, that he had made a wonderful discovery.

"Aye," replied the nobleman, staring; "a wonderful discovery, say you!"

"Yes, my lord, a wonderful discovery indeed! A discovery, my lord, beyond Gallileo, Friar Bacon, or even the great sir Isaac Newton himself."

"The d——l! what, beyond sir Isaac?"

"Yes, 'pon honour, my lord, beyond the great sir Isaac. 'Tis true his ATTRACTIONS and GRAVITATIONS and all that, are well enough; very clever things to be sure, my lord; but still nothing in comparison of this."

"Zounds, man, what can it be?"

"Why, my lord—please come a little this way—now, in confidence, my lord—I've been such a lucky dog as to discover the wondrous art of raising a breed of sheep *without wool*!"

The nobleman, who, it is thought, was not very nearly related to Solomon, had like to have gone into fits. "What sir," asked he, with a countenance wild-staring with amazement, "a breed of sheep without wool! impossible!"

"Pardon me, my lord, it is very possible, very true. I have indeed, my lord, discovered the adorable art of raising a breed of sheep without a lock of wool on their backs! not a lock, my lord, any more than there is here on the back of my hand."

"Your fortune is made, sir," replied the nobleman, smacking his hands and lifting both them and his eyes to heaven as in ecstasy—"Your fortune is made for ever. Government, I am sure, sir, will not fail suitably to reward a discovery that will immortalize the British nation."

Accordingly, a motion to that purpose was made in the *House of Lords*, and the empiric was within an ace of being created a peer of the realm; when, most unfortunately, the duke of Devonshire, a district famed for sheep, got up and begged a little patience of the house until it could be fully understood what great benefit the nation was to derive from a flock of sheep without wool. "Why, zounds! my lords," said the noble duke, "I thought all along that wool was the *main chance* in a flock of sheep."

A most learned discussion ensued. And it being made apparent to the noble lords, that wool is *actually* the basis of broadcloths, flannels, and most other of the best British manufactures—and it being also made apparent to the noble lords, which was another great point gained, that two good things are better than one, *i.e.* that wool and mutton together, are better than mutton by itself, or wool by itself, the motion for a TITLE was unanimously scouted: and in place of a pension the rascal had like to have got a prison, for daring thus to trump up a vile discovery that would have robbed the world of one its greatest comforts.

Just so, to my mind at least, it fares with all the boasted discoveries of our modern atheists. Admitting that these wonderful wizards could raise a nation of men and women without religion, as easily as this, their brother conjurer, could a breed of Merinos without wool—still we must ask *cui bono*? that is, what *good* would it be to the world? Supposing they could away at a dash, with all sense of so glorious a being as God, and all comfort of so mighty a hope as heaven, what benefit would it bring to man or beast?

But, God be praised, this dismal question about the consequence of discarding religion need not be asked at this time of day. These gentlemen without religion, like bell-wethers without wool, do so constantly betray their nakedness, I mean their want of morality, that the world, bad as it is, is getting ashamed of them. Here, for example, is master Ralph, who, for reasons abundantly convenient to himself, had accompanied Ben to London—Ben, as he himself confesses, had lent a liberal hand to make Ralph a sturdy infidel, that is, to free him from the restraints of the gospel. Now mark the precious fruits of this boasted freedom. Getting displeased with the parents of a poor girl, whom he had married, he determines to quit her for ever, as also a poor unoffending child he had by her, whom, by the ties of nature, he was bound to comfort and protect! Ben, though secretly abhorring this villany of Ralph, yet suffered himself to be so enamoured of his vivacity and wit, as to make him an inmate. "We were," says Ben, "*inseparable companions.*" Very little cause had he, poor lad! as he himself owns afterwards, to boast of this connexion. But it was fine sport for Ralph; for having brought no money with him from America but what just sufficed to pay his passage, and knowing what a noble drudge Ben was, and also that he had with him fifteen pistoles, the fruits of his hard labours and savings in Philadelphia, he found it very convenient to hang upon him; not only boarding and lodging at his expense, and at his expense going to plays and concerts, but also frequently drawing on his dear yellow boys, the pistoles, for purposes of private pleasure.

If the reader should ask, how Ralph, even as a man of honour, could reconcile it to himself, thus to devour his friend, let me, in turn, ask what business had Ben to furnish Ralph the very alphabet and syntax of this abominable lesson against himself? And, if that should not be thought quite to the point, let me ask again, where, taking the fear of God out of the heart, is the difference between a man and a beast? If man has reason, it is only to make him ten-fold more a beast. Ralph, it is true, did no work; but what of that? He wrote such charming poetry—and spouted such fine plays—and talked so eloquently with Ben of nights!—and sure this was a good offset against Ben's hard labours and pistoles. At any rate Ralph thought so. Nay, more; he thought, in return for these sublime entertainments, Ben ought to support not only him, but also his concubine. Accordingly he went and scraped acquaintance with a handsome young widow, a milliner, in the next street: and what with reading his fine poetry to her, and spouting his plays, he got so completely into her good graces, that she presently turned actress too; and in the "COMEDY OF ERRORS," or "ALL FOR LOVE," played her part so unluckily, that she was hissed from the stage, by all her virtuous acquaintance, and compelled to troop off with a big belly to another neighbourhood, where Ralph continued to visit her.

The reader will hardly wonder, when told that Ralph and his fair milliner soon found the bottom of Ben's purse. He will rather wonder what sort of love-powder it was that Ben took of this young man that could, for such a length of time, so fatally have befooled him. But Ben was *first in the transgression.* Like Alexander the coppersmith, he had done Ralph "*much harm,*" and "God, who is wiser than all, had ordained that he should be "*rewarded according to his works.*

CHAPTER XXVIII.

"Learn to be wise from others' ill,"

And you'll learn to do full well."

As nothing is so repellant of base minds as poverty, soon as Ralph found that Ben's pistoles were all gone, and his finances reduced to the beggarly ebb of living *from hand to mouth*, he "*cleared out*," and betook himself into the country to teach *school*, whence he was continually writing fine poetical epistles to Ben, not forgetting in every postscript, to put him in mind of his dear Dulcinea, the fair milliner, and to commend her to his kindness. As to Ben, he still persevered, after Ralph's departure, in his good old habits of industry and economy—never indulging in tobacco or gin—never sauntering to taverns or play houses, nor at any time laying out his money but on books, which he always visited, as frugal lovers do their sweethearts, at night. But still it would not all do. He could lay up nothing. The daily postage of Ralph's long poetical epistles, with the unceasing application of the poor milliner, kept his purse continually in a galloping consumption. At length he obtained a release from this unpleasant situation, though in a way that he himself never could think of afterwards without a blush.

After very frequent loans of money to her, she came, it seems, one night to his lodgings on the old errand—*to borrow half a guinea*! when Ben, who had been getting too fond of her, took this opportunity to offer freedoms which she highly resented.

This Ben tells himself, with a candour that will for ever do him credit among those who know that the confession of folly is the first step on the way to wisdom.

"Having, at that time," says he, "no ties of religion upon me, and taking advantage of her necessitous situation, I attempted liberties (*another great error of my life,*) which she repelled with *becoming indignation.* She informed Ralph; and the affair occasioned a breach between us. When he returned to London, he gave to understand that he considered all the obligations he owed me as annihilated by this proceeding; and that I was not to expect *one farthing of all the monies I had lent him.*"

Ben used to say, many years afterwards, that this conduct of his friend Ralph put him in mind of an anecdote he had some where heard, of good old Gilbert Tenant: the same that George Whitefield generally called HELL-FIRE TENANT. This eminent divine, believing *fear* to be a much stronger motive with the multitude than *love*, constantly made a great run upon that passion in all his discourses. And Boanerges himself could hardly have held a candle to him in this way. Nature had given him a countenance which he could, at will, clothe with all the terrors of the tornado. And besides he had a talent for painting the scenes of dread perdition in such colours, that when aided by the lightning of his eyes, and the bursting thunders of his voice, it was enough to start the soul of lion-hearted innocence; what then of rabbit-livered guilt? The truth is, he wrought miracles in New-Jersey: casting out devils—the devils of drunkenness, gambling, and lust, out of many a wretch *possessed.*

Among the thousands whom he thus frightened for their good, was a tame Indian of Woodbury, who generally went by the name of Indian-Dick. This poor savage, on hearing Mr. Tenant preach, was so terrified, that he fell down in the meeting house, and roared as if under the scalping knife.

He lost his stomach: and even his beloved bottle was forgotten. Old Mr. Tenant went to see Dick, and rejoiced over him as a son in the gospel;—heartily thanking God for adding this INDIAN GEM to the crown of his glory.

Not many days after this, the man of God took his journey through the south counties of New-Jersey, calling the poor clam-catchers of Cape May to repentance. As he returned and drew near to Woodbury, lo! a great multitude! He rejoiced in spirit, as hoping that it was a meeting of the people to hear the word of God: but the uproar bursting upon his ear, put him in doubt.

"Surely," said he, "this is not the voice of praise; 'tis rather, I fear, the noise of drunkenness." And so it was indeed; for it being a day of election, the friends of the candidates had dealt out their brandy so liberally that the street was filled with sots of every degree, from the simple *stagger* to the *dead drunk*. Among the rest, he beheld his Indian convert, poor Dick, under full sail in the street, reeling and hallooing, great as a sachem. Mr. Tenant strove hard to avoid him; but Dick, whose quick eye had caught the old pie-balled horse that Tenant rode on, instantly staggered towards him. Tenant put forth all his horsemanship to avoid the interview. He kicked old Pie-ball in one flank, and then in the other; pulled this rein and then that; laid on *here* with his staff, and laid on *there*; but all would not do; unless he could at once ride down the drunken beasts, there was no way of getting clear of them. So that Dick, *half shaved* as he was, soon got along side of old Pie-ball, whom he grappled by the rein with one hand, and stretching forth the other, bawled out, "*how do? how do, Mr. Tenant?*"

Tenant could not look at him.

Still, Dick, with his arm full extended, continued to bawl, "*how do, Mr. Tenant, how do?*" Finding that there was no getting clear of him, Mr. Tenant, red as crimson, lifted up his eyes on Dick, who still, bold as brandy, stammered out, "*High, Mr. Tenant! d-d-d-don't you know me, Mr. Tenant? Don't you know Indian Dick? Why, sure, Mr. Tenant, you are the man that converted me?*"

"I converted you!" replied Tenant, nearly fainting.

"*Yes*, roared Dick, *I'll be d-d-d-nd, Mr. Tenant, if you an't the very man that converted me.*"

"Poor fellow!" said Tenant, with a heavy sigh, "you look like one of my *handiworks.* Had God Almighty converted you, you would have looked like another guess sort of a creature."

From Ben's constantly relating this story of old Tenant and Indian Dick, whenever he mentioned the aforesaid case of Ralph's baseness, many of his acquaintance were of opinion, that Ben thereby as good as acknowledged, that at the time he took Ralph in hand, he did not altogether understand the art of converting; or, that at any rate, it would have been much better for Ralph, if, as Mr, Tenant said of Indian Dick, *God Almighty had converted him.* He would hardly, for the sake of a harlot, have so basely treated his best friend and benefactor.

CHAPTER XXIX.

Ben resolves to return to America.—Anecdote of a rare character.

"A wit's a feather, and a chief's a rod,

An *honest* man's the noblest work of God."

Ben used, with singular pleasure, to relate the following story of his Quaker friend Denham. This excellent man had formerly been in business as a Bristol merchant; but failing, he compounded with his creditors and departed for America, where, by his extraordinary diligence and frugality, he acquired in a few years a considerable fortune. Returning to England, in the same ship with Ben, he invited all his old creditors to a dinner. After thanking them for their former kindness and assuring them that they should soon be paid, he begged them to take their seats at table. On turning up their plates, every man found his due, principal and interest, under his plate, in shining gold.

This was the man after Ben's own heart. Though he never found in Denham any of those flashes of wit, or floods of eloquence, which used so to dazzle him in Ralph, yet he contracted such a friendship for him, on account of his honesty and Quaker-like meekness, that he would often steal an hour from his books at night, to go and chat with him. And on the other hand, Ben's steady and persevering industry, with his passion for knowledge, had so exalted him in Denham's esteem, that he was never better pleased than when his *young friend Franklin*, as he always called him, came to see him. One night Denham asked Ben how he would like a trip to America?

"Nothing on earth would so please me," replied Ben, "if I could do it to advantage."

"Well, friend Benjamin," said Denham, "I am just a-going to make up a large assortment of goods for a store in Philadelphia, and if fifty pounds sterling a year, and bed and board with myself, will satisfy thee, I shall be happy of thy services to go and live with me as my clerk."

The memory of his dear Philadelphia, and the many happy days he had spent there, instantly sprung a something at his heart that reddened his cheeks with joy. But the saddening thought of his total unacquaintedness with commerce, soon turned them pale again. "I should be happy indeed to accompany you," replied he, with a deep sigh, "if I were but qualified to do you justice."

"O! as to that, friend Benjamin, don't be uneasy," replied Denham: "If thou art not qualified *now*, thou soon wilt be. And then as soon as thou art fit; I'll send thee with a cargo of corn and flour to the West Indies, and put thee in a way wherein, with such talents and industry as thine, thee may soon make a fortune."

Ben was highly delighted with this proposal, for though fifty pounds a year was not so much as he could earn at printing, yet the prospects in other respects were so much greater. Added to this, he was getting heartily tired of printing. He had tried it five years at Boston, three at Philadelphia, and now nearly two in London. At all these places he had worked without ceasing; had lived most sparingly; had left no stone unturned; and after all was now, in his twenty-first year, just as indigent as when he began! "Scurvy, starving business!" thought he to himself, "'tis high time to quit you! and God be thanked for this fair opportunity to do it; and now we will shake hands and part for ever." Taking leave now of the printing business, and as he believed and wished, *for ever*, he gave himself up entirely to his new occupation, constantly going from house to house with Denham, purchasing goods and packing them. When every thing was safe on board, he took a little leisure to visit his friends, and amuse himself. This was a rule which he observed through life—to do business first, and then enjoy pleasure without a sting.

CHAPTER XXX.

On the 23d of July, 1726, Ben, with his friend Denham, took leave of their London acquaintance, and embarked for America. As the ebbing current gently bore the vessel along down the amber coloured flood, Ben could not suppress his emotions, as he looked back on that mighty city, whose restless din was now gradually dying on his ear, as were its smoke-covered houses sinking from his view, perhaps for ever. And as he looked back, the secret sigh would arise, for the many toils and heart aches he had suffered there, and all to so little profit. But virtue, like the sun, though it may be overcast with clouds, will soon scatter those clouds, and spread a brighter ray after their transient showers. 'Tis true, eighteen months had been spent there, but they had not been *misspent.* He could look back upon them without shame or remorse. He had broken no midnight lamps—had knocked down no poor watchman—had contributed nothing to the idleness and misery of any family. On the contrary, he had the exceeding satisfaction to know, that he had left the largest printing-houses in London in mourning for his departure—that he had shown them the blessings of temperance, and had proselyted many of them from folly to wise and manly living. And though, when he looked at those eighteen months, he could not behold them, like eastern maidens, dowered with gold and diamonds, yet, better still, he could behold them like the "Wise Virgins," whose lamps he had diligently fed with the oil of wisdom, for some great marriage supper—perhaps that between LIBERTY and his COUNTRY.

After a wearisome passage of near eleven weeks, the ship arrived at Philadelphia, where Ben met the perfidious Keith, walking the street alone, and shorn of all the short-lived splendours of his governorship. Ben's honest face struck the culprit pale and dumb. The reader hardly need be told, that Ben was too magnanimous to add to his confusion, by reproaching or even speaking to him. But as if to keep Ben from pride, Providence kindly threw into his way his old sweetheart, Miss Read. Here his confusion would have been equal to Keith's, had not that fair one furnished him with the sad charge against herself—of marrying during his absence. Her friends, after reading his letter to her, concluding that he would never return, had advised her to take a husband. But she soon separated from him, and even refused to bear his name; in consequence of learning that he had another wife.

Denham and Ben took a store-house, and displayed their goods; which, having been well laid in, sold off very rapidly. This was in October, 1726. Early in the following February, when the utmost kindness on Denham's part, and an equal fidelity on Ben's, had rendered them mutually dear, as father and son; and when also, by their extraordinary success in trade, they had a fair prospect of speedily making their fortunes, behold! O, vanity of all worldly hopes! they were both taken down dangerously ill. Denham, for his part, actually made a die of it. And Ben was so far gone, at one time, that he concluded it was all over with him; which afforded a melancholy kind of pleasure, especially when he was told that his friend Denham, who lay in the next room, was dead. And when he reflected that now, since his good patron had left him, he should be turned out again upon the world, with the same hard struggles to encounter, and no prospect of ever being able to do any thing for his aged father, he felt a secret regret, that he was called back to life again.

CHAPTER XXXI.

Some people there are who tell us that every man is born for a particular walk in life, and that whether he will or not, in that walk he must go; and can no more quit it than the sun can quit his course through the skies.

This is a very pleasing part of faith; and really there seems much ground for it. Certainly scripture, in many places, has a powerful squinting that way. And in the lives of many of our greatest men, we discover strong symptoms of it. The great Washington was, a dozen times and more within an ace of getting out of the only track that could have led him to the command of the American armies. But yet there seems to have been always some invisible hand to meet him at the threshold of his wanderings, and to push him back. Dr. Franklin also appears, on several occasions, to have been at the very point of breaking off from the printing business. But Heaven has decreed for him that walk in life, and in it he must move. And though blind at times, as Balaam's ass, he sought to turn out of the way, yet, crouch as he would, he still found at every turn a good angel to bring him back. First he was to have been a sailor out of Boston—then a swimming-master in London—then a merchant in America. But it would not all do. And though in this last brilliant affair, he seemed to have effected his escape, losing the black-fingered printer in the sprucely powdered merchant, yet, come back to the WORLD-ENLIGHTENING TYPES he must—for Denham dies, and with him all the grand castles which Ben had built in the air. Still averse to the printing business, he tries hard for another place *behind the counter*, but nobody will take him in. His money at length gone, and every avenue to honest bread hedged up against him, he is constrained to take refuge in his old trade.

Keimer, his former employer, who well knew his worth, waited on him, and made liberal offers if he would take charge of his printing-office. It must have been a sore trial to Ben to come under authority of a man whose ignorance and hypocrisy he so heartily despised; and who, he well knew, had nothing else in view, but just to get him to instruct his numerous apprentices, and then pick a quarrel and pack him off. But bad as he hated Keimer's vices, he still worse hated idleness and dependence, and therefore he accepted his invitation. He found Keimer's office in the old way, *i.e.* quite out of order, and miserably destitute of letters. There being at that time no such thing in America, as a type-foundry, this defect appeared at first utterly incurable. But Ben soon found a remedy. Having once, while he lived in London, glanced his eye on the practice of this art, he thought he could imitate it. And, by casting in clay, he presently created a fine parcel of letters in lead, which served at least, to keep the press from stopping. He also, on occasion, engraved a variety of ornaments for printing—made ink—gave an eye to the shop, and, in short, was in all respects the factotum of the establishment. But useful as he made himself, he had the mortification to find that his services became every day of less importance to Keimer, in proportion as his apprentices improved; and when Keimer paid Ben his second quarter's wages, he did it very grumblingly, and gave him to understand, that they were too heavy. By degrees he became less civil; was constantly finding fault, and seemed always on the point of coming to an open rupture.

Ben bore it all very patiently, conceiving that his ill humour was owing to the embarrassment of his affairs.

At length, however, the old wretch insulted him so grossly, and that under circumstances of all others the most provoking to a man of honest pride, *i.e.* in the presence of neighbours, that Ben could bear it no longer; but, after upbraiding him for his ingratitude, took up his hat and left him, begging a young man of the office to take care of his trunk, and bring it to him at night.

The name of this young man was Meredith, one of Keimer's apprentices. He had taken a great liking to Ben, because that while Keimer, ignorant and crabbed, taught him nothing, Ben was every day giving him some useful lesson in his trade, or some excellent hint in morals, conducive to the government and happiness of his life. In the evening he came and entreated Ben not to think of quitting the printing office while he continued in it. "My dear sir," said he to Ben, "I beg you will take no notice of what this Keimer does. The poor man is always, as you see, *half shaved*; and no wonder, for he is over head and ears in debt—often selling his goods at prime cost, for the sake of *cash*—constantly giving credit without taking any account; and therefore cannot help shortly coming out of the little end of the horn, which will leave a glorious opening for you to make your fortune."

Ben replied that he had nothing to begin with. "O, as to that difficulty," answered Meredith, "we can easily get over it. My father has a very high opinion of you, and will, I am sure, readily advance money to set us up, provided you will but go into partnership with me. I am no workman, but you are. And so, if you like, I will find the capital and you the skill, and let's go halves in the profits. By spring we can have in from London, our press, types, and paper, and then, as my time with Keimer will be out, we can fall to work at once, and make our *jacks*."

As this was an offer not to be met with every day, Ben readily agreed to it, as also did old Mr. Meredith.

But the old gentleman had a better motive in view than the pecuniary profits. He had marked, with great pleasure, Ben's ascendancy over his son, whom he had already wonderfully checked in his passion for tobacco and brandy. And he fondly hoped, that by this connexion his son would be perfectly cured.

With this hope, he desired Ben to make him out the list of a *complete* printing-office, which he immediately took to his merchant, with orders to import it without loss of time. Keimer was to know nothing of all this; and Ben, in the interim, was to get work with Bradford.

On application, Bradford had no room. Ben, therefore, had to rest on his oars. This, however, was but for a short season: for Keimer getting a hint that he should be employed to print some New-Jersey paper money, that would require engravings and types which he knew nobody in Philadelphia but Ben could make; and fearful that Bradford, by engaging Ben, might deprive him of the job, sent a very civil message to Ben, telling him that "*old friends ought not to part on account of a few hasty words dropt in a passion*," and concluding with a pressing invitation to come back.

Ben went back; and Keimer met him with a most cordial welcome. Although there was nothing in this poor old man to excite his esteem, yet Ben could not help feeling happy to see smiles of joy brightening over his withered face; and he then felt, though not for the first time, that though learning is a pleasant thing, yet one touch of "*kindred sentiment warm at the heart*," outweighs, in pure delight, all the learning in the world.

CHAPTER XXXII.

Keimer presently obtained what he so ardently wished, the printing of the New-Jersey paper-money, and flew into the office with the news to Ben, who immediately set about constructing a copper-plate press, the first that had ever been seen in Philadelphia. He also engraved various ornaments and devices for the bills; and putting every thing in readiness for their paper-money coinage, he set out with Keimer for Burlington, where the New-Jersey legislature held their session.

At the first sight of Ben's paper-money, every eye was struck with its beauty. "*Why this Keimer must be a very clever old fellow!*" was the cry. But others who were deeper in the secret, replied, "not so; young Franklin is the man." Hereupon great attention was paid to Ben. And he was sensibly taught, that though he had been grievously tried and held back in the world, yet he had much cause of gratitude. Presently another affair arose, furnishing him fresh matter of congratulation, that he had ever paid such attention to the improvement of his mind.

Fearing that our Philadelphia printers might strike off *more money bills* than they had been desired, the New-Jersey Assembly thought proper to send two or three commissioners to superintend the press. These gentlemen, all of the shrewd sort, and constantly with them while at work, soon found out the difference between the master and his young journeyman. Keimer, though a printer, had never been a reader. Ben had devoted all his leisure hours to reading. The one had ever courted pleasure in the furniture of his mind: the other, popularity in the decorations of his body. The shape of his whiskers; the cock of his hat; the cut of his coat, were great things with Keimer. Every trick at easy outside show was caught up by him. Among other dashes at popularity, he pretended to be a freemason, and was constantly grinning and making his signs. But it would not all do. The New-Jersey commissioners knew nothing of Jachin and Boaz. So that though, while Ben, stripped to the buff, was heaving at the press, old Keimer would stand by, stately as a prince at his levee, his attitude perpendicular as the *plummet*, and his feet perfectly on the *square*, with his gilt snuff-box nicely poised in his left hand, and his right, bespangled with rings, tastily carrying the fragrant Maccabau to his nostrils, courting the commissioners—yet, as before said, it would not all do. The commissioners wanted new ideas, and Keimer had none to give them. He had a pompous way of saying yes or no. And this was all they could get from him in answer to their questions. Presently they turned to Ben, whom by the by, they hardly thought it worth while to interrogate, considering the character of his master, and his own young and raw appearance. But in place of the old YES and NO of master Keimer, Ben gave them such answers to their questions, as at once surprised and delighted them. He was slow to speak, but when the commissioners, curious to explore his intellect, which had so unexpectedly startled them, purposely put a number of deep questions to him on the subject of their paper-money, such as its effects on agriculture and commerce, and the laws that should regulate its quantity, he answered all in his own peculiar way of sagacious brevity, that made them declare he must have studied nothing else all his life. The reports which these gentlemen made in his favour, produced their natural effect. Ben was invited every where, and treated with the most flattering attention; while Keimer, though his employer, was entirely neglected, or invited only as a compliment to Ben.

Among the many wealthy and great ones, his admirers, was the inspector general, Isaac Deacon, a cunning old fox, and rich as a Jew. He could never rest without Ben at his house. "*Young man,*" said he one day, as Ben was hard at work, "*I am mightily taken with you*, and let me tell you, I never look at you without thinking of myself, as I was at your time of life. Now, do you know what was my first employment, when I was a boy?"

Ben replied that that was a question beyond his reach.

"Well then, I will tell you, sir, if you can but believe me. I'll tell you. My first employment was to carry clay to the brick-makers!"

"Impossible!" said Ben.

"No, indeed, not impossible at all, but very certain. Yes, many a hot day have I carried the clay, and so daubed with it all over, that my own mother would hardly have told me from her house pig. Well, after that I became an underling to a surveyor, and dragged his chain many a day through the woods; and all the time did not know '*B from a bull's foot.*' But the surveyor was a good man, sir, and taught me to read and write. Ah! *them were dark times*, sir, *dark times*; all living here like Indians in the woods. A young man, printing his books and pictures like you, would have been looked on as a conjurer. And now let me tell you one thing. Don't you be discouraged, but keep up a good heart. A *little*, making every day, makes a great deal in a long life. And I am mistaken if you don't make a fortune, and come out a great man yet some of these days."

CHAPTER XXXIII.

Having finished printing the New-Jersey money, Ben, accompanied by Keimer, set out for Philadelphia, where he had scarcely arrived before in came Meredith, with a face of joy, and taking Ben aside, told him that their press and types were all come. Immediately the two friends went forth in search of a good house and stand, which they were so lucky as to find near the market, at twenty-four pounds *a year*! The fixing and putting all their things to rights, having consumed every penny of their money, our young beginners were at their wit's end what to be at. In this extremity, one of their acquaintance, a Mr. George House, brought them a countryman who wanted some advertisements for a cow he had lost. Ben soon had the old cow up for him in a "*staring*" shape, which so pleased the honest rustic, that he instantly counted them down their *five shillings*. Never did five shillings come more acceptably. The gratitude which Ben felt towards George House for this little kindness, fixed on him a determination from that day, "*never to miss an opportunity to lend a helping hand to young beginners.*"

His favourite young Hercules, the PRINTING-OFFICE, which had been so long labouring in his brain, being now happily brought to birth, Ben determined immediately to give it the countenance and support of another noble bantling of his own. I allude to his famous club, called the "Junto," a kind of Robinhood society, composed of young men desirous of improving themselves in knowledge and elocution, and who met one night every week, to discuss some interesting question in morals, politics, or philosophy.

The members at first were but few; but Ben, now a complete master of his pen, made such a dash with their speeches in his *newspaper*, that the Junto soon got to be the talk of the town; and members were added to it daily. Ben was unanimously appointed moderator of the club; and in reward for the great pleasure and profit derived from this noble, mind-improving institution, the members all agreed to support his printing-office. This was of service; but its principal support was derived from a still higher source; I mean his own astonishing industry. No sooner was it known in town that Ben had set up a new paper and press, under the very nose of two others, Keimer's and Bradford's, than it became a matter of speculation whether it could possibly stand. The generality gave into the negative. But Dr. Bard, a shrewd old Scotchman, who well knew the effect of persevering industry on young men's fortunes, laughed heartily at the doubters. "*Stand*," said he, "*gentlemen*! Yes, take my word it *will stand.* The industry of that young Franklin will make any thing stand. I see him still at work when I return from my patients at midnight, and he is at it again in the morning before his neighbours are out of bed." Ben was fairly entitled to his praise. He generally composed and corrected ten to twelve thousand m's a day, though it constantly took him till near midnight. But so intent was he on finishing this incredible task, that when accident had deranged a good half of his hard day's work, he has been known to fall to work and set it up again before he went to bed.

The reputation acquired by this industry, made such an impression in his favour, that the merchants, many of them, made him liberal offers of their stationary on *credit.* But, not wishing to have "*too many irons in the fire*," he declined their offers, which added to his reputation of an *industrious* young man, that of an *upright* and *cautious* one. This is mentioned, not so much for praise of the *dead*, as for a *hint* to the living.

Business began now to make a flood-tide movement in the new printing-office, and Ben made such good use of it, and picked up money so fast, that he was in hopes he had nearly thrown all his troubles over the "*left shoulder.*" But in this he was miserably mistaken; for presently, as if there was to be no end to troubles, there leaped out another, more alarming than all before. Old Meredith, finding that Ben had not cured his son of his drunken fits, *took a miff*, and all at once *backed out* of his promise to pay for their press and printing materials! and the merchant who imported these costly articles, and who had for some time been expecting his money, commenced a suit, and threatened immediate execution!

Poor Ben! Imagination sees him, at first, standing like a luckless merchant, who, after two noble ventures swallowed up, now beholds the breakers that are to swallow up his third, and *last* hope—"Yes," thought he, "but a few short weeks and my press and type will be under the hammer; all my delightful hopes annihilated; and myself turned adrift on the wide world again!"

At this perilous moment, when nothing but infamy and ruin stared him in the face, God was pleased to cause his OWN VIRTUES to leap forth like an armed Minerva, with shield and buckler for his defence. His INDUSTRY and PRUDENCE having, as aforesaid, been trumpeted through the town, the public feelings were greatly excited by his misfortunes. "*Shame*," *said they*, "*that such a young man should fall. As to that drunken fellow, that Meredith, no matter how soon he is stripped and sent to jail. But this Franklin must not fall for want of a little help. It were a disgrace to the town.*" Accordingly several gentlemen, two at least are recorded, Coleman and Grace, without each other's knowledge, called on him, and tendered whatever sum he should want!—but hoping at the same time he would, if possible, get quit of Meredith, who only served to disgrace and injure him; being often seen at *taverns* and *gambling tables.*

A relief so unexpected, and in a manner too so flattering, produced on the mind of Ben, a satisfaction beyond expression. After making the best acknowledgments he could to such noble benefactors, he begged they would allow him a day or two to effect, if possible, an honourable separation from Meredith. Fortunately he found no difficulty in this: for Meredith, heartily sick of the business, readily agreed, for a small consideration, to give him up the printing-office to himself. Ben then called on his two friends, accepted the proffered supply, taking exactly one half from each for fear of offending either, and making full settlement with the Merediths, took the whole business into his own hands.

Ben's extreme alarm from the danger of having his printing-office seized, and its fortunate rescue by the amiable Coleman and Grace, has been very briefly narrated. But transient as this event may seem in our narrative, it produced on his feelings a glow of gratitude which kings might envy; and it led to an *act* which Angels would glory in. The reader shall hear all in good time.

CHAPTER XXXIV.

Having now got the printing-office in his own hands, Ben began to find the unspeakable advantage of his past labours to acquire ideas, and to convey them handsomely by his pen. The town and country getting at this time prodigiously excited about a PAPER CURRENCY, Ben came out with a most luminous pamphlet, on "THE ADVANTAGES and DISADVANTAGES of a PAPER CURRENCY." The pamphlet gave such satisfaction to the legislature, that they rewarded him with the *printing* of all their money bills. His pamphlet producing the same effect on the legislature of Delaware, they rewarded him in the same way—as also did both these legislatures by throwing into his way several other jobs of public printing.

Money now coming in, he went at once, and paid his good friends Coleman and Grace what they had so nobly lent him. With a light heart he then wiped off that old score of VERNON'S, which had given him so much uneasiness, but which now receipted in *full*, *principal* and *interest*, made him feel himself the freest, and therefore the happiest man in Pennsylvania. Money still coming in, he fitted up a few shelves in the front room of his printing-office, where he spread out an assortment of Books, Blanks, Paper and Quills; but all in the small way—for he always thought, that though

"Vessels large may venture more,

Yet little boats should keep near shore."

Like a ship that after long tacking against winds and tides, through dangerous straits and shallows, has at last got safely out on the main ocean flood, and at liberty to lay her own course; such was now the condition of Ben; who hereupon felt it his duty immediately to take on board those two grand guides and guardians of his voyage—RELIGION and a GOOD WIFE.

As to religion—the grum looks and bitter sectarian animosities of the christians in those wretched days, had early made a deist of him; and he, in turn, had made deists of others, as Collins and Ralph. But on coming to test the thing by its fruits, he found that this new religion (deism) was not yet the religion he could admire. He found that poor Collins, with all his deism, was but a drunkard—Ralph, an ungrateful swindler—governor Keith, a great rascal—and even himself, though a prime deist, yet in his treatment of Miss Read, as culpable as any of them all. This led him to a train of thought which resulted in the conclusion, that though he could not conceive that *bad actions are bad, merely because revelation forbids them; nor good actions good, because revelation enjoins them*: yet he doubted not but the former were forbidden, because they are *hurtful*, and the latter enjoined because they are *beneficial* to us—all things considered. On this grand principle then, the inseparable connexion between VICE and MISERY, and VIRTUE and HAPPINESS, he determined from that day to shun the one, and embrace the other; thus summing up his religion in those beautiful lines:—

"What CONSCIENCE dictates to be done,"

Or warns me not to do;"

This teach me more than HELL to shun,"

That more than HEAVEN pursue."

So much for his religion. As to his wife, his behaviour in this respect seems to have shown that there was some substance in the religious ground he had taken. Having, at the time of his sad disappointment in London, and when he despaired of ever marrying her, neglected his old sweetheart Miss Read, he resolved, now that he was getting into better circumstances, to make her all the amends in his power. 'Tis true, her mother, who had prevented the marriage before he set off for England, and during his absence had prevailed on her to marry another lover, was most in fault, and actually acquitted him, laying the blame altogether at her own door.—But Ben never acquitted himself; he felt condemned, and would therefore accept no *absolution* while he could make *reparation*. He renewed his visits to the family, who were rejoiced to see him. He saw his old sweetheart, Miss Read; but O how altered from her who, formerly bright with love and joy, used to fly to the door to welcome his coming! How altered from her, whose rosy cheeks crimsoned with blushes, he so fondly kissed at taking leave for England, with sweetest promises of speedy return and blissful marriage. Pale and wan were her looks, where she sat silent, and retired, and often deeply sighing, like one much troubled in mind, or crossed in hopeless love. She never reminded him of his "*troth and broken vows*." But such patient suffering served but the more to harrow up his feelings. Each stifled sigh sounded in his ear as a death bell; and each tender glance carried a point keener than the lightning's fork. In a word, his heart was completely torn, and he had wisdom to seek its only cure—*reconciliation with the injured.* 'Tis true, pride whispered that Miss Read, having treated him with great disrespect by marrying in his absence, ought to be *punished*. But how could he think of revenge on a poor girl, whom his own neglect had driven to that desperate act! Avarice, too, remonstrated against marrying a woman, whose last husband had left debts which he might be ruined to pay. But Ben felt resolved, that as he had rendered this dear woman unhappy, he would restore her peace, whatever might be the cost. As the coming forth of the sun after clouds, such was the shining of conscious virtue on Ben's face, after such noble resolving. As a flower after long mourning its absent sun, rejoices again in his returning beams; so the soul of Miss Read rejoiced in the smiles of her returning lover. The hearts of her aged parents revived with the cheerful rose once more blooming on her pallid cheek; and heaven itself shed choicest blessings on their happy union.

No debts of the former husband were ever exhibited against them. No foe was permitted to triumph. And while old Keimer, after all his roguery, was fain to run away from his creditors to the West Indies, where he died in poverty—and while his successor, Harry, elated with a puff of prosperity, and affecting the FINE GENTLEMAN, soon came out at the little end of the horn, Ben and his lovely bride, going on in their virtuous toils, prospered together like twin trees planted by the rivers of water. Lured by her pleasant looks, the book-store, over which she presided, was constantly thronged; and equally pleased with the neatness and fidelity of his printing, Ben's press was always at work. Happy in the tender wish to please, "each was to the other a dearer self." And whether their duties called them to the kitchen, the book-store, or the printing-office, they still found, in their mutual love, that divine cordial which lightened every burden and sweetened every care. Their table, though frugal, was delicious, because seasoned with smiles of mutual fondness. And doubly welcome the return of night, where Hymen, unreproved, had lighted up his sacred torch; and where pressed to the soft bosom of his affectionate spouse, the happy husband could take his fill of pure connubial bliss, without remorse or dread of danger. Such were the benefits which Ben derived from his generous dealings with the afflicted Miss Read; and as a farther reward, it was in this self same year, that Ben was enabled to *incorporate* his grand library-company.

This first of social blessings, a PUBLIC LIBRARY, was set on foot by Franklin, about the year 1731. Fifty persons subscribed forty shillings each, and agreed to pay ten shillings annually. The number increased; and in 1742, the company was incorporated, by the name of "The Library Company of Philadelphia." It now contains eight thousand volumes on all subjects, a philosophical apparatus, and a good beginning towards a collection of natural and artificial curiosities. The company have lately built an elegant house in Fifth street, on the front of which is erected a marble statue of their founder, Benjamin Franklin. [2]

The beneficial influence of this institution was soon evident. The cheapness of terms rendered it accessible to every one. Hence a degree of information was extended among all classes of people, which is very unusual in other places. The example was soon followed. Libraries were established in various places, and they are now become very numerous in the United States, and particularly in Pennsylvania. It is to be hoped, that they will be *still more widely extended*, and that information will be every where increased. This will be the best security for our liberties. *A nation who has been taught to know and prize the rights which God has given them, cannot be enslaved. It is in the regions of ignorance alone that tyranny reigns.*

In 1732, Franklin began to publish POOR RICHARD'S ALMANAC.

The eloquent Charles Fox used to say, that had Doctor Franklin written nothing else, his "Poor Richard's Almanac" were alone sufficient to immortalize him. Instead of being taken up, as too many Almanacs are, with trifling stories and fool-born jests, it abounds with the finest maxims on Industry, Temperance, and Frugality, thrown together with astonishing conciseness, and written with that happy mixture *of gravity* and gaiety that captivates every body, and never tires. It took a wonderful run. From 10 to 15,000 a year were generally sold in Pennsylvania. And to this Almanac, in a considerable measure, may be ascribed that wonderful start which Pennsylvania has taken of the middle and southern states in all the REPUBLICAN VIRTUES, of INDUSTRY and ECONOMY, which point the WAY to WEALTH.

Even the finest girls there, worth their thousands, don't think it beneath them, to "*lay hold on the distaff*," like Solomon's accomplished daughter, to swell the riches of the family *wardrobe* and to improve the *savoury dishes* of their parents.

A foppish young fortune-hunter from the south, ventured sometime ago to pay his respects to the beautiful Miss Dickenson, one of the first fortunes in the state. Instead of finding her, as he had expected, idly lolling in a room of state, and bedizened in ribbands and laces, like a fairy queen, he found her attired in that simple dress of exquisite neatness which best sets off the rosy freshness of youthful beauty; and he found her, too, busied in some piece of domestic industry. He blushed to find her "*at work*!" After a world of compliments, all tending to make her out far too *divine a creature* for such disparaging employments, he gave her to understand that she should not thus demean herself if she were in Carolina.

"*What!*" replied she, with sarcastic pleasantry, "*don't the young ladies with you, read* POOR RICHARD'S ALMANAC?"

Thus was this little annual visitor of Doctor Franklin's, a general blessing to the Pennsylvanians, making them all fond of industry. And Jacob did not more naturally beget Joseph and his twelve brethren than does industry beget INNOCENCE, and HEALTH, and WEALTH, and CHEERFULNESS, and all that lovely train of virtues, which tend to make men happy by driving away their vices. For who, for example, will ever get drunk who has no *debts* nor *duns* nor vices of any sort to make him *uneasy*? And who will ever *sell his birthright* of an *honest vote* for an electioneering dinner and a drink of grog, when he has fatted calves and wine of his own at home? This is Pennsylvania all over.

In the Almanac for the last year that doctor Franklin ever published, he compressed the choicest sentiments of all the preceding editions, and entitled it "THE WAY TO WEALTH." It is not easy to do justice to this little work. American writers need not eulogize it. The British, and even the French into whose language it was quickly translated, have paid it the most flattering attention. Doctor Knox gave it a place in his "ELEGANT EXTRACTS;" and Lewis XV. on hearing it read, was so charmed with the admirable sense and humour of Poor Richard, that he gave orders for a new frigate, just launching, to be named, in honour of this famous nosegay of Franklin's, LE BON HOMME RICHARD, or "POOR RICHARD." I have heard nothing of this frigate or of any exploits of her's, while she was a new ship, and in the French service. But this I know, that in her latter days she was covered over with glory. This was the ship on which that gallant Scot, Paul Jones, hoisted the American flag in the great war of the revolution. Though the Poor Richard mounted but 36 guns, and was old and crazy besides, yet her commander had the audacity to carry her alongside of the SERAPIS, a British 44, and a new ship. It is true, the Alliance, an American frigate of the smallest class, was in company with the POOR RICHARD; but as Jones and his officers all declare, rendered him no assistance whatever. But though thus basely deserted by her consort in the hour of conflict with a mightier foe, yet did not the POOR RICHARD despair, but bravely grappled with her enemy at once, and after one of the bloodiest contests recorded in history, gloriously succeeded in hauling down her colours. The Poor Richard, however, but barely survived this dreadful four hours' conflict with such a heavy adversary. For as if only waiting to see the modest stars of liberty waving where the proud jack of tyranny had waved before, she bowed her head beneath a mountainous billow and went down—the glorious tomb of many of her gallant crew, embalmed, for dear liberty's sake, in their own heart's blood.

As the reader might think it hard, after so much said about it to whet his curiosity, if we did not give him a squint at this famous "POOR RICHARD'S ALMANAC," we hasten now to do ourselves the pleasure to lay it before him, in the last and best form wherein doctor Franklin gave it to the public, and under the same title, viz. "THE WAY TO WEALTH," or "POOR RICHARD," *improved*—which runs thus:—

COURTEOUS READER,

I have heard that nothing gives an author so great pleasure as to find his works respectfully quoted by others. Judge, then, how much I must have been gratified by an incident I am going to relate to you. I stopped my horse lately, where a great number of people were collected at an auction of merchant's goods. The hour of the sale not being come, they were conversing on the badness of the times; and one of the company called to a plain, clean old man, with white locks, "Pray, father Abraham, what think you of the times? Will not these *heavy taxes*, quite ruin the country? How shall we be ever able to pay them? What would you advise us to do?" Father Abraham stood up, and replied, "If you would have my advice, I will give it you in short; 'for a word to the wise is enough,' as poor Richard says." They joined in desiring him to speak his mind, and gathering round him, he proceeded as follows:—

Friends, said he, the taxes are, indeed, very heavy; and, if those laid on by the government, were the only ones we had to pay, we might more easily discharge them; but we have many others, and much more grievous to some of us. We are taxed twice as much by our *idleness*, three times as much by our *pride*, and four times as much by our *folly*; and from these taxes the commissioners cannot ease or deliver us, by allowing an abatement. However let us hearken to good advice, and something may be done for us; "God helps them that help themselves," as poor Richard says.

I. It will be thought a hard government that should tax its people one tenth part of their time, to be employed in its service: but idleness taxes many of us much more; sloth, by bringing on diseases, absolutely shortens life. "Sloth, like rust, consumes faster than labour wears, while the used key is always bright," as poor Richard says. "But dost thou love life, then do not squander time, for that is the stuff life is made of," as poor Richard says. How much more than is necessary do we spend in sleep? forgetting that the sleeping fox catches no poultry, and that "there will be sleeping enough in the grave," as poor Richard says.

"If time be of all things the most precious, wasting time must be," as poor Richard says, "the greatest prodigality;" since, as he elsewhere tells us, "lost time is never found again; and what we call time enough, always proves little enough;" let us then up and be doing, and doing to the purpose; so by diligence shall we do more with less perplexity. "Sloth makes all things difficult, but industry all easy; and he that riseth late, must trot all day, and shall scarce over take his business at night; while laziness travels so slowly, that poverty soon overtakes him. Drive thy business, let not that drive thee; and early to bed and early to rise, makes a man healthy, wealthy and wise," as poor Richard says.

So what signifies wishing and hoping for better times? we may make these times better, if we bestir ourselves. "Industry need not wish, and he that lives upon hope will die fasting. There are no gains without pains; then, help hands for I have no lands," or if I have they are smartly taxed. "He that hath a trade, hath an estate; and he that hath a calling, hath an office of profit and honour," as poor Richard says; but then the trade must be worked at, and the calling well followed, or neither the estate nor the office will enable us to pay our taxes. If we are industrious, we will never starve; for at the working man's house, "hunger looks in but dares not enter." Nor will the bailiff or the constable enter, for "industry pays debts, while despair increaseth them." What, though you have found no treasure, nor has any rich relation left you a legacy, "diligence is the mother of good luck, and God gives all things to industry. Then plough deep while sluggards sleep, and you shall have corn to sell and to keep."

"Work while it is called to-day, for you know not how much you may be hindered to-morrow. One to-day is worth two to-morrows," as poor Richard says; and farther, "never leave that till to-morrow, which you can do to-day." If you were a servant, would you not be ashamed that a good master should catch you idle? Are you then your own master? be ashamed to catch yourself idle when there is so much to be done for yourself, your family, your relations, and your country. Handle your tools without mittens: remember that "the cat in gloves catches no mice," as poor Richard says. It is true, there is much to be done, and, perhaps, you are weak-handed; but stick to it steadily, and you will see great effects; for "constant dropping wears away stones; and by diligence and patience the mouse ate in two the cable; and little strokes fell great oaks."

Methinks I hear some of you say, "must a man afford himself no leisure?" I will tell thee, my friend, what poor Richard says; "employ thy time well, if thou meanest to gain leisure; and, since thou art not sure of a minute, throw not away an hour. Leisure is time for doing something useful; this leisure the diligent man will obtain, but the lazy man never; for, a life of leisure and a life of laziness are two things. Many, without labour would live by their wits only, but they break for want of stock: whereas industry gives comfort, and plenty, and respect. Fly pleasures, and they will follow you. The diligent spinner has a large shift; and now I have a sheep and a cow, every body bids me good-morrow."

II. But with our industry, we must likewise be steady, settled and careful, and oversee our own affairs with our own eyes, and not trust too much to others; for, as poor Richard says,

"I never saw an oft removed tree, Nor yet an oft removed family,

That throve so well as those that settled be."

And again, "three removes are as bad as a fire;" and again, "keep thy shop, and thy shop will keep thee;" and again, "if you would have your business done, go; if not, send." And again,

"He that by the plough would thrive,

Himself must either hold or drive."

And again, "the eye of a master will do more work than both his hands;" and again, "want of care does us more damage than want of knowledge:" and again, "not to oversee workmen is to leave them your purse open." Trusting too much to others' care is the ruin of many; for, "in the affairs of this world, men are saved, not by faith, but by the want of it; but a man's own care is profitable;" for, "if you would have a faithful servant, and one that you like, serve yourself. A little neglect may breed great mischief; for want of a nail the shoe was lost; for want of a shoe the horse was lost; and for want of a horse the rider was lost, being overtaken and slain by the enemy: all for want of a little care about a horse-shoe nail."

III. So much for industry, my friends, and attention to one's own business; but to these we must add frugality, if we would make our industry more certainly successful. A man may, if he knows not how to save as he gets, "keep his nose all his life to the grindstone, and die not worth a groat at last. A fat kitchen makes a lean will;" and,

"Many estates are spent in the getting,

Since women for tea forsook spinning and knitting,

And men for punch forsook hewing and splitting."

If you would be wealthy, think of saving as well as of getting. The Indies have not made Spain rich because her outgoes are greater than her incomes.

Away then with your expensive follies, and you will not then have so much cause to complain of hard times, heavy taxes, and chargeable families; for,

"Women and wine, game and deceit,

Make the wealth small, and the want great."

And farther, "what maintains one vice will bring up two children." You may think, perhaps, that a little tea, or a little punch now and then, diet a little more costly, clothes a little finer, and a little entertainment now and then, can be no great matter; but remember, "many a little makes a mickle."

Beware of little expenses; "a small leak will sink a great ship," as poor Richard says; and again, "who dainties love, shall beggars prove;" and moreover, "fools make feasts, and wise men eat them." Here you are all got together to this sale of fineries and nicknacks. You call them *goods*, but if you do not take care they will prove *evils* to some of you. You expect they will be sold cheap, and, perhaps, they may, for less than they cost; but, if you have no occasion for them, they must be dear to you. Remember what poor Richard says, "buy what thou hast no need of, and ere long thou shalt sell thy necessaries." And again, "at a great pennyworth pause awhile;" he means that perhaps the cheapness is apparent only, and not real or the bargain, by straitening thee in thy business, may do thee more harm than good. For in another place he says, "many have been ruined by buying great pennyworths." Again, "it is foolish to lay out money in a purchase of repentance:" and yet this folly is practised every day at auctions, for want of minding the Almanac. Many a one, for the sake of finery on the back, have gone with a hungry belly, and half starved their families; "silks and sattins, scarlet and velvets, put out the kitchen fire," as poor Richard says. These are not the necessaries of life, they can scarcely be called the conveniences: and yet only because they look pretty, how many want to have them. By these, and other extravagances, the genteel are reduced to poverty, and forced to borrow of those whom they formerly despised, but who through industry and frugality have maintained their standing; in which case it appears plainly, that "a ploughman on his legs is higher than a gentleman on his knees," as poor Richard says. Perhaps they have had a small estate left them, which they knew not the getting of: they think "it is day, and will never be night;" that a little to be spent out of so much is not worth minding: but "always taking out of the meal-tub, and never putting in, soon comes to the bottom," as poor Richard says; and then, "when the well is dry, they know the worth of water." But this they might have known before, if they had taken his advice. "If you would know the value of money, go and try to borrow some; for he that goes a borrowing goes a sorrowing," as poor Richard says; and, indeed, so does he that lends to such people, when he goes to get it again. Poor Dick farther advises, and says,

"Fond pride of dress is sure a very curse,

Ere fancy you consult, consult your purse."

And again, "pride is as loud a beggar as want, and a great deal more saucy." When you have bought one fine thing, you must buy ten more, that your appearance may be all of a piece; but poor Dick says, "it is easier to suppress the first desire, than to satisfy all that follow it." And it is as truly folly for the poor to ape the rich, as for the frog to swell to equal the ox.

"Vessels large, may venture more, But little boats should keep near shore."

It is, however, a folly soon punished; for, as poor Richard says, "pride breakfasted with plenty, dined with poverty, and supped with infamy." And, after all, of what use is this pride of appearance, for which so much is risked, so much is suffered? It cannot promote health, nor ease pain; it makes no increase of merit in the person, it creates envy, it hastens misfortune.

But what madness must it be to run in debt for these superfluities? We are offered, by the terms of this sale, six months credit; and that, perhaps, has induced some of us to attend it, because we cannot spare the ready money, and hope now to be fine without it. But ah! think what you do when you run in debt; you give to another power over your liberty. If you cannot pay at the time, you will be *ashamed to see your creditor*; you will *be in fear when you speak to him*; you will make *poor, pitiful, sneaking excuses*, and by degrees, come to *lose your veracity*, and sink into *base, downright lying*; for "the second vice is lying, the first is running in debt," as poor Richard says; and again, to the same purpose, "lying rides on debt's back;" whereas a free American ought not to be ashamed, nor afraid to see or speak to any man living. But poverty often deprives a man of all spirit and virtue. "It is hard for an empty bag to stand upright." What would you think of that nation, or of that government, who should issue an edict, forbidding you to dress like a gentleman or gentlewoman, on pain of imprisonment or servitude? Would you not say that you were free; have a right to dress as you please, and that such an edict would be a breach of your privileges, and such a government tyrannical? And yet you are about to put yourself under that tyranny when you run into debt for such a dress! your creditor has authority, at his pleasure, to deprive you of your liberty, by confining you in jail for life, or by selling you for a servant, if you should not be able to pay him: when you have got your bargain, you may perhaps think little of payment; but as poor Richard says, "creditors have better memories than debtors; creditors are a superstitious set, great observers of set days and times." The day comes round before you are aware, and the demand is made before you are prepared to satisfy it; or, if you bear your debt in mind, the term, which, at first seemed so long, will, as it lessens, appear extremely short; time will seem to have added wings to his heels, as well as his shoulders. "Those have a short Lent, who owe money at Easter." At present, perhaps, you may think yourself in thriving circumstances, and that you can bear a little extravagance without injury; but,

"For age and want save while you may,

No morning suns last the whole day."

Gain may be temporary and uncertain, but ever while you live, expense is constant and certain; and "it is easier to build two chimneys, than to keep one in fuel," as poor Richard says: so "rather go to bed supperless, than rise in debt."

"Get what you can, and what you get, hold, 'Tis the stones that will turn lead into gold."

And when you have got the philosopher's stone, sure you will no longer complain of bad times, or the difficulty of paying taxes.

IV. This doctrine of my friend's is reason and wisdom; but after all, do not depend too much upon your own industry and frugality, and prudence, though excellent things; for they may all be blasted without the blessing of heaven; and therefore ask that blessing humbly, and be not uncharitable to those that at present seem to want it, but comfort and help them. Remember Job suffered, and was afterwards prosperous.

And now to conclude, "experience keeps a dear school, but fools will learn in no other," as poor Richard says, and scarce in that; for it is true, "we may give advice, but we cannot give conduct;" however, remember this, "they that will not be counselled cannot be helped;" and farther, that "if you will not hear reason, she will surely wrap your knuckles," as poor Richard says.

Thus the old gentleman ended his harangue. The people heard it and approved the doctrine, and immediately practised the contrary, just as if it had been a common sermon; for the auction opened, and they began to buy extravagantly. I found the good man had thoroughly studied my Almanacs, and digested all I had dropt on those topics during the course of twenty-five years. The frequent mention he made of me must have tired any one else; but my vanity was wonderfully delighted with it, though I was conscious, that not a tenth part of the wisdom was my own, which he ascribed to me; but rather the gleanings that I had made of the sense of all ages and nations. However I resolved to be the better for the echo of it; and though I had at first determined to buy stuff for a new coat, I went away, resolved to wear my old one a little longer. Reader, if thou wilt do the same, thy profit will be as great as mine. I am, as ever thine to serve thee.

RICHARD SAUNDERS.

CHAPTER XXXV.

"*When poverty comes in at the door*," said a shrewd observer, "*love flies out at the window*." When foolish families, "*wasting their substance in riotous living*," have fairly run their estates through the girt, and brought a host of hungry sheriffs and constables to the door, seizing on all their trumpery of fine carpets and curtains, and side-boards, and looking-glasses for *auction*, oh what sudden palpitations and blank looks ensue! what bitter upbraidings between husbands and wives, parents and children! what lyings, and perjuries, and secret transfers of property to *cheat creditors*! with universal wreck of character, and conscience, and every thing else that can give dignity or pleasure to life!

But while Franklin, by his famous Almanack "*poor Richard*," was generously striving to prevent all these curses of *sloth* and *extravagance*, his wide spread newspapers were scattering thousands of the finest lectures on that *honest industry* and *prudence*, which makes nations wealthy and glorious. And his lecturing, like one born to be the moralist of nations, was in that style of brevity, sprightliness, and nerve, that young and old, men, women, and children were never tired of reading. And to give more value to these beautiful little essays, they were always written under the smarting recollection of what himself had suffered, from the follies which he wished to guard others against. Witness first, his celebrated little story, entitled

THE WHISTLE.

A TRUE STORY.

WRITTEN TO HIS NEPHEW.

When I was a child, about seven years old, my friends, on a holiday, filled my pocket with coppers. I went directly to a shop, where they sold toys for children, and being charmed with the sound of a *whistle*, that I met by the way, in the hands of another boy, I voluntarily offered him all my money for it. I then came home, and went whistling all over the house, much pleased with my *whistle*, but disturbing all the family. My brothers, and sisters, and cousins, understanding the bargain I had made, told me I had given four times as much for it as it was worth. This put me in mind what good things I might have bought with the rest of my money; and they laughed at me so much for my folly, that I cried with vexation; and the reflection gave me more chagrin than the *whistle* gave me pleasure.

This, however, was afterwards of use to me. The impression continued on my mind; so that, often, when I was tempted to buy some unnecessary thing, I said to myself, *don't give too much for the whistle*; and so I saved my money.

As I grew up, came into the world, and observed the actions of men, I thought I met with many, very many who *gave too much for the whistle.*

When I saw any one too ambitious of court favours, sacrificing his time in attendance on levees, his repose, his liberty, his virtue, and perhaps his friends, to attain it; I have said to myself, *this man gives too much for his whistle.*

When I saw another fond of popularity, constantly employing himself in political bustles, neglecting his own affairs, and ruining them by that neglect; *he pays indeed*, says I, *too much for his whistle.*

If I knew a miser, who gave up every kind of comfortable living; all the pleasures of doing good to others, all the esteem of his fellow-citizens, and the joys of benevolent friendship, for the sake of accumulating wealth; *poor man*, says I, *you do, indeed, pay too much for your whistle.*

When I meet a man of pleasure, sacrificing every laudable improvement of the mind, or of his fortune, to mere corporeal sensations—*Mistaken man*, says I, *you are providing pain for yourself, instead of pleasure. You give too much for your whistle.*

If I see one fond of fine clothes, fine furniture, fine equipages, all above his fortune, for which he contracts debts, and ends his career in prison; *alas*, says I, *he has paid dear, very dear, for his whistle.*

When I see a beautiful sweet-tempered girl, married to an ill-natured brute of a husband; *what a pity it is*, says I, *that she has paid so much for her whistle.*

In short, I conceived, that great part of the miseries of mankind were brought upon them, by the false estimates they had made of the value of things, and by their giving too much for their *whistle.*

The following admirable satire against *prejudice*, can never be too often read by the ill-natured and hypochondrical.

THE HANDSOME AND UGLY LEG.

There are two sorts of people in the world, who, with equal advantages of life, become, the one happy, and the other miserable. This arises, very much, from the different views in which they consider things, and the effect of those different views upon their own minds.

In every situation men can be placed, they may find conveniences and inconveniences; in every company, persons and conversation more or less pleasing; at every table, meats and drinks of better or worse taste; dishes better and worse dressed; in every climate, good and bad weather; and under every government, good and bad laws, and a good and bad administration of those laws; in every poem, faults and beauties; in almost every face, and every person, fine features and sad defects, good and bad qualities.

Under these circumstances, the two classes above mentioned, fix their attention—those who are disposed to be *happy*, on the *conveniences* of things, the *pleasant parts* of conversation, the *well dressed* dishes, the *goodness* of the wine, the *fine weather*, &c. and enjoy all with *cheerfulness*. Those who are to be *unhappy*, think and speak only of the contraries. Hence they are continually discontented themselves, and, by their remarks, sour the pleasures of society, and make themselves every where disagreeable.

Nobody loves this sort of people; no one shows them more than the commonest civility, and scarcely that; and this frequently puts them out of humour, and draws them into disputes. If they aim at obtaining any advantage in rank or fortune, nobody wishes them success, or will stir a step to favour their pretensions. If they incur public censure or disgrace, no one will defend or excuse, and many join to aggravate their misconduct, and render them completely odious. If these poor gentlemen will not change this bad habit, condescend to be pleased with what is pleasing, without fretting themselves and others about the contraries, it is good to avoid an acquaintance with them, which is always disagreeable, and sometimes very inconvenient, especially when one finds one's self entangled in their quarrels.

An old philosophical friend of mine was grown, from experience, very cautious in this particular, and carefully avoided any intimacy with such people. He had, like other philosophers, a thermometer, to show him the heat of the weather, and a barometer, to mark when it was likely to prove good or bad; but there being no instrument invented to discover, at first sight, this unpleasing disposition in a person, he, for that purpose, made use of his legs, one of which was remarkably handsome; the other, by some accident, crooked and deformed. If a stranger, at the first interview, kept his eyes on his ugly leg more than the handsome one, he doubted him; if he spoke of it, and took no notice of the handsome leg, that was sufficient to determine my philosopher to have no further acquaintance with him. Every body has not this two-legged instrument; but every one, with a little attention, may observe signs of that carping, fault-finding disposition, and take the same resolution of avoiding the acquaintance of those infected with it. I therefore advise those critical, querulous, discontented, unhappy people, that if they wish to be respected and beloved by others, and happy in themselves, they should *leave off looking at the ugly leg.*

"*A good wit will turn every thing to advantage,*" says Shakespeare; and the following will show what a singular passion Dr. Franklin had to turn every little cross incident of his own life into pleasure and profit to others. He calls it

STOOP, AND GO SAFE.

To the late Dr. Mather, of Boston.

REV. SIR,

When I was a boy, I met with a book, entitled, "*Essays to do good,*" which, I think, was written by your father. It had been so little regarded by a former possessor, that several leaves of it were torn out: but the remainder gave me such a turn for thinking, as to have an influence on my conduct through life; for I have always set a greater value on the character of a doer of good than any other kind of reputation; and if I have been, as you seem to think, a useful citizen, the public owes the advantage of it to that book.

The last time I saw your father was in the beginning of 1724, when I visited him after my first trip to Pennsylvania. He received me in his library; and on my taking leave, showed me a shorter way out of the house, through a narrow passage, which was crossed by a beam over head. We were still talking, as I withdrew; he accompanying me behind, and I turning partly towards him, when he said hastily, "*stoop! stoop!*" I did not understand him, till I felt my head hit against the beam. He was a man, who never missed any occasion of giving instruction; and upon this he said to me, "*you are young, and have the world before you.* STOOP, *as you go through, and you will miss many hard thumps.*" This advice, thus beat into my head, has frequently been of use to me; and I often think of it, when I see pride mortified, and misfortune brought upon people, by carrying their heads too high.

I long much to see again my native place; and did hope to have been there in 1783; but could not obtain my dismission from employment here. And now I fear I shall never have that happiness. My best wishes, however, attend my dear country. It is now blessed with an excellent constitution. *May it last for ever!*

This powerful monarchy continues its friendship for the United States. It is a friendship of the utmost importance to our security; and should be carefully cultivated. Britain has not yet digested the loss of its dominion over us, and has still, at times, some flattering hopes of recovering it. Accidents may increase those hopes, and encourage dangerous attempts. A breach between us and France would infallibly bring the English again upon our backs: and yet, we have some wild beasts among our countrymen, who are endeavouring to weaken that connexion.

Let us preserve our reputation, by performing our engagements; our credit, by fulfilling our contracts; and our friends, by gratitude and kindness: for we know not how soon we may again have occasion for all of them.—With great and sincere esteem, I have the honour to be—Reverend sir,

Your most obedient and most humble servant,

B. FRANKLIN.

Passy, May 12, 1784.

The witty little essay that follows, will show how very closely Dr. Franklin observed every thing around him, and what gross errors in education yet remain to be corrected.

THE HUMOUROUS PETITION.

I address myself to all the friends of youth, and conjure them to direct their compassionate regard to my unhappy fate, in order to remove the prejudices of which I am the victim. There are twin sisters of us, and the two eyes of man do not more resemble, nor are capable of being upon better terms with each other, than my sister and myself, were it not for the partiality of our parents, who make the most injurious distinctions between us. From my infancy I have been led to consider my sister as being of a more elevated rank. I was suffered to grow up without the least instruction, while nothing was spared in her education. She had masters to teach her writing, drawing, music, and other accomplishments, but if, by chance, I touched a pencil, a pen, or a needle, I was bitterly rebuked; and more than once, I have been beaten for being awkward, and wanting a graceful manner. It is true, my sister associated me with her upon some occasions; but she always made a point of taking the lead, calling upon me only from necessity, or to figure by her side.

But conceive not, sirs, that my complaints are instigated merely by vanity—no, my uneasiness is occasioned by an object much more serious. It is the practice in our family, that the whole business of providing for its subsistence falls upon my sister and myself. If any indisposition should attack my sister—and I mention it in confidence, upon this occasion, that she is subject to the gout, the rheumatism, and cramp, without making mention of other accidents—what would be the fate of our poor family? Must not the regret of our parents be excessive, at having placed so great a distance between sisters who are so perfectly equal? Alas! we must perish from distress: for it would not be in my power even to scrawl a suppliant petition for relief, having been obliged to employ the hand of another in transcribing the request which I have now the honour to prefer to you.

Condescend, sirs, to make my parents sensible of the injustice of an *exclusive tenderness*, and of the necessity of distributing their care and affection among all their children equally. I am, with profound respect, Sirs,

Your obedient servant,

THE LEFT HAND.

The following essays strikingly illustrate the admirable wisdom and philanthropy of Dr. Franklin; and, if read *practically*, would, no doubt, greatly lessen the number both of PHYSICIANS and PATIENTS.

THE ART OF PROCURING PLEASANT DREAMS.

As a great part of our life is spent in sleep, during which we have sometimes pleasing, and sometimes painful dreams, it becomes of some consequence to obtain the one kind, and avoid the other; for whether real or imaginary, pain is pain, and pleasure is pleasure. If we can sleep without dreaming, it is well that painful dreams are avoided. If, while we sleep, we can have pleasing dreams, it is so much clear gain to the pleasures of life.

To this end, it is, in the first place, necessary to be careful in preserving health—for, in sickness, the imagination is disturbed; and disagreeable, sometimes terrible ideas are apt to present themselves. But for health, our main dependence is on EXERCISE and TEMPERANCE. These render the appetite sharp, the digestion easy, the body lightsome, and the temper cheerful, with sweet sleep and pleasant dreams. While indolence and full feeding never fail to bring on loaded stomachs, with night-mares and horrors—we fall from precipices—are stung by serpents—assaulted by wild beasts—murderers—devils—with all the black train of unimaginable danger and wo. Temperance, then, is all-important to sweet sleep and pleasant dreaming. But a main point of temperance, is to *shun hearty suppers*, which are indeed not safe, even when dinner has been missed; what then must be the consequence of hearty suppers after full dinners? why only restless nights and frightful dreams; and sometimes *a stroke of the apoplexy*, after which they sleep till doomsday. The newspapers often relate instances of persons, who, after eating hearty suppers, are found dead in their beds next morning.

Another grand mean of preserving health, is to admit a constant supply of *fresh air* into your chamber. A more sad mistake was never committed than that of sleeping in tight rooms, and beds closely curtained. This has arisen from the dread of night air. But, after all the clamour and abuse that have been heaped on *night air*, it is very certain that no outward air, that may come in, is half so unwholesome as the air often breathed in a close chamber. As boiling water does not grow hotter by longer boiling, if the particles that receive greater heat can escape; so living bodies do not putrify, if the particles, as fast as they become putrid, can be thrown off. Nature expels them by the pores of the skin and lungs, and in a free open air they are carried off; but, in a *close room*, we receive them again and again, though they become more and more corrupt. A number of persons crowded into a small room, thus spoil the air in a few minutes, and even render it mortal, as in the black hole at Calcutta. [3] A single person is said to spoil a gallon of air per minute, and therefore requires a longer time to spoil a chamber full; but it is done, however, in proportion, and many putrid disorders hence have their origin. It is recorded of Methusalem, who, being the longest liver, may be supposed to have best preserved his health, that he slept always in the open air; for when he had lived five hundred years, an angel said to him, "*arise, Methusalem, and build thee an house, for thou shalt live yet five hundred years longer.*" But Methusalem answered and said, "*If I am to live but five hundred years longer, it is not worth while to build me an house—I will sleep in the air, as I have been used to do.*" Physicians, after having for ages contended that the sick should not be indulged with fresh air, have at length discovered that it may do them good. It is therefore to be hoped that it is not hurtful to those who are in health, and that we may be then cured of the *acrophobia* that at present distresses weak minds, and makes them choose to be stifled and poisoned, rather than leave open the windows of a bed chamber, or put down the glass of a coach.

Confined air, when saturated with perspirable matter, [4] will not receive more; and that matter must remain in our bodies, and occasions diseases; but it gives some previous notice of its being about to be hurtful, by producing certain uneasinesses which are difficult to describe, and few that feel know the cause. But we may recollect, that sometimes, on waking in the night, we have, if warmly covered, found it difficult to get asleep again. We turn often without finding repose in any position. This *fidgetiness*, to use a vulgar expression for the want of a better, is occasioned wholly by an uneasiness in the skin, owing to the retention of the perspirable matter, the bed-clothes having received their quantity, and, being saturated, refusing to take any more.

When you are awakened by this uneasiness, and find you cannot easily sleep again, get out of bed, beat up and turn your pillow, shake the bed-clothes well, with at least twenty shakes, then throw the bed open, and leave it to cool; in the meanwhile, continuing undrest, walk about your chamber, till your skin has had time to discharge its load, which it will do sooner as the air may be drier and colder. When you begin to feel the cool air unpleasant, then return to your bed, and you will soon fall asleep, and your sleep will be sweet and pleasant. All the scenes presented by your fancy, will be of the pleasing kind. I am often as agreeably entertained with them, as by the scenery of an opera. If you happen to be too indolent to get out of bed, you may instead of it, lift up your bed-clothes so as to draw in a good deal of fresh air, and, by letting them fall, force it out again. This, repeated twenty times, will so clear them of the perspirable matter they have imbibed, as to permit your sleeping well for some time afterwards. But this latter method is not equal to the former.

Those who do not love trouble, and can afford to have two beds, will find great luxury in rising, when they wake in a hot bed, and going into the cool one. Such shifting of beds, would be of great service to persons ill in a fever; as it refreshes and frequently procures sleep. A very large bed, that will admit a removal so distant from the first situation as to be cool and sweet, may in a degree answer the same end.

These are the rules of the art. But though they will generally prove effectual in producing the end intended, there is a case in which the most punctual observance of them will be totally fruitless. This case is, when the person who desires to have pleasant dreams has not taken care to preserve, what is necessary above all things—A GOOD CONSCIENCE.

ON THE ART OF SWIMMING.

The exercise of swimming is one of the most healthy and agreeable in the world. After having swam for an hour or two in the evening, one sleeps coolly the whole night, even during the most ardent heat of summer. Perhaps the pores being cleansed, the insensible perspiration increases, and occasions this coolness. It is certain that much swimming is the means of stopping a diarrhœa and even of producing a constipation. With respect to those who do not know how to swim, or who are affected with a diarrhœa at the season which does not permit them to use that exercise, a warm bath, by cleansing and purifying the skin, is found very salutary, and often effects a radical cure. I speak from my own experience, frequently repeated, and that of others, to whom I have recommended this.

You will not be displeased if I conclude these hasty remarks by informing you, that as the ordinary method of swimming is reduced to the act of rowing with the arms and legs, and is consequently a laborious and fatiguing operation, when the space of water to be crossed is considerable; there is a method in which a swimmer may pass a great distance with much facility, by means of a sail. This discovery I fortunately made by accident, and in the following manner.

When I was a boy, I amused myself one day with flying a paper kite; and approaching the bank of a pond, which was near a mile broad, I tied the string to a stake, and the kite ascended to a very considerable height, above the pond, while I was swimming. In a little time, being desirous of amusing myself with my kite, and enjoying at the same time the pleasure of swimming, I returned, and loosing from the stake the string, with the little stick fastened to it, went again into the water, where I found, that, lying on my back, and holding the stick in my hands, I was drawn along the surface of the water in a very agreeable manner. Having then engaged another boy to carry my clothes round the pond to the other side, I began to cross the pond with my kite, which carried me quite over without the least fatigue, and with the greatest pleasure imaginable. I was only obliged occasionally to halt a little in my course, and resist its progress, when it appeared that, by following too quick, I lowered the kite too much, by doing which occasionally I made it rise again. I have never since that time practised this singular mode of swimming, though I think it not impossible to cross, in this manner, from Dover to Calais. The packet boat, however, is still preferable.

NEW MODE OF BATHING.

The cold bath has long been in vogue as a tonic, but the shock of the cold water has always appeared to me, generally speaking, as too violent, and I have found it much more agreeable to my constitution to bathe in another element—I mean cold air. With this view, I rise, early every morning and sit in my chamber, without any clothes whatever, half an hour or an hour, according to the season, either reading or writing, This practice is not the least painful, but, on the contrary, agreeable; and if I return to bed afterwards, before I dress myself, as sometimes happens, I make a supplement to my night's rest of one or two hours of the most pleasing sleep that can be imagined. I find no ill consequences whatever resulting from it, and that at least I do not injure my health, if it does not, in fact, contribute much to its preservation. I shall, therefore, call it for the future a *tonic air bath.*

The common saying, "*lazy people take the most pains,*" was never more clearly exemplified than in the following squib.

STRENUOUS IDLENESS.

Passing the Schuylkill, one day, he saw a man sitting on the bridge, very earnestly looking on the cork of his fishing line. "*What luck? What luck?*" cried the doctor. "*O none! none!*" answered our fishing hawk; "*none yet; I have not been here over a couple of hours or so.*" The doctor pushed on. Near sun-down he returned. The man was still sitting and staring at his cork, like a spaniel at a dead set. "Well," said the doctor, "I hope you have had a fine haul among the fish." "Not a single one," replied the man. "*Not a single one!*" quoth the doctor, amazed. "No, not one, sir," answered the fisher, "not one; but I've had a most *glorious nibble*!"

The following is a fine hint to such as have learned useful trades, but have not learned what is infinitely more valuable, I mean that divine philanthropy which alone can make their trades their delight, and thus strew life over with roses.

THE SILVER HOOK.

Doctor Franklin observing one day a hearty young fellow, whom he knew to be an extraordinary blacksmith, sitting on the wharf, bobbing for little mud-cats and eels, he called to him, "Ah Tom, what a pity 'tis you don't fish with a *silver* hook." The young man replied, "he was not able to fish with a silver hook." Some days after this, the doctor passing that way, saw Tom out at the end of the wharf again, with his long pole bending over the flood. "What, Tom," cried the doctor, "have you not got the silver hook yet?"

"God bless you, doctor," cried the blacksmith, "I'm hardly able to fish with an iron hook."

"Poh! poh!" replied the doctor, "go home to your anvil; and you'll make silver enough in one day to buy more and better fish than you would catch here in a month."

But few have it so much in their power to do good or evil as the PRINTERS. I know they all glory in Dr. Franklin as a FATHER, and are wont to name his name with *veneration*; happy would it be for this country if they would read the following with *imitation*.

TRUE INDEPENDENCE.

Soon after his establishment in Philadelphia, Franklin was offered a piece for publication in his newspaper. Being very busy, he begged the gentleman would leave it for consideration. The next day the author called and asked his opinion of it. "Why, sir," replied Franklin, "I am sorry to say that I think it highly scurrilous and defamatory. But being at a loss on account of my poverty whether to reject it or not, I thought I would put it to this issue—at night, when my work was done, I bought a two-penny loaf, on which with a mug of cold water I supped heartily, and then wrapping myself in my great coat, slept very soundly on the floor till morning; when another loaf and a mug of water afforded me a pleasant breakfast. Now, sir, since I can live very comfortably in this manner, why should I prostitute my press to personal hatred or party passion, for a more luxurious living?"

One cannot read this anecdote of our American sage without thinking of Socrates' reply to King Archilaus, who had pressed him to give up preaching in the dirty streets of Athens, and come and live with him in his splendid courts—"*Meal, please your majesty, is a half penny a peck at Athens, and water I can get for nothing.*"

The letter ensuing was from Dr. Franklin to a friend of his, who having displeased some of his relatives by marrying very early, wrote to him for his opinion on that subject. Young bachelors would do well to read it once a month.

ON EARLY MARRIAGES.

DEAR JACK,

From the marriages that have fallen under my observation, I am rather inclined to think that *early* ones stand the best chance for happiness. The temper and habits of the young are not yet become so stiff and uncomplying, as when more advanced in life; they form more easily to each other, and hence, many occasions of disgust are removed. And if youth has less of that prudence which is necessary to manage a family, the parents and elder friends of young married persons are generally at hand to afford their advice, which amply supplies that defect. By early marriage youth is sooner formed to regular and useful life; and possibly some of those accidents or connexions that might have injured the constitution, or reputation, or both, are thereby happily prevented. Particular circumstances of particular persons, may sometimes make it prudent to delay entering into that state; but in general, when nature has rendered our bodies fit for it, the presumption is in nature's favour, that she has not judged amiss in making us *desire* it. Late marriages are often attended too, with this inconvenience, that there is not the same chance that the parents shall live to see their offspring educated. "*Late children*," says the Spanish proverb, "*are early orphans*." A melancholy reflection to those whose case it may be! With us in America, marriages are generally in the morning of life; our children are educated and settled in the world by noon; and thus, our business done, we have an evening of cheerful leisure to ourselves.

By these early marriages we are blessed with more children; and from the mode among us, founded in nature, of every mother suckling her own child, more of them are raised. Thence the swift progress of population among us, unparalleled in Europe. In fine, I am glad you are married, and congratulate you most cordially upon it. You are now in the way of becoming a useful citizen; and you have escaped the unnatural state of celibacy for life—the fate of many who never intended it, but who having too long postponed the change of their condition, find, at length, that it is too late to think of it, and so live all their lives in a situation that greatly lessens a man's value. An odd volume of a set of books bears not the value of its proportion to the set: what think you of the *half* of a pair of scissors? it can't well cut anything; it may possibly serve to scrape a trencher.

Pray make my best wishes acceptable to your bride. I am old and heavy, or I should ere this have presented them in person. I shall make but small use of the old man's privilege, that of giving *advice to younger friends*. Treat your wife always with respect; it will procure respect to you, not only from her, but from all that observe it. Never use a slighting expression to her even in *jest*; for slights in *jest*, after frequent bandyings, are apt to end in angry *earnest*. Be studious in your profession, and you will be learned. Be industrious and frugal, and you will be rich. Be sober and temperate, and you will be healthy. Be virtuous, and you will be happy. At least, you will, by such conduct, stand the best chance for such consequences. I pray God to bless you both!

Your affectionate friend,

B. FRANKLIN.

As next to a GOOD WIFE, there is but "ONE THING" to be compared to a *handsome fortune*, we advise our young countrymen to read the following. It needs but be read to be valued, and it can hardly be read and valued enough by all who know the value of INDEPENDENCE.

ADVICE TO A YOUNG TRADESMAN.

Remember that time is money. He that can earn ten shillings a day, by his labour, and goes abroad, or sits idle one half of that day, though he spends but six-pence during his diversion or idleness, ought not to reckon *that* the only expense; he has really spent, or rather thrown away five shillings besides.

Remember that *credit* is money. If a man let his money lie in my hands, after it is due, he gives me the interest, or so much as I can make of it, during that time. This amounts to a considerable sum where a man has good and large credit, and makes good use of it.

Remember that money is of a very breeding prolific nature. Money begets money; and its offspring can beget more: and so on. Five shillings turned is six. Turned again it is seven and three-pence; and so on, till it becomes hundreds and thousands of pounds. The more there is of it, the more it produces, every turning; so that the profits rise quicker and quicker. He, who kills a breeding sow, destroys all her offspring, to the thousandth generation. He, who murders a crown, destroys all that it might have produced; even scores of pounds.

Remember that six pounds a year is but a groat a day. For this little sum, which may be daily wasted either in time or expense, unperceived, a man of credit may, on his own security, have the constant possession and use of an hundred pounds. So much in stock, briskly turned by an industrious man, produces great advantages.

Remember this saying, "the good paymaster is lord of another man's purse." He who is known to pay punctually and exactly to the time he promises, may, at any time, and on any occasion, raise all the money his friends can spare. This is sometimes of great use. After industry and frugality, nothing contributes more to the raising of a young man in the world, than punctuality and justice in all his dealings. Therefore never keep borrowed money an hour beyond the time you promised, lest a disappointment shut up your friend's purse for ever.

The most trifling actions, that affect a man's credit, are to be regarded. The sound of your hammer at five in the morning, or nine at night, heard by a creditor, makes him easy six months longer; but if he see you at a billiard table, or hears your voice at a tavern, when you should be at work, he sends for his money next day; and demands it before he can receive it in a lump.

It shows, besides, that you are mindful of what you owe. It makes you appear a careful as well as an honest man; and that still increases your credit.

Beware of thinking all your own, that you possess; and of living accordingly. It is a mistake that many people, who have credit, fall into.

To prevent this, keep an exact account, for some time, both of your expenses and your income. If you take the pains at first to mention particulars, it will have this good effect:—you will discover how wonderfully small, trifling expenses mount up to large sums; and will soon discern, what might have been, and may for the future be saved, without occasioning any great inconvenience.

Again: he, who sells upon credit, asks a price, for what he sells, equivalent to the principal and interest of his money, for the time he is to be kept out of it. Therefore, he who buys upon credit, pays interest for what he buys; and, he who pays ready money, might let that money out to use. So, that he who possesses any thing he has bought, pays interest for the use of it.

Yet, in buying goods, it is best to pay ready money; because, he who sells upon credit, expects to lose five per cent, by bad debts. Therefore, he charges, on all he sells upon credit, an advance that shall make up that deficiency.

Those who pay for what they buy upon credit, pay their share of this advance.

He who pays ready money, escapes, or may escape that charge.

A penny sav'd is two-pence clear,

A pin a day's a groat a year.

In short, the way to wealth, if you desire it, is as plain as the way to market. It depends chiefly on two words: *Industry* and *Frugality*. Waste neither *time* nor *money*; but make the best use of both. Without industry and frugality, nothing will do; but with them every thing. He who gets all he can, honestly, and saves all he gets, necessary expenses excepted, will certainly become *rich*; if that Being who governs the world, to whom all should look for a blessing on their honest endeavours, doth not, in his wise providence, otherwise determine.

AN OLD TRADESMAN.

Every reader will be diverted with the following.

IDLE CURIOSITY CURED.

On his first trip, by land, to see his father in Boston, he was worried almost to death by the abominable inquisitiveness of the New England tavern-keepers.

Neither man nor beast could travel among them in comfort. No matter how wet or weary, how hungry or thirsty, the poor traveller might be, he was not to expect an atom of refreshment from these silly publicans until their most pestiferous curiosity was first gratified. And then Job himself could not stand such questions as they would goad him with; such as, *where he came from—and where he might be a-going—and what religion he might be of—and if he was a married man*—and so on. After having been prodigiously teazed in this way for several days, until at last the bare sight of a public house almost threw him into an ague, he determined to try the following remedy at the very next tavern. Soon as he alighted from his horse he desired the tavern keeper to collect his whole family, wife, children, and servants, every soul of them; for that he had something *vastly important* to communicate. All being assembled and wondering what he had to say, he thus addressed them. "My name is Benjamin Franklin. I am a printer by trade. I live, when at home, in Philadelphia. In Boston I have a father, a good old man who taught me, when I was a little boy, to read my book and say my prayers. I have, ever since, thought it my duty to visit and pay my respects to such a father; and I am on that errand to Boston now. This is all that I can at present recollect of myself that I think worth telling you. But if you can think of any thing else that you wish to know about me, I beg you to out with it at once, that I may answer, and so give you opportunity to get me something to eat; for I long to be on my journey that I may return as soon as possible to my family and business, where I most of all delight to be."

Forty thousand sermons against IDLE CURIOSITY could hardly have driven it so effectually out of New England as did this little squib of ridicule.

The following jeu d'esprit is peculiarly in character with Dr. Franklin. It proves that his wit and his benevolence were equal to every emergence, and that if he carried the Old Testament language in his head, he carried the New Testament spirit in his heart.

WIT AND PERSECUTION.

The conversation turning, one day, on *persecution*, a doctor of divinity, distinguished for his wit, but, unfortunately, a little too much infected with that acrimony which is caught by reading books of religious controversy, took the part of persecution and contended that it was *sometimes* right to employ it. Franklin said, he could not think of any case wherein *persecution* was *admissible* among rational creatures. It might be very excusable in *error* to persecute, whose nature it was to see things wrong, and to get angry; but that for such a "*divinity as* TRUTH," to persecute, was, in his opinion, a sin against the *Holy Ghost, never to be forgiven.* After using, in his facetious manner, a variety of arguments honourable to wit and philanthropy, and the clergyman still remaining unconvinced, Franklin called out to him with an air of great surprise, "Why, my dear sir, I am astonished that you plead thus for persecution when it is so diametrically opposite to your *Bible.*"

The clergyman replied, that he did not know what doctor Franklin meant. He thought, he said, he knew something of his *Bible*, but he did not recollect any chapter in point.

"*No, sir!*" answered Franklin, still with the look and voice of surprise, "*not that memorable chapter concerning Abraham and the poor man! Pray, sir, favour us with your Bible a minute or two.*"

"With all my heart," replied the clergyman, "I should like to see that *memorable chapter.*"

The company manifested a solicitude for the issue of the pending controversy—the family Bible was brought and laid on the table by the side of doctor Franklin. "Well, reverend sir," said he, looking at the preacher, as he took up the Bible, "shall I read this chapter?"

"Certainly," replied the divine, settling himself in his chair to listen.—The eyes of all were fixed on Franklin; when, opening the Bible and turning back the leaves as to find the place, he thus audibly began:—

The twenty-seventh chapter of the first book of Moses, commonly called the book of Genesis.

1. And it came to pass, after these things, that Abraham sat in the door of his tent, about the going down of the sun.

2. And behold a man, bowed with age, coming from the way of the wilderness, leaning on a staff.

3. And Abraham arose, and met him, and said unto him, turn in, I pray thee, and wash thy feet, and tarry all night, and thou shalt arise early in the morning and go on thy way.

4. But the man said, nay, for I will abide under this tree.

5. And Abraham pressed him greatly; so he turned, and they went into the tent; and Abraham baked unleavened bread, and they did eat.

6. And when Abraham saw that the man blessed not God, he said unto him, wherefore dost thou not worship the most high God, Creator of heaven and earth.

7. And the man answered and said, I do not worship thy God, neither do I call upon his name; for I have made to myself a God, which abideth always in mine house, and provideth me all things.

8. And Abraham's zeal was kindled against the man, and he arose and fell upon him, and drove him forth with blows into the wilderness.

9. And at midnight God called unto Abraham, saying, where is the stranger?

10. And Abraham answered, and said, Lord, he would not worship thee, neither would he call upon thy name, therefore have I driven him out from before my face into the wilderness.

11. And God said, have I borne with him these hundred and ninety and eight years, and nourished him and clothed him, notwithstanding his rebellion against me; and couldest not thou, that art thyself a sinner, bear with him one night?

12. And Abraham said, let not the anger of my Lord wax hot against his servant; lo, I have sinned: forgive me, I pray thee.

13. And he arose, and went forth into the wilderness, and sought diligently for the man and found him:

14. And returned with him to his tent; and when he had entreated him kindly, he sent him away in the morning with gifts.

15. And God spake again unto Abraham, saying, for this thy sin, shall thy seed be afflicted four hundred years in a strange land:

16. But for thy repentance, will I deliver them; and they shall come forth with power, and with gladness of heart, and with much substance.

That witty but splenetic old bachelor, Dean Swift, used to say, that "there was no dispute which a man of a tolerably good head and heart might not easily avoid falling into, or honourably get out of; and, therefore, as none but fools and rascals fought duels, the sooner such beasts cut each other's throats, the better for the community." This, no doubt, is very true, but still it is too much like striking with a war club, or *tomahawk*, to be allowed among christians. The following *impromptu* on duelling, by Dr. Franklin, claims a far higher admiration. It is an arrow pointed with the diamond of wit, dipt in the oil of kindness, that wounds but to heal.

THE FOLLY OF DUELLING.

This most pusillanimous practice was one day made the theme of conversation in a large party in London, where Doctor Franklin dined. The philosophers and divines of the company joined unanimously to execrate it; and so many sensible and severe things were said against it, that everybody seemed willing to give it up to its father, the devil, except a young officer, whose ugly distortions showed plainly enough that he did not at all relish their strictures. Soon as they were done, he called aloud, "well, gentlemen, you may preach as much as you please against duelling, but I'll never pocket an insult for all that. No, if any man affront me, I'll call him to an account, if I lose my life for it."

The philosophers and divines looked at each other in silence, like fools who had shot their last bolt.

Here Franklin took up the cudgels; and looking at the young officer with a smile, said, "This, sir, puts me in mind of an affair that lately happened in a Philadelphia coffee-house."

The young fellow, rather pertly, said he should like to hear what had lately happened in a Philadelphia coffee-house.

"Why, sir," continued the doctor, "two gentlemen were sitting together in the coffee-house, when one said to the other, for heaven's sake, sir, sit further off, and don't poison me; you smell as bad as a pole-cat."

"Sir," resorted the other, "what do you mean? Draw, and defend yourself."

"O, sir," quoth the first, "I'll meet you in a moment, if you insist on it; but let's see first how that's to *mend the matter*. If you kill me, I shall smell as bad as a pole-cat too. And if I kill you, you will *only smell ten times worse*."

In short, that divine motto,

"Homo sum, nil humani a me alienum puto."

In English thus,

A man I am, in man I take a part,

And good of man is ever next my heart.

has seldom been more justly applied than to Dr. Franklin. He seems to have been all eye, all ear, all touch, to every thing that affected human happiness. Did he, even at the early age of twenty-five, form an acquaintance with young persons fond of reading, but unable to purchase books? Instantly he suggested the plan for obviating that great, great misfortune, by founding a PUBLIC LIBRARY; whereby, at a *small expense* in hand, and a much smaller paid annually, a subscriber might have his choice of books, on all subjects, whether of pleasure or profit. This Library, which was commenced in 1731, by Franklin and only thirty-seven members, and no more than one hundred volumes, consisting of much little parcels of books as each subscriber possessed, is now, 1820, enlarged to six hundred members, and upwards of twenty thousand volumes.

The great advantages arising from this library became so sensibly felt that others were soon founded; and they have now kindled up their salutary lights not only in several parts of the city, but in almost every county in the state. From the choicest books on Religion, Morals, History, Voyages, Travels, &c. thus brought home to their fire-sides and constantly lying on their mantlepieces, the citizens derive advantages incalculable. Their idle hours, formerly so dangerous, were now innocently filled up; solitude was cheered with a succession of new ideas; company enlivened by witty conversation, and labour itself sweetened by the thought of a beloved book at night.

With their taste thus exalted to *better pleasures*, the youth of all classes were saved from the brutalizing sensualities that destroy character and health. Having their understandings enlightened, they were led to greater virtues and usefulness. And being thus taught to enjoy life, they felt the strongest inducements to preserve it. Hence the astonishing prosperity of Philadelphia in industry and morals, population and wealth.

The mother Library now displays its twenty thousand volumes, in an elegant building, on the corner of Fifth and Chestnut. In a niche on the wall above the door is a fine marble likeness of Dr. Franklin at full length, presented by William Bingham, Esq.

Again:—Did Franklin catch a glimpse of those poor pusillanimous creatures, who rather than live nobly independent in the pure aired country, by cultivating their own sweet vegetables, and raising fat poultry, will run into the sickly towns to sell whiskey and apples in the summer, and take their chance to starve and freeze in the winter? Did he, I say, catch a glimpse of these poor spiritless creatures with their children, shivering over small fires kindled by a little "*charity wood*?" Instantly his bowels of compassion were stirred within him. Although he was no friend to such *lazy self-made paupers*, nor to the miserable policy that winks at them, yet it was impossible for him to remain unconcerned at their sufferings. In a letter to one of his friends, he says, "since we can get no more wood for the poor, we must try from that wood to get more warmth for them." He set himself to examine the principles of the stoves generally in use. His genius, as usual, discovered such room for amendment, that he soon came out with a stove, which to this day, in honour of him, is called "THE FRANKLIN STOVE," and wherein one cord of charity oak would afford as much heat and comfort to those poor people, as two cords in the old way!

Did he hear the shrill midnight cry of FIRE! and mark the deep distress of the citizens, as with tearful eyes they beheld the flames swallowing up their pleasant habitations and furniture? Instantly he set himself to call up all the energies of the public against this dire calamity, and to point them to the only adequate remedy, MUTUAL INSURANCE COMPANIES.

"*Man*," said he, in his calls to the citizens through his popular newspaper, "*Man separate* from man, is but a feeble creature; and like the filament of flax before the thread is formed, he is without strength, because without connexion. But UNION will make us strong, and *enable us to do all things essential to our safety. The houses burnt every year are, compared with all the houses in the city, but few. And were all the housekeepers in the city, joined for mutual security, to pay a certain sum; and were that sum put to interest, it would not only cover all the losses by fire, but would bring in every year, clear profit on his money to each subscriber.*"

Numbers of the citizens came into his scheme; and a large "*Mutual Insurance Company*," was immediately formed. The great benefits, foretold to flow from it, being soon realized, several others were presently set on foot: and now (in 1820,) there are, in Philadelphia, no fewer than forty engines, with eight thousand feet of hose, (strong leather pipes,) to convey the water from the pumps or hydrants to the engines; whereby in less than *two minutes* they are in full play, pouring their watery cataracts on the flames. Hence, while for lack of one Franklin, one intelligent and public spirited philanthropist, many of our promising young towns are suddenly turned to ashes, and their hapless families, driven out naked into the weather; the favoured citizens of Philadelphia, guarded by forty engines, and hundreds of well trained young firemen, seldom suffer any thing beyond a momentary pang from this most alarming element!

CHAPTER XXXVI.

"*To him who hath shall be given, and he shall have abundance.*"

The life of Dr. Franklin appears to have been one continued exemplification of this most animating promise; for scarcely had he finished that noble work just mentioned, before he was called to another which acquired him a still higher reputation, I mean his wonderful discoveries in electricity, and his application of them to the preservation of human life and property. The manner in which this honour was conferred on Dr. Franklin, is enough to convince all honest minds that there is a kind Providence over the ways of men, that often turns their "*seeming evils into real good.*"

Among the many benefits which he derived from the dangerous scenes of London, where he was so severely tried, and where he so gloriously triumphed, was his acquaintance with a Mr. Collinson, of that city. This gentleman had a soul of uncommon sensibility to the charms of virtue. His first interview with Franklin, was in Watts's printing-office. The sight of a youthful stranger, not yet out of his teens, exhibiting such practical lessons of virtue to the deluded young PORTER DRINKERS of London, filled him with admiration of his character. On getting acquainted with him, he was in pleasing doubt, whether most to esteem his heart or admire his head.

When Franklin left England, the generous Collinson accompanied him on board the ship, and at parting, the two friends exchanged *canes*, with promises of everlasting friendship and constant correspondence by letters. Soon as all London had become filled with the aforesaid rage for electricity, and electrical experiments, Collinson wrote the whole history of them to Franklin, with a compliment to his genius, and an earnest request that he would turn it to that subject, and accompanied all with the present of a small electrical instrument. Franklin's curiosity was excited. He immediately set to work; and presently made discoveries that far exceeded all that Collinson had promised himself. He discovered the power of metallic points to draw off the electrical matter—he discovered a *positive* and a *negative* state of electricity—he explained on electrical principles, the phenomena of the famous Leyden vial—he explained the phenomena of the aurora borealis, and of thunder-gusts—he showed the striking resemblance in many respects between electricity and lightning.

1 st. In giving light.

2 d. In colour of the light.

3 d. In crooked direction.

4 th. In swiftness of motion.

5 th. In being conducted by metals.

6 th. In cracking in exploding.

7 th. In subsisting in water or ice.

8 th. In rending the bodies it passeth through.

9 th. In killing animals.

10 th. In melting metals.

11 th. Firing inflammable substances.

12 th. Emitting a sulphurous smell.

13 th. In being attracted by iron points.

"We do not, indeed," says he, "know that this property is in lightning, but since electricity and lightning agree in so many other particulars, is it not probable that they agree also in this?"

He resolved at any rate to make the experiment. But foreseeing what a blessing it would be to mankind, to disarm the lightnings of their power to harm, he did not in the pitiful spirit of ordinary inventors, cautiously conceal the dawnings of a discovery that promised so much glory to his name. On the contrary, and with a philanthropy that throws eternal loveliness over his character, he published his ideas, inviting all the philosophers to make experiments on this important subject, and even pointed the way, *i.e.* by insulated bars of iron raised to considerable heights in the air.

Immediately, metallic bars, some of them forty feet high, were raised towards the heavens, by sundry philosophers, both in France and England. But God, as if pleased with such disinterested virtue, determined to reserve to Franklin the honour of confirming the truth of his own great theory. His plan to accomplish this, was in that simplicity which characterizes all his inventions.

To a common kite, made of silk rather than paper, because of the rain, he fixed a slender iron point. The string which he chose for his kite was of silk, because of the fondness of lightning for silk; and for the same reason, at the lower end of the string he tied a key. With this simple preparation, he went out on the commons back of Philadelphia, as a thundergust was coming on, and raised his kite towards the clouds. The lightning soon found out his metallic rod, as it soared aloft on the wings of the kite, and greeted its polished point with a cordial kiss. With joy he beheld the loose fibres of his string raised by the fond salute of the celestial visitant.

He hastened to clap his knuckle to the key, and behold, a smart spark! having repeated a second, and a third time, he charged a phial with this strange visitor from the clouds, and found that it exploded gunpowder, set spirits of wine on fire, and performed in all respects as the electrical fluid.

It is not easy to express the pleasure which this clear confirmation of his theory must have given to our benevolent philosopher, who had already counted up some of the great services which he should thereby render to the world.

He lost no time in communicating these discoveries to his friend Collinson in London, by whom they were read with unimaginable joy. Collinson instantly laid them before the Royal Society, not doubting but they would be printed among their papers, with the same enthusiasm which he had felt. But to his great mortification they were utterly rejected. Upon this, Collinson went in high dudgeon and printed them himself, which was looked on as a very desperate kind of undertaking, especially as he chose for his book, a title that seemed to carry a death warrant on its face, *viz.* "NEW EXPERIMENTS ON ELECTRICITY, MADE AT PHILADELPHIA, IN NORTH AMERICA." Some ventured however to read the EXPERIMENTS ON ELECTRICITY MADE IN NORTH AMERICA, though with pretty nearly such motives as usually lead people to see the learned pig, or to hear a woman preach. But the scoffers were soon turned into admirers. Discoveries so new and astonishing, presented in a manner so simple, struck every reader with admiration and pleasure. The book soon crossed the British channel, and was translated into most of the languages of Europe. A copy of it, though miserably translated, had the fortune to fall into the hands of the celebrated Buffon, who immediately repeated the experiments and with the most complete success. Lewis XV. hearing of these curious exhibitions, expressed a wish to be a spectator of them. A course of experiments was made before him and his court, to their exceeding surprise and diversion, by Buffon and De Lor. The history of electricity has not recorded those experiments. But it is probable, that they were not of so comic a character as the following, wherewith Dr. Franklin would sometimes astonish and delight his Philadelphia friends, during the intervals of his severer studies.

I. In the presence of a large party at his house, he took up a pistol which he had beforehand charged with inflammable air, well stopped with a cork, and presented it to Miss Seaton, a celebrated belle in those days. She took it from the doctor, but could not help turning pale, as though some conjuration was brewing. "*Don't be afraid, madam,*" said he, "*for I give you my word that there is not a grain of powder in it; and now turn it against any gentleman in the room that you are angry with.*" With a sudden blush, she turned it towards a gentleman whom she soon after married. In the same instant, the doctor drew a charged rod near the mouth of the pistol, the electric spark rushed in, and set fire to the inflammable air; off went the pistol; out flew the cork, and striking her lover a smart shock in the face, fell down on the floor, to the exceeding terror at first, but afterwards, to the equal diversion of the young lady and the whole company. This he called THE MAGIC PISTOL.

II. At another time, in a large party at his house, all eager, as usual, to see some of his ELECTRICAL CURIOSITIES, he took from the drawer a number of little dogs, made of the pith of elder, with straw for feet and tails, and set them on the table. All eyes were fixed on him. "*Well, Miss Eliza,*" said he, addressing the elegant Miss E. Sitgreaves, "*can you set these little dogs a dancing?*" "*No indeed, I can't,*" replied she. "*Well,*" replied he, "*if I had such a pair of eyes as you have, I think I could do it.*" She blushed. "*However, let us see,*" continued he, "*if we can't do something.*" He then took a large tumbler from the table, which he had previously charged with the electric fluid, and clapped the tumbler over the dogs; whereupon they instantly fell to skipping and jumping up the sides of the tumbler, as if they were half mad to get out of it. This he called "THE DANCING DOGS."

III. During something like a *levee*, at his house, one night, a couple of ladies who had been at London and Paris, were speaking in rapturous terms of the splendours of those royal courts, and of the diamond stars which they had seen, glittering with more than solar lustre on the breasts of the Prince of Wales and the Dauphin. At length one of the fair orators, as if wrought up to a perfect adoration of the wondrous stars which she had been so elegantly depicting, turned to the doctor, and smartly asked him if he would not like mightily to have such a star. "*To be sure, madam,*" replied he with his usual gallantry, "*and suppose we order one?*" She looked surprised. "*Boy,*" continued he, "*bring me down one of my electrical jars, and put it on the sideboard.*" While the servant was gone, the doctor took a plate of tin, and cutting it into a dozen angles, like a star, poised it on a wire projecting from his prime conductor. "*Well now, ladies, put out the candles, and you shall see a star not inferior to that of the prince of Wales.*" The candles were put out, and a turn or two of the jar being made, the lightning flew to the plate of tin, and appeared at the extremities of its angles, in a blaze of light beautiful as the morning star. This he called "THE ELECTRIC STAR."

IV. On his sideboard was placed an electrical jar, concealed behind a large picture of a man dressed in purple and fine linen. At a short distance stood a little brass pillar, in front of which was the picture of a poor man lying down ragged and wan as Lazarus. From the ceiling, and reaching down to the sideboard, was suspended by a fine thread, the picture of a boy, with a face benevolent and beautiful as a youthful cherub. "*Well, now, gentlemen, do you know who these are?—This is the proud, unfeeling Dives; that, the poor dying Lazarus; and here is a beautiful boy, that for humanity's sake, we will call the son of Dives. Now gentlemen, can any of you make this lovely child the minister of Dives' bounty to poor Lazarus?*"

They all confessed their inability; regarding him at the same time with an eye of expectation. Without being noticed by his company, he charged the jar behind the picture of Dives with electric fluid from his prime conductor. Instantly, the beauteous youth flew to it, and getting charged flew to the brass pillar behind Lazarus, which possessed no electricity, and imparted to it his whole load. He then flew back to the jar of Dives, and receiving a second supply, hastened to poor Lazarus and emptied himself again. And thus it went on to the astonishment of the spectators, alternately receiving and imparting until it had established a balance between them, and then, as if satisfied, it came to a pause.

Seeing their surprise, the doctor thus went on. "Well, now, gentleman, here is a fine lesson for us all. This electric fluid, which you saw animating that youth, came down from heaven to teach us that men were as assuredly designed to be helpmates to men, as were the two eyes, the two feet, or the two hands, to assist one another. And if all who are overcharged with this world's riches would but imitate this good little electrical angel, and impart of their superabundance to the empty and the poor, they would, no doubt, even in this world, find a much higher pleasure than in hoarding it up for ungrateful heirs, or spending it on vanity." This he called "DIVES AND LAZARUS."

But it were an endless task to enumerate all the rare and beautiful phenomena, wherewith he would surprise and delight the vast circles of friends and citizens, whose curiosity was so pressing, that, as he says, *it almost wore him out.*

Sometimes, in order to show them the force of electricity he would turn his wires against a pack of cards, or a quire of paper, and the subtle fluid would instantly dart through, leaving a beautiful perforation like the puncture of a large needle.

Sometimes, to show the wondrous qualities of electricity, he would let them see it darting, like a diamond bead, through a long cylinder of water, not hurt, like other fires, by that element.

Sometimes he would place a young lady, generally the handsomest of the company, on his electrical stool; then by slily touching her dress with his magic wand, he would so fill her lovely frame with the electric fluid, that, on the approach of any young gentleman to kiss her, a spark from her ruby lips would suddenly drive him frightened and staggering back. This was called the "MAGIC KISS."

Sometimes he would fix figures of horses cut in paper, on wires nicely poised, so as to move in circles round his prime conductor, then, from his magic wand, he would dash on them a stream of mimic lightning, which, potent as the whips and spurs of Newmarket, would set them all in full speed, bending and buckling with glorious emulation in the beautiful contest, to the great amusement of the spectators. The public named this the "ELECTRICAL HORSE RACE."

Sometimes he would suspend, near the ceiling, a large flock of finely picked cotton, or place on a distant table, a paper of gunpowder; then from his wires, artfully directed, he would send a flash of lightning, instantly exploding the powder, and wrapping the cotton into a blaze.

Sometimes he would take the model of a double-geared water mill, turning two pair of stones, and placing it near his prime conductor, direct a stream of electric fire against the large wheel, setting it in motion, and with it the whole machinery of his mill, to the equal surprise and pleasure of the beholders.

Sometimes he would take the figures of the sun, moon, and earth, cut in papers, and fix them on wires, nicely balanced. Then, by the force of the electric fluid, he would set them a-going in most harmonious style—the earth revolving round her own axis; the moon round the earth; and both round the sun; all exactly according to the course which the hand of the Creator had prescribed to these mighty orbs.

For the sake of those who have never considered this wonderful attraction of lightning to iron rods, I beg leave to relate the following very extraordinary and daring experiments of Dr. Franklin.

In a large chamber, which he kept for his electrical apparatus and experiments, he suspended a number of bells, all connected by wires, and communicating, through the gable end of the house, with the large lightning rods that descended along the chimney to the ground. His aim in this contrivance was, that he might know whenever a lightning cloud passed over his house in the night; and also what freight of electrical fluid it carried about with it. For, as it seldom passes, without paying a loving visit to his rod, so it always told, with great honesty, the amount of its inflammable cargo, especially if it was ample; in which case, it was always sure to set the bells a ringing at a terrible rate.

And besides these, he had numbers of men and women of the Lilliputian stature, cut in paper, and so artfully attached to the clappers, that as soon as the bells began to ring, the men and women began to dance also, and all of them more and more merrily, according as this extraordinary kind of music played up more briskly. But though, for the amusement of his friends, Franklin would sometimes set his bells and dolls to ringing and dancing, by his electricity, yet his main object was, to invite the lightnings to be the bell ringers, and dancing masters to his puppets, that, as before observed, he might become better acquainted with the nature of lightning, and thus extend his electrical experiments and knowledge.

But it must be owned, that when the lightnings were drawn down for this purpose among the bells and wires of his chamber, the entertainment was almost too terrible to be agreeable to any but philosophers.

The elegant J. Dickinson, Esq. informed me, that he was at Dr. Franklin's one evening, with a large party, when a dreadful cloud began to rise, with distant thunder and lightning. The ladies, panic struck, as usual, were all in a prodigious bustle for their bonnets, to get home. The doctor entreated them not to be frightened; for that they were in the safest house in Philadelphia; and indeed, jokingly offered to underwrite their lives at the low premium of a groat a head.

When the storm was near its worst, he invited his company up into his large chamber. A glimmering light faintly showed them his electrical apparatus of globes, cylinders, bells, wires, and the Lord knows what, conveying to those of the superstitious sort, a strong idea of a magic cell, or a haunted castle, at least. Presently a dreadful clap of thunder shook the house over their heads, the chamber was filled with vivid lightnings, darting like fiery serpents, crackling and hissing along the wire all around them, while the strong smell of sulphur, together with the screams of the poor ladies, and the ringing of the bells, completed the terribleness of the scene, inspiring a fearful sense of the invisible world.

"*But all these things, gentlemen,*" he would say, smiling all the time on his crowding and gaping friends, as a parent on his children, whom he saw surprised at small matters, "*all these things are mere nothings; the childish sportings of an art but yet in its cradle.* ELECTRICITY, gentlemen, is of the terrible family of lightning, that most powerful of the works of God on this globe, and the chosen instrument of most of his operations here below. It is the electric fluid, (passing from a full cloud to an empty one,) that makes his voice, and that, as the scripture says, *a terrible voice*, even the THUNDER, to terrify the guilty, and to increase in the virtuous a becoming reverence of the Creator.

For if the electric fluid passing from a small jar, cause so loud a crack, why should we wonder at the dreadful peals of thunder that are occasioned, when thousands and myriads of acres of clouds are throwing off their electric fluid in rivers of living fires, sufficient to blow up the globe itself, if the Almighty were but to let loose his hold on these furious agents. And this electric fluid is that same lightning which, as David says, *shines out from one end of Heaven to another*, and that so instantaneously, that were all the men, women, and children, on earth, joining hands, to form a ring round this great globe, an electric shock given to the first person in that ring, would so suddenly reach the last, that they themselves would probably be at a loss to determine which of them received it first.

"Thus the electric fluid, in the form of lightning, serves also in the hand of heaven as the *red rod* to restrain the vicious. Does the benevolent governor of the world seek to impress a salutary awe on the gambler, the drunkard, and such immoral characters, whose lives are in constant opposition to their own and the happiness of others? He but speaks to his ready ministers, the lightnings. Quickly, from the sultry cloud, coming up with muttering thunder, black and terrible as nature's approaching pall, the frightening flash bursts forth, rending the trees and houses over their heads; killing their flocks and herds; and filling the air with smoking sulphur, a strong memento of that dismal place to which their evil practices are leading them. And when, to unthinking mortals, he sees fit to read instruction on a wider scale, he only needs but beckon to the ELECTRIC FLUID. Straightway this subtle servant of his power rushes forth, clad in various forms of terror, sometimes as the roaring WHIRLWIND, unroofing the palaces of kings, and desolating the forests in its course. Sometimes with dreadful stride it rushes forth upon the 'howling wilderness of waves,' in shape of the funnelled water-spout, with hideous roar and foam, whirling the frightened billows to the clouds, or dashing them back with thundering crash into their dismal gulphs; while the hearts of the seamen, looking on, sink with terror at the sight, and even sharks and sea-monsters fly for refuge to their oozy caverns.

"Sometimes, with the bolder aim of the earthquake, it strikes both sea and land at once, sending the frightened globe bellowing and trembling along her orbit, sadly pondering the coming day, when the measure of sin being filled up, she shall be wrapt in these *same electric fires*, perhaps, and lose her place for ever among the starry train."

But though the experiments above mentioned are highly curious; and also Dr. Franklin's reflections on them abundantly philosophical and correct, for what I know, yet the world should learn that the gratification of public curiosity formed but a very small part of his many and grand discoveries in electricity. For soon as he had ascertained that lightning was the same thing with the electric fluid, and like it, so passionately fond of iron that it would forsake every thing else in its course, to run along upon that beloved metal, he conceived the plan of putting this discovery to those beneficent uses for which alone he thought the power of discovery was given to man, and which alone can consecrate it to the divine Giver.

"*The* GRAND *practical use*," says the learned Mr. Immison, who, though a Scotch monarchist himself, had the extraordinary virtue to be a profound admirer of our republican American,—"the grand practical use which Dr. Franklin made of this discovery was to secure houses and ships from being damaged by lightning; a thing of vast consequence in all parts of the world, but more especially in North America, where thunder gusts are more frequent and their effects, in that dry air, more dreadful than they are ever known to be with us. This great end he accomplished by the cheap, and seemingly trifling, apparatus of a pointed metallic rod, fixed higher than any part of the building, and communicating with the ground, or rather the nearest water. This rod the lightning is sure to seize upon preferably to any other part of the building, unless it be very large; in which case, rods may be erected at each extremity; by which means this dangerous power is safely conducted to the earth, and dissipated without doing any harm to the edifice."

Had any thing more been necessary to convince the world of the value of lightning rods to buildings, it was abundantly furnished by several very terrible instances of destruction which took place about this time in several parts of America, for no other reason upon earth, as every one must admit who reads the account, but the want of lightning rods.

There, for example, was the affair of the new church, in the town of Newberry, New-England. This stately building was adorned on its north end with an elegant steeple or tower of wood, running up in a fine square, seventy feet from the ground to the bell, and thence went off in a taper spire of wood, likewise seventy feet higher, to the weathercock. Near the bell was fixed an iron hammer to strike the hours; and from the tail of the hammer, a wire went down through a small gimblet hole in the floor that the bell stood upon, and through a second floor in like manner; then horizontally under the plaistered ceiling of that floor to a plaistered wall, then down that wall to a clock which stood about twenty feet below the bell.

Now come, gentlemen, *you* who have no faith in lightning rods—you who think it *blasphemy* to talk of warding off GOD ALMIGHTY'S LIGHTNING!—as if it were not just as pleasing to him to see you warding off the lightning by steel rods, as warding off the ague and fever by jesuit's bark; come, I say, and see how very visibly he approbates our works of wisdom, which make us like himself. You have read the structure of this steeple—the top, a *seventy feet spire without any rod*—then a rod that went down zigzag, about thirty feet; then a plaistered brick and stone wall without any rod, to the ground. A dreadful cloud came over the steeple. At the first flash, away went the whole of the seventy foot wooden spire, scattered all over the church yard in splinters fit to boil the preacher's tea kettle. The lightning then found the iron wire which it instantly seized on, quitting all things else for that, and darting along with it in so close an embrace, as barely to widen a little the gimblet holes through which it passed. It then followed the wire in all its meanders, whether perpendicular or horizontal—never turning either to the right or to the left, to hurt the building, but passed through it the whole length of the wire, which was about thirty feet, as harmlessly as a lamb. But soon as its dear chain was ended, it assumed the furious lion again; attacking the building with the most destructive rage, dashing its foundation stones to a great distance, and in other respects damaging it dreadfully.

Now what can be more reasonable than doctor Franklin's remarks on this very remarkable occurrence?

"I. That lightning, in its passage through a building, will leave wood, brick, or stone, to pass as far as it can in metal; and not enter those again, till the metal conductor ceases.

"II. The quantity of lightning that passed through this steeple must have been very great, by its effects on the lofty spire, &c., and yet great as this quantity was, it was conducted by a small wire without the least damage to the building as far as the wire extended.

"III. Hence it seems probable, that if even such a small wire had been extended from the top of the steeple to the earth, before the storm, no damage would have been done by that stroke of lightning."

A fate exactly similar to this attended the great Dutch church, of New York, in 1750. As far as the wire was extended, which was from the top of the steeple, to within a few feet of the earth, the lightning closely accompanied it, passing with it through small holes in the floors, without doing the least damage. But the instant it quitted the wire, it commenced its ravages on the building.

The summer of 1760 was dreadfully hot in Pennsylvania; and the thunder gusts frequent and terrible. Several ships at the wharves were struck and greatly injured. One of them in particular, a very large ship, had her mainmast torn to pieces, and her captain and three seamen killed. Of houses, both in town and country, many were struck; and some of them, as barns with large quantities of hay, and warehouses with hemp, were set on fire and destroyed to the great detriment and terror, both of the unfortunate sufferers and their neighbours.

These things, though melancholy in themselves, were not without their good effects. They served to place in the strongest point of view, the admirable efficacy of the newly invented lightening rods. For, while buildings destitute of them, were often struck, and sometimes with great loss of lives and property, those houses that had them, were hardly ever known to be hurt, though the neighbours who saw the dismal clouds when they bursted, with such hideous peals of thunder and streams of lightning, were sickened with horrid apprehension that all was lost. And even the house keepers themselves, when recovered from their terrors and faintings, would fly shrieking from chamber to chamber, amidst the clouds of sulphur to see who were *dead.* But behold, to the delicious wonder of themselves and congratulating friends, all were safe. But still the cry was, *certainly the house was struck! the house was surely struck! let us examine the conductors.*

The conductors were resorted to and examined, and behold! the wondrous laws imposed of God on the most powerful of his creatures! The furious lightnings had fallen on the houses in torrents of fire, threatening a wide destruction. But the iron rods, faithful to their trust, had arrested the impending bolts, and borne them in safety to the ground.

But it was found that the cataracts of lightning had proved too powerful for the rods; in some instances melting them in two at their slenderest parts, and in others entirely consuming them into smoke. But though these GUARDIAN RODS had perished in their conflict with the rude lightnings, yet they had succeeded in parrying the dreadful stroke with perfect safety to the buildings and their terrified inhabitants; thus impressing all men with joy and thankfulness, *that God had given such complete victory over one of the most terrible of all our natural enemies.*

In short, to use the handsome language of president Adams, "nothing perhaps that ever occurred on earth, could have better tended to confer universal celebrity on man, than did these lightning rods of doctor Franklin's. The idea was certainly one of the most sublime ever suggested to the human imagination. That mortal man should thus be taught to disarm the clouds of heaven, and almost snatch from his hand '*the sceptre and the rod*!'"

The ancients would, no doubt, have enrolled among their gods, the author of so wonderful an invention. Indeed the reputation which Franklin acquired by it, not only in America, but in Europe also, far transcended all conception. His *lightning rods*, or as the French called them, his "*paratonerres*," erected their heads, not only on the temples of God and the palaces of kings, but also on the masts of ships and the habitations of ordinary citizens. The sight of them every where reminded the gazing world of the name and character of their inventor, who was thought of by the multitude as some *great magician* dwelling in the *fairy lands* of North America, and to whom God had given controul over the elements of nature.

And equally wonderful was the change produced by them in the state of general comfort. The millions, who had hitherto trembled at the cloud rising in the heat of summer, could now look on it with pleasing awe as it rose dark and solemn, with all its muttering thunders. And even amidst the mingled flash and crash of the earth shaking tornado, the very women and children, if they had but Franklin *paratonerres* to their chimnies, would sit perfectly composed, silently adoring God for teaching such great salvation to men.

But the pleasure which doctor Franklin found in these plaudits of an honest world was not without an alloy. Though the end of his labours had been to do good; yet he soon discovered that there were some who sickened at his success. Alas!

"Among the sons of men, how few are known

Who dare be just to merit, not their own."

Certain invidious scribblers, in London and Paris, began to decry his well-earned glory, by pretending that it was all due to the Abbe Nollet, to doctor Gilbert, or some other wonderful Frenchman or Englishman, as the real father of electricity. Franklin took no notice of all this impotent malice; nor indeed was it necessary; for soon as it dared to present its brazen front in print, it was attacked by the first-rate philosophers of Europe, who nobly taking the part of Franklin, soon showed, to the general satisfaction, that whatever others may have dreamed about the late wonderful discoveries in electricity, they were all due, under God, to the great American philosopher, who for these, and many other important discoveries, had a good right to share with Newton in the following bold compliment.

"Nature and nature's works lay hid in night,

God said, let Franklin be, and all was light."

CHAPTER XXXVII.

A curious demonstration of Dr. Franklin's philosophy of lightning. About thirty-four years after this date, when Doctor Franklin, by his opposition to Lord North's measures, had become very unpopular, George III. was persuaded to pull down the *sharp points* of that "HOARY REBEL," and set up the *blunts* of an impudent quack, because, forsooth, he was a *loyal subject*! Scarcely were the *sharps* taken down from the palace, to which, during thirty four years, they had been an excellent safeguard, before a dismal cloud rose upon the city, black as midnight, and when right over the palace discharged a cataract of electric fluid, with horrid glare and thunder, stunning all ears, blinding all eyes, and suffocating every sense with the smell of sulphur. The famous *blunt conductors* presented no point to catch the bolt, which, dashing at the stately edifice, tore away all its gable end, marring the best apartments, and killing several of the king's servants.

Shortly arrived the packet from New York, with news of a far more dreadful thunder-clap which had bursted on poor George in America—the capture of his grand Canada army! which Lord North had promised him should soon bring the rebels to their marrow bones. The next day the following pasquinade made its appearance in the newspapers:

"While you, great George, intent to hunt,

Your sharp Conductors change to blunt,

The nation's out of joint;

Franklin a wiser course pursues,

And all your thunder fearless views,

By sticking to the POINT."

I cannot quit this subject without observing, that from Dr. Franklin's experiments it appears, that death by lightning, must be the easiest of all deaths.

"In September, 1752," says he, "six young Germans, apparently doubting the truth of the reported force of electricity, came to me to see," as they said, "if there was *any thing in it.* Having desired them to stand up side by side, I laid one end of my discharging rod on the head of the first; this laid his hand on the head of the second, that on the head of the third, and so on to the last, who held in his hand the chain that was attached to the lightning globe. On being asked if they were ready, they answered *yes*, and boldly desired that I would give them a *thumper*; I then gave them a shock; whereat they all dropped down together. When they got up, they declared that they had not felt any stroke; and wondered how they came to fall. Nor did any of them *hear* the crack, or *see* the light of it."

He tells another story equally curious. "A young woman, afflicted with symptoms of a palsy in the foot, came to receive an electrical shock. Heedlessly stooping too near the prime conductor, she received a smart stroke in the forehead, of which she fell like one perfectly lifeless on the floor. Instantly she got up again complaining of nothing, and wondering much why she fell, for that nothing of the sort had ever happened to her before."

Nay, he also tells us of himself, that by accident, he received a shock which in an instant brought him to the floor, without giving him time to *see, hear, or feel any thing of the matter*! Hence he concludes, and I think with good reason, that all who dread the idea of pain in dying, would do well to pray, if it be God's will, to die of *coelatactio*n, as the ancients called it, or a *touch from heaven.*

It is worthy of remark, that persons thus knocked down, do not *stagger*, or fall *lengthwise*, but as if deprived instantaneously of strength and firmness, they sink down at once, doubled or folded together, or as we say, "*all in a heap*."

Dr. Franklin seldom suffered any thing to escape him. From the power of lightning to dissolve the hardest metals, he caught an idea favourable to cooking and matrimony. First, an old dunghill cock killed in the morning by a shock from his electrical jar, by dinner was become so tender that both the doctor and several of his literary friends pronounced it equal to a young pheasant. Second, an old bachelor thought to be far gone in a consumption, had hardly received more than a couple of dozen smart shocks of electricity, before he turned into courting with great spirit, and presently got himself a wife.

If electrical jars could be had cheap, this discovery concerning the old dunghill cock might prove a good hint to those gentlemen in the *tavern-keeping* line, who are so very frugal that they will not keep up a coop full of young poultry, fat and fine, and always ready for the traveller, but prefer giving him the pain, long after his arrival at their door, to hear the lean tenants of the dunghill flying and squalling from the pursuit of the barking dogs and noisy servants.

And as to the experiment on the other kind of old CAPON, the grunting wheezing old bachelor, it clearly points to the wish often expressed by Dr. Franklin, viz. "*that the legislature would order an electrical machine, large enough to kill a turkey cock at least, to be placed in every parish, at the cost and for the benefit of all the old bachelors of the same.*"

CHAPTER XXXVIII.

I have been told that Dr. Franklin on his death bed often returned thanks to God for having so kindly cast his lot of life in the very time when of all others he would have chosen to live for the great purposes of usefulness and pleasure. And so indeed it appears; for scarcely had he matured, as above, his most useful discoveries in electricity, before a new door was opened to him for another noble charity to his country.

Some there are who for a good work begun by themselves will do every thing; but for the same work begun by others will do nothing; and yet will call themselves christians. Franklin lived to set the example of a better christianity. A notable instance of this occurred about this time, 1754.

A Dr. Thomas Bond, having noticed a number of families so extremely poor, as to be in imminent danger not only of suffering grievously in case of sickness, but of actually perishing for want of wholesome food and medicine, generously undertook, by subscription, to build a hospital for these sufferers. Meeting with but little encouragement, and knowing Dr. Franklin's influence and public spirit, he applied to him for assistance. Perfectly indifferent who got the praise, provided he but shared the pleasure of founding so god-like an institution, Franklin entered very heartily into the plan with Dr. Bond, and inserted in his newspaper, a series of essays, "*on the great duty of charity to the sick and miserable*," which made such an impression on the public mind, that the noble sum of twelve thousand dollars was quickly subscribed. With this the trustees bought a lot, and finished one wing of their hospital, for immediate use. On the foundation stone is to be seen the following inscription by Dr. Franklin:

"In the year of Christ MDCCLV,
George the Second, *happily reigning*,
(For he sought the HAPPINESS OF HIS PEOPLE,)
Philadelphia *flourishing*,
(For its inhabitants were *public spirited*,)
This Building
By the bounty of the Government
And of many private persons
Was piously founded
For the relief of the *sick* and *miserable*.
MAY THE GOD OF MERCIES BLESS THE UNDERTAKING!"

Never did benevolence put up an ejaculation more fervent. And never was one more signally answered. Indeed the blessings of heaven have been so signally showered on this excellent charity, that it now forms one of brightest ornaments of the fairest city in America, presenting to the delighted eye of humanity a noble front, of elevation and extent far beyond that of Solomon's temple, even a royal range of buildings, two and three stories high, two hundred and seventy-eight feet long, and forty wide, containing about one hundred and thirty spacious well-aired rooms, for the accommodation of the sick, wounded, and lunatic of every description; affectionately waited on by skilful physicians and active nurses; comforted by refreshing baths both hot and cold; and abundantly supplied with the best loaf bread, nice vegetables, fresh meats, soups, wines and medicines.

And while other parts of the city have been very sickly; and especially in the summer of 1793, when no fewer than 4000 persons perished of the yellow fever, not a single case of disease occurred in this hospital. The destroying angel as he passed along, smelt the odour of that precious grace (charity) which embalmed the building, and let fall his avenging sword.

Gentlemen travellers falling sick in Philadelphia, will please be informed of this famous hospital, that if they wish excellent physicians, experienced nurses, pleasant chambers, pure air, and sweet retirement, they may here have all those of the first quality at *half price*; and *even* THAT a *donation* to the *Institution.*

CHAPTER XXXIX.

Dr. Franklin, about this time, 1756, commenced his political career.

When we see some peerless *Childers*, (whose figure almost proves the divinity of matter, and who in matchless speed leaves the stormy winds behind him,) bending under the weight of a miller's bag, or tugging at the hames of some drunken carman, how can we otherwise than mourn such a prostitution of excellences; so how can we but mourn, when we see such a man as Franklin, born for those divine arts which widen our empire over nature, and multiply a thousand-fold the comforts of life, wasting his precious time in combatting the unreasonable claims of selfish and wicked man?

This, for a portion of his eventful life, was the sad destiny of Dr. Franklin. Scarcely had he passed his first forty years in his favourite philosophical labours, equally useful to the world, and delightful to himself, when he was at once stopped short—stopped by the voice of public gratitude. The wise and virtuous people of Pennsylvania, chiefly quakers, who estimate a man, not by the fineness of his coat, but the *usefulness* of his life, were not to overlook such a man as Franklin. His astonishing industry, and his many valuable inventions, had long made him the favourite theme of their talk. But it was not for approbation so general and hearty, to be satisfied with *mere talk.*

What shall be done for the man whom the people delighteth to honour? was the question in every circle. *God, they said, has lighted up this candle for our use, it must not be hid under a bushel. Let it be placed on the great candlestick of the nation, the* LEGISLATURE. So strong, indeed, was the public feeling in his favour, that from several of the wards, deputations were appointed to wait upon him, to beg he would serve the city as their representative in the house of burgesses.

The sight of his name in the papers, as a candidate at the next election, to serve the city of Philadelphia, gave a general joy. Among his opponents were several of the wealthiest citizens, who had long served as representatives, and whose numerous friends could not bear the idea of their being turned out. Great exertions were made on both sides; and the polls were uncommonly crowded. But when the contest came to issue, it was found that the Philadelphia printer, and son of the good old psalm-singing Boston tallow-chandler, carried the day with great ease.

O ye simple ones, how long will you love simplicity! you, I mean, who can once a year look sweetly on your constituents, and once a year invite them to barbacues, and make them drunk with whiskey, thus ignobly begging those votes which you feel you have not the sense to deserve, O learn from this your great countryman, wherein consists the true art of electioneering; not in ignoble tricks like these, to court the little, but in high qualifications, like Dr. Franklin's, to be courted by the great.

The exalted expectations formed of him by the public were not disappointed. Heartily a lover of man and the friend of equal rights, he had scarcely taken his seat in the legislature before he had to turn the torrent of his honest indignation against the *proprietaries* and their creatures the *Governors*.

The reader will please here be reminded that in the year 1680, that great GOOD man, William Penn, a quaker, was paid off a large claim against Charles II. of England, by a grant of lands in North America. To make the best of a bad bargain, honest William gathered together a caravan of his poor persecuted brethren, and taking ship came over to North America.

The good angel that guided the steps of pious Jacob as he sojourned from Padan-aram to the land Uz, seeking a rest, guided Penn and his gentle followers to the mouth of the Delaware bay. He followed the stately flood in all its wanderings among the green marshes and forests of the new found world, until he reached the pleasant spot where now Philadelphia stands. The majestic grove that shaded the extended level on the western bank, bordered on the back by the beautiful serpentine river called by the natives, the SCHUYLKILL, struck his eye as a fine site for his future city.

Abhorring the idea of killing his fellow men, the poor natives, and taking away their lands, he sent around among them the Calumet, or *pipe of peace*, inviting them to "A FRIENDLY TALK." Painted in red ochre, and decked in all the savage pomp of wild skins and feathers, the kings of the soil with all their simple tribes assembled themselves together. The meeting was in the summer of 1681, under the trees near the margin of the great river. The scene was lovely to the eye of humanity. The red and white men from different continents were seen to meet, not as enemies for mutual slaughter, but as brothers for loving commerce. The shores were covered with British merchandize. The eyes of the simple children of nature sparkled on those rich wares, the like of which they had never seen before.

Penn gave them every thing. He gave them precious axes to master the forests; and still more magic guns to master the wolves and panthers. He gave them warm clothes for defence against the cold, and plough-shares and hoes for plentiful harvests. In return they gave him that large tract of land in their country, which, in honour of this good man, has been called Pennsylvania. Instantly the aged forests began to resound with the strokes of axes and the crash of falling trees. And the corner stone was laid of the new city, which, with great propriety, was named of Penn, PHILADELPHIA, or the city of *brotherly love.*

Having thus laid, the foundation of this colony in JUSTICE to the poor natives, and in generosity to his own followers in the great cheapness of his lands, in perfect liberty of conscience, and in the exceeding moderation of his government, this wise statesman then looked to God for his blessings. Nor did he look in vain, The fame of "PENN COLONY" resounded throughout Great Britain. An immense emigration were quickly on their way to Pennsylvania. The young city grew apace, and farms and fair buildings in the country, spread in every direction with a rapidity unequalled in history.

But alas! when honest William fell asleep, there rose after him a race of heirs "*who knew not Joseph*;" who not content, *like him*, with modest drab, and simple dinners, and aspiring to the true happiness of imitating God in godlike loves and deeds, basely prostituted their hearts to carnal lusts and pride.

The worship of these gods, though contemptible, is costly; and to these *wet-quaker* successors of the good William Penn, nothing promised such a swelling revenue as a bold rise in the price of their lands. And in this pitiful kind of management they soon gave the Pennsylvanians to understand that like Rehoboam of old, "*their little fingers were heavier than their father's loins.*" I have not been able to procure any thing like certainty as to the sum that GOOD William Penn gave to the natives for the vast tract of land he purchased of them. But that he hardly gave at the rate of a *hatchet* for what is now a noble farm, may be very fairly inferred. In 1754, which was seventy years later than the first purchase, the house of Penn bought of the Indians seven millions of acres lying within the ROYAL GRANT. And what do you suppose they gave for it? what do you suppose they gave for seven millions of acres of rich, heavy timbered Pennsylvania land? why not quite two thousand dollars! not *three cents* the hundred acres! And what do you suppose they immediately asked for it? why *fifteen pounds ten shillings!* near fifty thousand cents per hundred acres! And yet with such a bank of millions in hand they were not willing to bear their part of the taxes for public good!!

Like the starched Pharisees of old, they could throw heavy weights on other men's shoulders, but not suffer a fly to light on theirs. They could smile when they saw the officer going round with his ink horn and pen, noting down the poor man's paddock, but if he but looked at their princely manors and parks they would make the whole colony ring with it.

Grown beyond calculation rich by the sales and rents of their lands in America, they scorned the country of their illustrious predecessor, and went over to London, where they mimicked the pride and pageantry of princes.

Thinking they did the obscure Pennsylvanians honour enough to govern them by *proxy*, they washed their hands of the poor colony government, and sent them over deputies. These, hirelings, to augment their salaries, soon commenced a course of oppressions on the people, whom they treated with great insolence.

It were too great an honour to those wretches to set the people of the present day to reading their insolent messages to the legislature. They were always, however, very properly chastised by Dr. Franklin; sometimes in the columns of his own popular newspaper, and sometimes in the assembly. Not, indeed, by long and eloquent orations, for which he either had no talent, or declined it, preferring the pithy and pungent *anecdote* or *story*, which was always so admirably appropriate, and withal so keen in wit and truth, that like a flash from his own lightning rods, it never failed to demolish the fairest fabric of sophistry, and cause even its greatest admirers to blush that they had been so fascinated by its false glare.

In 1756, he was appointed deputy post-master general for the British colonies. It is asserted that in *his* hands, the post-office in America yielded annually thrice as much as did that of Ireland. An extraordinary proof of our passion for reading and writing beyond the Irish. Perhaps it was owing to this that we saved our liberties, while they lost theirs.

Several of the middle colonies suffering much at this time from Indian depredations on their frontiers, it was agreed among them to send commissioners to Albany to devise means for mutual defence. Dr. Franklin, commissioner on the part of Pennsylvania, had the honour to draw up a plan, which was thought excellent. Knowing the colonists to be the best marksmen in the world, and supposing it infinitely safer that the defence of their own firesides should be entrusted to them than to British hirelings, he had with his usual sagacity recommended that muskets and powder should be put into their hands.

But when his plan was presented to the KING and COUNCIL for ratification, it was indignantly rejected. It was thought by some that hardly could Satan and his black janisaries have been more seriously offended, had a cargo of Bibles and hymn books been recommended for their pandemonium.

The truth is, the British ministry had for a long time depressed the unfortunate Americans into mere *hewers of wood and drawers of water*, by making them bring all their rich produce of tobaccos, furs, &c. to English ports, and there give them the meanest prices; sometimes a penny, and even half a penny a pound for their brightest tobacco, which they would the next hour sell to the Dutch merchants for two shillings a pound. To preserve such a trade as this, as Lord Howe ingenuously confessed, from going into any other channel, was a grand object to the ministry. But this they could not long count on, if the Americans were furnished with muskets, cannon, and powder. They therefore, very prudently, determined to leave Dr. Franklin's *excellent marksmen* out of the question, and confide to their own creatures the protection of a country whose trade could so *well repay them for it.*

But their folly in preferring such troops was soon made evident, as Franklin had predicted. In the spring of 1755, two thousand veterans, the elite of the British military, were sent over to drive the French from the Ohio. One half that number of Virginia riflemen would have done the business completely. But such was the ministerial jealousy of the American riflemen, and so great their dread to embody and arm that kind of troops, that they permitted no more than three companies to join the army. And even these were so ludicrously scrimped up by governor Dinwiddie, in jackets scarcely reaching to their waists, that they became a mere laughing stock of the British army, who never called them by any other name than the "VIRGINIA SHORT RUMPS." Many believed that this was done purposely, that by being thus constantly laughed at, they might be *cowed* thereby, and be led to think meanly of themselves, as quite an inferior sort of beings to the MIGHTY ENGLISH. But blessed be God whose providence always takes part with the oppressed. A few short weeks only elapsed when this motley army was led, by an incautious commander, into a fatal ambuscade of the French and Indians—general Braddock, at the head of his 2000 British veterans, and young George Washington at the head of his two hundred "*Virginia short rumps*." Then was displayed the soundness of Dr. Franklin's judgment, in the wide difference, as to *self-possession and hard fighting*, between these two kind of troops.

The conceited Englishmen behaved no better than WILD TURKIES; while the despised "*Virginia short rumps*" fought like lions, and had the glory of saving the wreck of the British army.

This sad defeat had like to have ruined doctor Franklin, by whose credit with the Pennsylvanians, colonel Dunbar of the rear guard of his army, had been furnished with fifty wagons, which were all burnt on the retreat. His escape from this danger was owing to the generosity of governor Shirley, who learning that Franklin had incurred this debt on account of the British government, undertook to discharge it.

Seeing no end to the vexation and expense brought on the colony by those selfish beings, the PROPRIETARIES, the assembly came at length, to the resolution to petition the king to abolish the proprietary government, and take the colony under his own care. Doctor Franklin was appointed to the honour of presenting this petition to his majesty George II. and sailed for England, June, 1757.

Learning at last that by obstinately contending for *too much*, they might possibly lose *all*, the proprietaries signified to doctor Franklin a willingness that their land should be *taxed.*

After the completion of this important business, Franklin remained at the court of Great Britain as agent for the province of Pennsylvania. The extensive knowledge which he possessed of the situation of the colonies and the regard which he always manifested for their interests, occasioned his appointment to the same office by the colonies of Massachusetts, Maryland and Georgia.

He had now an opportunity of visiting those illustrious Englishmen, whom his useful writings and discoveries had strongly bound to him, though they had never seen his face. The high opinion which they had formed of him at a distance, was greatly increased by a personal acquaintance.

Such vastness of mind with such sweetness of spirit and simplicity of manners, formed a spectacle as rare as it was lovely. And as a proof that SUPERIOR SENSE and superior benevolence will always prevail against prejudice, he was now courted by those learned societies who formerly affected to deride his discoveries in philosophy and electricity. The Royal Society of London, which had at first refused his performances admission into its transactions, now deemed it an honour to class him among its fellows. The universities of St. Andrews, of Edinburgh, and Oxford, conferred on him the degree of doctor of laws; and the most distinguished philosophers of Europe sought his correspondence. In reading his letters to those great men, we are at a loss which most to admire, the majesty of his sense, or the simplicity of his style. While in England, which was from July, 1757, to July, '62, he suggested to the British ministry the duty of dispossessing the French of that great country on the north of our colonies called Canada. To this end, he published his famous *Canada pamphlet*, exhibiting in strong colours the many mischiefs and murders committed on his countrymen, even in times of peace, by the Indians in French pay. This little tract served to rouse the British nation to the pitch he desired.

An army of English regulars and New-England militia were sent under the command of general Wolfe, who presently succeeded in driving the French out of a fine country, of which, by their cruelties, they had rendered themselves utterly unworthy.

About this time the celebrated doctor Cullen, of Scotland, made some curious discoveries in the art of producing cold by evaporation. Hoping that the genius of Franklin might throw some lights on this dawning science, a friend of doctor Cullen's wrote a statement of the facts to Franklin. The American philosopher, though now immersed in political pursuits, took a little leisure to repeat doctor Cullen's experiments on cold, which he so improved as easily to produce ICE in the *dog days*. But it was one of those discoveries, which, as he says, he *never valued, because it was too expensive to be of general utility.*

About the autumn of 1761, he rendered himself prodigiously popular among the ladies in London, by completing that sweet toned little instrument of music, the HARMONICA.

I have been told that his fame at court on this account, so awakened the recollection of George III. that he caused it to be signified to Dr. Franklin, that he felt a disposition to "*do something for him.*" Our philosopher replied, that he wanted nothing for himself, but—that, *he had a son in America.* The king took the hint, and immediately made out a commission of "*Governor of his colony of New Jersey, for his beloved subject, Temple Franklin, Esq.*" On such small things are the fortunes of men sometimes founded!

Doctor Franklin was now become so great a favourite that the people of all classes seemed to take a pride in talking of him, and his sayings, insomuch that not a word of the brilliant sort could fall from his lips but it was sure to be caught up instantly and re-echoed through every circle, from proud St. James to humble St. Giles. The following impromptu made a great noise in London about this time.

One evening in a large party at his friend Vaughan's he was, laughingly, challenged by a very beautiful girl, a Miss Gun, to make her a couplet of verses *extempore.* Well, madam, replied he, with great gallantry, since every body is offering a tribute to your graces, let me tender the following:

"Cupid now to ensure his fun,

Quits his *bow* and takes to *gun.*"

This handsome play on her name instantly suffused the cheeks of Miss Gun with celestial roses, making her look much more like an angel than before.

I mention this merely to show what an extraordinary mind that man must have possessed, who with such equal ease, could play the *Newton* or the *Chesterfield*, and charm alike the lightnings and the ladies.

In the summer of 1762, he took leave of his friends in England to return to his native country. On his voyage he discovered in oil or grease thrown on the water, a property, which few people ever dreamt of. When we learn of *gold* that it may by beating, be expanded into a leaf of such incredible fineness, that a guinea might in that way be made to cover Solomon's temple, or deck Noah's ark, we are filled with wonder of such a metal. Doctor Franklin tells us of equal wonders in oil. He informs us, that a wine glass full of pure oil poured on a mill pond, will presently spread over it, with a film inconceivably thinner than a cobweb, and so adhesive that the winds shall not excite it to mad-caps and breakers. Hence, he infers, that oil might be made a mean of saving ships during a violent storm at sea.

In this voyage he made also another discovery, which ought to be known to all going by sea, viz. that if persons perishing of thirst on a voyage, would but bathe half a dozen times a day in the sea water, which they easily might, by using their empty water casks as bathing tubs, they would obtain great relief from their thirst, and live several days longer; thence enjoying a better chance for their lives, by getting into port, or falling in with some friendly sail.

On his arrival in Philadelphia doctor Franklin was welcomed with marks of the most flattering respect by the citizens universally—handsome addresses and dinners were given him by literary societies and clubs—and the assembly, in the most public manner voted him their thanks for "the great honour and services he had rendered the country in general during his residence in England; and especially to the province of Pennsylvania." And they accompanied their thanks with a present of five thousand pounds.

Ye blind parents who can think hard of laying out a few dollars for books and education of your children, O think of this, and learn a course of conduct more to your own credit and to their temporal and eternal welfare.

In a few weeks after his return to Philadelphia there occurred in that neighbourhood an affair that serves to show the popularity of doctor Franklin in a very strong light.

In consequence of a number of murders committed on the frontiers by some villanous Indians, about a hundred and twenty young men of Dauphin county, christians in *name* but perfect savages in nature, bound themselves by a horrid oath to exterminate a little tribe of about twenty tame Indians, who lived very harmlessly among the whites in York county. Mounted on horses, and with rifles and tomahawks in their hands, they set off very deliberately on this hellish errand towards the settlements of the poor Indians. The old men, women, and children, in the cabins, soon fell weltering in their blood. The rest, who were at work, getting notice, fled to Lancaster, and were lodged in the jail as in a place of security. The blood thirsty whites broke open the jail and butchered every soul. All smeared with innocent blood, and furious as demons, they then pushed off for Philadelphia, to massacre the feeble remains of a friendly tribe who had fled into that city for protection. The governor issued his proclamation. The rioters paid no regard to it, but moved on rapidly, well armed, and determined to cut their way to the hated Indians over the bodies of all who should oppose them. They are now on this side of Germantown, only one hour's march from Philadelphia. The inhabitants are all in terror. The governor quits his palace, and for safety flies to the house of doctor Franklin. He, calm as he was wont to be amidst the lightnings as they darted around him on his rods, went out to meet the rioters. We sincerely regret that we cannot give the speech which he made on this memorable occasion. It must have been impressive in a most extraordinary degree; for on hearing it they instantly abandoned their hellish design and returned peaceably to their homes!

CHAPTER XL.

Had the fatal sisters, even now, put forth their shears and clipped his thread, yet would not the friend of man "*have fallen without his fame.*" Admiring posterity would still have written on his tomb,

Here lies the GREAT FRANKLIN.

But though great now, he is destined to be much greater still. A crisis is approaching that is to call forth all his talents, and to convince even the most unthinking, that in the dark day of trouble the "*wise shall shine forth like the firmament.*" By the crisis here mentioned, I mean the events leading to the American revolution.

The British cabinet, as if entire strangers to that divine philosophy which commands its disciples to be "*no respecters of persons,*" allowed themselves in the most fatal policy of sparing the British subjects in *England* at the expense of the British subjects in *America.* After having drained much money from them in a variety of unconstitutional ways, they came at length to the resolution of taxing *the colonies without their consent.*

This dark design was hinted in 1754, by the minister, to governor Shirley, of the Massachusetts-Bay colony. The governor, well knowing his extraordinary penetration and judgment, broke this ministerial plan to Dr. Franklin; requesting *his* opinion of it. Dr. Franklin answered this question of the governor, by urging an "*immediate union of the colonies with great Britain, by allowing them representatives in parliament,*" as the only thing that could prevent those ceaseless encroachments on the one side, and those bitter animosities on the other, which, *he feared,* would one day prove the ruin of both countries. As to the ministerial plan of taxing the colonies by act of parliament, where they have no representation, he assured the governor that it would prove utterly abominable. "His majesty, sir," said he to the governor, "has no subjects in all his wide dominions, who more heartily love him than do his American subjects. Nor do there exist on earth, the Englishmen who hold more dear the glory of old England than they do. But the same spirit of their gallant forefathers, which makes them ready to lay down their lives and fortunes, in a constitutional way, for their king and country, will for ever secure them from being slaves. We exult, sir, in the recollection, that of all the governments on earth, that of Great Britain has long been the *freest*; and that more blood has been shed for freedom's sake in England in one week, than on the whole continent for fifty years. Now, on the bright face of that government, the first and fairest feature is this: that no king can touch a penny belonging to the poorest subject, without his own consent, by his representative in parliament. For, if, say they, '*a king can at pleasure take our money, he can take every thing else; since with that he can easily hire soldiers to rob, and then murder us if we but open our lips against him.*' As Americans glory in being Englishmen on the western side of the Atlantic, they very naturally claim the common right of Englishmen, not to be taxed without their own consent, by their representatives in parliament. But the British ministry, though they obstinately refuse to the Americans the sacred rights of representation, yet as wickedly insist on the right of *taxation*; and accordingly have brought into parliament the famous *stamp act bill*, whereby no business that requires a record on paper, as *deeds*, *bonds*, *wills*, *marriages*, *&c.* can be legally done but on paper that has received the *royal stamp*. Now, sir, you well know that the same minister who proposes this most iniquitous and unconstitutional act, would not dare propose to any the most drunken tavern-keeper in England, a farthing tax on a pot of his ale without the consent of his representative in parliament; and yet, without being allowed a hearing in parliament, *three millions* of free-born Americans, sons of Englishmen, are to be taxed at the pleasure of a distant minister! Not, honoured sir, that the Americans care a fig for the *pence* imposed on this bit of stamp paper, but for the *principle*. For they well know that if parliament claim a *right* to take from us a penny in the pound, there is no line drawn to bound that right; and what shall hinder their calling whenever they please for the other *nineteen shillings and eleven pence*? And besides, sir, where is the necessity for this *most degrading* measure? Have not the Americans ever shown themselves the warmest friends of their king and country? Have they not, in all cases of danger, most readily voted both their men and money to the full extent of their means, and sometimes far beyond?

"And in addition to all this, are they not daily paying large monies in secret taxes to Great Britain?

"I. We are not *permitted to trade with foreign nations*! All the difference in the price of what we could buy cheaper from them, but must buy dearer from Britain, is a clear *tax* to Britain.

"II. We are obliged to *carry our produce to Britain*! All that it sells for less *there* than it would in any other market, is a clear *tax* to Britain.

"III. All the manufactures that we could make, but are *forbidden* and must buy of British merchants, is a clear *tax* to Britain.

"And what *freeborn* Englishman can, without indignation, think of being so daringly defrauded of his *birthright*, that if he wants a pipe of good wine, he cannot go to the island of Madeira and get it on easy exchange for his bread stuff, and return at once to his home and business; but must go a thousand miles farther from his family, even to Great Britain, and there run the gauntlet, through so many ruinous charges, as to bring his wine up to almost double what it ought to have cost? And all this most flagrant injustice done to the whole people of the colonies, just to enrich half a dozen British merchants engaged in the Portugal wine trade!

"A similar outrage on another of the dearest rights of Englishmen, *i.e.* '*to make the most that they honestly can of their property*,' is committed on the British subjects in America, for the sake of favouring a few hatters and nail makers in England. No country on the globe, furnishes better iron or better beaver than does North America. But the Americans must not make a hob-nail or a felt hat for themselves. No; they must send all their iron and fur to England for the hatters and nail makers *there*; who may give them their own price for the raw materials, and ask their own price for the manufactures.

"All that a wise government wishes, is, that the people should be numerous and wealthy enough to *fight the battles* of their country, and to *pay the taxes.* But they care not so much whether the fighting be done by John or Thomas, or the tax paid by William or Charles.

"What imports it to the government, whether a merchant, a smith, or a hatter, grows rich in Old England or New England? And if, through increase of the people, *two* smiths are wanted for *one* employed before, why may not the *new* smith be allowed to live and thrive in the *new* country, as well as the *old* in the *old*? In short, why should the countenance of a state be *partially* afforded to its people, unless it be most in favour of those who have most merit?"

The whig papers in London soon got this letter, and laid it before the public.

Among a high-minded people like the British, who pride themselves in their love of liberty and their perfect scorn of *foul play*, such sentiments could not be read without the liveliest emotions. And though some, the ministerial junto for example, with the merchants and manufacturers, did not like such plain truths, yet the nation in general gave him great credit both for his singular honesty and abilities; and the name of Dr. Franklin became very dear to thousands of the most enlightened and virtuous patriots of Britain.

But the pleasure of admiration was dashed with fear, that the minister would suffer no good to be done to the nation by all this divine counsel, merely because the giver was not an *Englishman.*

The lights, however, which Dr. Franklin had thrown on this great subject, were pressed upon the minister with such courage by numbers of honest English writers, that he prudently delayed ordering the collection of the tax until he could get further information. It was not long before an opportunity was offered him to obtain this information in a way highly complimentary to Dr. Franklin, *i.e.* by summoning him, then in London as colony agent from Pennsylvania, February 2, 1766, *to appear before the Bar of the British House of Commons, to answer certain questions, &c.*

The next day, accompanied by Mr. Strahan, afterwards member of parliament, with several illustrious Englishmen, his warm friends, he went to the house. The concourse was immense. *To see Dr. Franklin*—the American, whose philosophical discoveries and political writings had filled the world with his name, excited universal curiosity. The galleries were filled with ladies of the first distinction, and every seat below was occupied by the members from the house of lords. At ten o'clock he appeared at the bar before the eager waiting crowd. The profoundest silence ensued. All eyes were fixed on him; and, from their deep regard, it appeared, that though they beheld no stars nor garters glittering on his breast, no burning velvets nor flaming diamonds adorning his person, yet they were not disappointed. They beheld a spectacle still more interesting and novel.—The spectacle of a man whose simple dress evinced that he asked no aid of the tailor and silkworm to recommend him, but stood solely on the majesty of his mind. The hour for examination being come, and the attendant officer beckoning him thereto, he arose—

"And in his rising seemed a pillar of state—deep on his brow engraven deliberation sat and public care. His looks drew audience and attention still as night, or summer's noontide air."

Who can paint the looks of the minister, as with darkly scowling eye-balls, he beheld this terror of aristocracy! or who can paint the NOBLE LORDLINGS, as lost in equal *stare*, they gazed and gazed at the wondrous American, forgetting the while, "*to quiz*," as they were wont, "*his homespun coat and simple shoe-strings*."

But never did the mind-illumined looks of man shine more divinely bright than did those, that day, of the generous Barry, the godlike Chatham, and the high-minded Dunning, when they beheld the noble form of Franklin. Though born in North America, he shines before their eyes as a true born son of Britain—the luminous and brave interpreter of her SACRED CONSTITUTION, and the wise politician who seeks to exalt her glory, lasting as the skies, on the broad base of impartial justice to all her children. With eyes sparkling with esteem unutterable, they hail him as a brother; and breathe the ardent wish that in the impending examination he may succeed in diverting the minister from that unconstitutional course which may involve the ruin both of England and America.

The moment for trial being come, and the minister giving the signal to begin, the speaker thus commenced:—

Q. What is your name and place of abode?

A. Franklin, of Philadelphia.

Here followed nearly *three hundred questions* and *answers*, which were once read with exceeding interest by men, women, and children in America. But as they turn altogether on that great quarrel which the British ministry formerly excited in this country; and which God, to his endless glory, was pleased to put asleep in our favour near half a century ago, then let all these questions and answers lie asleep with it. However, it is but justice to Dr. Franklin to observe, that when we consider these questions, what a wide range they take both of the British and American *relations* and *interests*—together with the *luminous*, prompt, and decisive manner in which they were solved, we are lost in astonishment at the extent of his information and the powers of his mind, and are almost tempted to believe that the *answers*, and not the *questions* must have been studied with the nicest discrimination of circumstances.

Charles Fox, an honest Englishman, and an excellent judge in these matters, being asked his opinion of Dr. Franklin and the *ministers* in the late examination, replied, in his strong way, "*Dwarfs*, sir, mere *dwarfs in the hand of a giant*!"

Edmund Burke used to say, that this examination of Dr. Franklin before the ministers, always put him in mind of a "*Master examined before a parcel of school-boys.*"

But though his abilities on this occasion excited the admiration of generous enemies, while his more partial friends set no bounds to their praise, yet it would appear from the following that all afforded *him* but little pleasure. In a letter to a friend in Philadelphia, he has these remarkable words: "You have, no doubt, heard that I have been examined before the HOUSE OF COMMONS in this country. And it is probable you have also been told that I did not entirely disappoint the expectations of my friends, nor betray the cause of truth. This, to be sure, gives me some pleasure; and, indeed it is the only thing that does; for, as to any good being done by my honest statement to ministers, of what I firmly believe to be the best interests of the two countries, 'tis all, I fear, *a lost hope.* The people of this country are too proud, and too much despise the poor Americans, to allow them *the common rights of Englishmen*, that is, *a representation in parliament.* And until this be done, I apprehend that no taxes laid by parliament, will ever be collected, but such as must be stained with blood. How lamentable it is that two people, sprung from the same origin, speaking the same language, governed by the same laws, and worshipping at the same altar of God, and capable, by a wise use of the extraordinary means he has now put into their hands, of becoming the greatest nation on earth, should be stopped short and perhaps reduced to insignificance by a civil war, kindled by ministers obstinately contending for what they cannot but know to be utterly unconstitutional and eternally inadmissible among the *free-born sons of Englishmen.* But I suppose the repeal will not now be agreed to, from what I think a mistaken opinion, that the honour and dignity of government are better supported by persisting in a wrong measure, once entered into, than by rectifying an error as soon as it is discovered."

Differently, however, from the apprehensions of Franklin, the stamp act was repealed, and even in the course of the same year!

But though so little expected by him, yet was this event ascribed, in a great measure, to Dr. Franklin. His famous examination, printed in a shilling pamphlet, had been distributed by myriads throughout Britain and America. In America it served to brighten up the *old land marks* of their rights as *free-born sons of Englishmen*, and to quicken their sensibilities to ministerial frauds. In England, it served to show the ignorance of the ministers; the impolicy of their measures towards America; and the utter inexpediency of the stamp act. The stamp act of course fell to the ground. The reader, if a good man, exults, no doubt, in this as a most fortunate event, and already hails this removal of strife, as a certain prelude to that return of love between the mother country and her colonies, which will make them both, glorious and happy. He may hope it, but alas! he is never to see the accomplishment of that good hope. Death is whetting his scythe; and civil wars and slaughters are now just as near at hand as though the stamp act had never been repealed. For a pamphlet in some popular style that should unrip the black budget of ministerial injustice and lay naked to view the causes of the coming war; that unnatural war that is to sever England and her colonies for ever! Brighter than a thousand sermons it would illustrate to politicians that "*the Lord is King*"—that the sole end of his government, is to *glorify himself in the happiness of his creatures*—that thereunto he hath *established his throne in justice*—the eternal justice of men "*doing unto others as they would that others should do unto them,*" and that none, however great, shall ever violate this blessed order with impunity. The British ministry are destined to illustrate this. They are fond of power—to preserve this, they must continue in place—in order thereunto they must please the merchants and manufacturers—to accomplish this they must favour their trade and lighten their taxes. And how is this to be done? why, by a little peccadillo of INJUSTICE. They have only to sweat the "CONVICTS *on their American plantations,*"—the rascals live a great way off, and have no *representative* in parliament to make a noise about it. Accordingly, soon as the Americans were supposed to have gotten a little over their fever about the stamp act, the minister, lord North, of famous memory, determined to try them again. However it was but a small affair now—only a *three penny excise* on the pound of tea.

When Dr. Franklin, our ARGUS, then in London, discovered the designs of minister North, he exerted himself to point that purblind gentleman to the horrible gulf that was yawning at his feet. He wrote letters to several members of parliament, his friends; and he published a number of luminous pieces in the patriotic gazettes, all admirably calculated to rouse the friends of the nation to a sense of the impending dangers.

In three letters to the honourable Mr. W. Strahan, he has, in the extract, these remarkable words:—

"*London, November, 1768.*

"DEAR SIR,

"With respect to the present dispute between Great Britain and the colonies, there is nothing I wish for more than to see it amicably settled. But *Providence* brings about its own ends by its own means; and if it intends the downfall of a nation, that nation will be so blinded by its pride and other passions as not to see its danger, or how its fall may be prevented.

"The friends of the ministry say that this tax is but a *trifle*; granted. But who does not see what will be the consequence of submitting to it? Is it not the more dangerous for being a trifle? Is it not in this way that the devil himself most effectually works our ruin? If he can but prevail on a poor thoughtless youth to shake hands with innocence, and to *steal*, he is abundantly satisfied. To get the boy's *hand in*, is all he wants. And he would as leave the simpleton should begin with stealing a halter as a horse. For he well knows that if he but begins with the one he is sure to end with the other. Just so the minister, angling for American liberty, artfully covers his hook with this delicate bait. But the truth is, I have talked and written so much and so long on the subject of this unhappy quarrel, that my acquaintance are weary of hearing, and the public of reading, any more of it; which begins to make me weary of talking and writing; especially as I do not find that I have gained any point in either country, except that of rendering myself suspected, by my impartiality, in England of being too much an *American*, and in America of being too much an *Englishman*. However, as in reply to your polite question, "*what is to be* done *to settle this alarming dispute?*" I have often told you what I think the minister *ought* to do: I now go a step farther, and tell you what I fear he will do.

"I apprehend he will, ere long, attempt to enforce this obnoxious tax, whatever may be the consequences.—I apprehend that in the mean time, the colonies will continue to be treated with contempt, and the redress of their grievances be neglected—that, this will inflame matters still more in that country—that, further rash measures there, may create more resentments here—that, their assemblies will be attempted to be dissolved—that, more troops will be sent to oppress them—that, to justify these measures of government, your newspapers will revile them as *miscreants*, *rogues*, *dastards*, and *rebels*—that, this will alienate the minds of the people here from them, and theirs from you—that, possibly too, some of their warm patriots may be distracted enough to do some *mad* act which will cause them to be sent for hither—and that government may be indiscreet enough to hang them for it—that mutual provocations will thus go on to complete the separation, and instead of that cordial affection which so long existed, and which is so necessary to the glory and happiness of both countries, an implacable malice, dishonourable and destructive to both, may take place. I hope, however, that this may all prove *false prophecy*, and that you and I may live to see as sincere a friendship established between our countries, as has so many years subsisted between W. Strahan, Esq. and his truly affectionate old friend,

"B. FRANKLIN."

But notwithstanding his prayer to the contrary, every body recollects how, exactly as Dr. Franklin had predicted, the minister continued to blunder and blunder on with his face constantly towards war—how nothing was trumpeted by the ministerial party, like the ingratitude and baseness of the Americans—how *certain* newspapers perpetually vilified them as *miscreants*, *rascals* and *rebels*—how the public mind was so set against them that even the *shoe-blacks*, as Mr. Wilkes said, talked of the colonies as *their plantations*, and of the people there as if they had been their *overseers* and *negroes*—how the minister determined at last, to enforce the *tea-tax*—how, on hearing the news of this, as of the stamp act, the yankees muffled their drums, and played the *dead march*—how they took the sacrament never to submit to it—how the minister, to test their valour, sent three ships laden with this three-penny tea—how the yankees, dressed like Mohawks, boarded their ships and destroyed their cargoes—how the minister, waxing more in wrath, sent more soldiers to quell the rebels—how the rebels insulted the soldiers—how the soldiers fired on the rebels—how the port of Boston was shut by royal proclamation—how, in spite of the royal proclamation, the colonies would trade with her and send monies to her relief—how the LORDS and COMMONS petitioned the king that, any rebel opposing the officers of his sacred majesty, should be instantly hung up without judge or jury—how the king *thanked* his noble lords and commons, and was graciously pleased to decree that all rebels thus offending should be thus hung up without judge or jury—how that, notwithstanding this gracious decree, when his majesty's troops attempted to destroy the rebel stores at Concord, the rebels attacked and killed them, without any regard to his majesty's decree.

This unpardonable sin against the "Lord's anointed," which happened on the 19th of April 1775, served as the double bolting and barring of the door against all hope of peace. Throughout America, it struck but one deep and awful sentiment, "*the sword is drawn, and we must now throw the scabbard away.*" In May, the news got to England, where it excited emotions that beggar all description. They somewhat, however, resembled the effects of the trumpet of the great angel spoken of in the *Revelations*, that sounded "*wo! wo! wo! to the inhabitants*" of America, and proclaimed the pouring forth of *fire* and sword. But, reserving this tragedy for the next chapter, we will conclude the present with the following anecdote. It will show at least, that doctor Franklin left no stone unturned to carry his point; and that where logic failed he had recourse to wit.

THE CAT AND EAGLE.

A FABLE, BY DOCTOR FRANKLIN.

Lord Spencer was a great admirer of Dr. Franklin, and never missed sending him a card when he intended a quorum of learned ones at his table. The last time that our philosopher enjoyed this honour, was in 1775, just before he was driven from England by lord North. The conversation taking a turn on fables, lord Spencer observed, that it had certainly been a very lucky thing, especially for the YOUNG, that this mode of instruction had ever been hit on, as there was a something in it wonderfully calculated to touch a favourite string with them, *i.e.* novelty and surprise. They would listen, he said, to a fox, when they would not to a father, and they would be more apt to remember any thing good told them by an owl or a crow, than by an uncle or an aunt. But I am afraid, continued his lordship, that the age of fables is past. Æsop and Phædrus among the ancients, and Fontaine and Gay among the moderns, have given us so many fine speeches from the birds and beasts, that I suspect their budgets are pretty nearly exhausted.

The company concluded with his lordship, except Franklin, who was silent.

"Well, doctor," said lord Spencer, "what is your opinion on this subject?"

"Why, my lord," replied Franklin, "I cannot say that I have the honour to think with you in this affair. The birds and beasts have indeed said a great many wise things; but it is likely they will say a great many more yet before they are done. Nature, I am thinking, is not quite so easily exhausted as your lordship seems to imagine."

Lord Spencer, evidently confused, but still with that countenance of pleasure which characterizes great souls, when they meet superior genius, exclaimed—"Well, doctor, suppose you give us a fable? I know you are good at an impromptu." The company all seconded the motion. Franklin thanked them for the compliment, but begged to be excused. They would hear no excuses. They knew, they said, he could *go it,* and insisted he should gratify them. Finding all resistance ineffectual, he drew his pencil, and after scribbling a few minutes, reached it to Spencer, saying—"Well, my lord, since, you will have it so, here's a something fresh from the brain, but I'm afraid you'll not find Æsop in it."

"Read it, doctor, read it!" was the cry of the noble lord and his friends. In a mood, spriteful and pleasant, Franklin thus began—"Once upon a time—hem!—as an Eagle in the full pride of his pinions, soared over a humble farm-yard, darting his fiery eyes around in search of a pig, a lamb, or some such pretty tit-bit, what should he behold but a plump young rabbit, as he thought, squatted among the weeds. Down at once upon him, he pounced like thunder, and bearing him aloft in his talons, thus chuckled to himself with joy—Zounds, what a lucky dog I am! such a nice rabbit here, this morning, for my breakfast!

"His joy was but momentary; for the supposed rabbit happened to be a stout cat, who, spitting and squalling with rage, instantly stuck his teeth and nails, like any fury, into the eagle's thighs, making the blood and feathers fly at a dreadful rate.

"HOLD! HOLD! *for mercy's sake, hold!* cried the eagle, his wings shivering in the air with very torment.

"Villain! retorted the cat, with a tiger-like growl, dare you talk of *mercy* after treating me thus, who never injured you?"

O, God bless you, Mr. CAT, is that you? rejoined the eagle, mighty complaisant; 'pon honour, I did not intend, sir. I thought it was only a rabbit I had got hold of—and you know we are all fond of rabbits. Do you suppose, my dear sir, that if I had but dreamt it was you, I would ever have touched the hair of your head? No, indeed: I am not such a fool as all that comes to. And now, my dear Mr. CAT, come let's be good friends again, and I'll let you go with all my heart.

"Yes, you'll let me go, scoundrel, will you—here from the clouds—to break every bone in my skin!—No, villain, carry me back, and put me down exactly where you found me, or I'll tear the throat out of you in a moment.

"Without a word of reply, the eagle stooped at once from his giddy height, and sailing humbly down, with great complaisance restored the cat to his simple farm-yard, there to sleep, or hunt his rats and mice at pleasure."

A solemn silence ensued. At length, with a deep prophetic sigh, lord Spencer thus replied: "*Ah! Dr. Franklin I see the drift of your fable; and my fears have already made the application. God grant,* that Britain may not prove the eagle, and America the cat." This fable paraphrased in the WHIG papers of that day, concludes in this way:

"Thus Britain thought in seventy-six,

Her talons in a hare to fix;

But in the scuffle it was found,

The bird received a dangerous wound,

Which, though pretending oft to hide,

Still rankles in his Royal side."

CHAPTER XLI.

Doctor Franklin now began to find his situation in London extremely unpleasant. For twelve years, like heaven's own minister of peace, he had pressed the olive-branch on the British ministry; and yet after all, their war-hawks could hardly tolerate the sight of him. They even went so far as to call him "*the hoary headed villain, who first stirred up the Americans to rebellion.*" As soon as he could obtain his passports he left England.

His old friend, Strahan, advised him to continue in that country, for that America would soon be filled with tumult and bloodshed. He replied, "*No, sir, where liberty is, there is my country.*"

Unbounded was the joy of the Americans on the return of so great a patriot and statesman. The day following he was elected by the legislature of Pennsylvania, a member of Congress. The following letters, in extract, to his constant friend, and the friend of science and liberty, the celebrated doctor Priestley, will show how full his hands were

"*Philadelphia, July 7, 1775.*

"DEAR FRIEND,

"Britain has begun to burn our sea port towns; *secure*, I suppose, *that we shall never be able to return the outrage in kind.* She may doubtless destroy them all. But is this the way to recover our friendship and trade? She must certainly be distracted; for no tradesman out of Bedlam ever thought of increasing the number of his customers by knocking them on the head; or of enabling them to pay their debts, by burning their houses.

"My time was never more fully employed. I breakfast before six. At six I hasten to the COMMITTEE of SAFETY for putting the province in a state of defence. At nine I go to Congress, which sits till after four. It will scarcely be credited in Britain, that men can be as diligent with us, from zeal for the public good, as with you, for *thousands* per annum. Such is the difference between uncorrupted new states, and corrupted old ones.

"Great frugality and great industry are now become fashionable here: gentlemen, who used to entertain with two or three courses, pride themselves now in treating with simple beef and pudding. By these means, and the stoppage of our consumptive trade with Britain, we shall be better able to pay our voluntary taxes for the support of our troops. Our savings in the article of trade, amount to near five millions of sterling per annum.—Yours, most affectionately,

"B. FRANKLIN."

In another letter to the same, dated October 3d, he says:

"Tell our dear good friend, doctor Price, who sometimes has his doubts and despondencies about our firmness, that America is determined and unanimous: a very few tories and placemen excepted, who will probably soon export themselves. Britain, at the expense of three millions has killed in this campaign, *one hundred and fifty yankees!* which is 20,000 pounds sterling a head; and at Bunker's hill she gained half a mile of ground! During the same time she lost, at one place, near one thousand men, and we have had a good sixty thousand children born in America. From these data, with the help of his mathematical head, lord North will easily calculate the time and expense necessary to kill us all, and conquer our whole territory.—

"I am yours, B. FRANKLIN."

In another letter to the same, and of the same date, he says:

"Britain still goes on to goad and exasperate. She despises us too much; and seems to forget the Italian proverb, that '*there is no little enemy.*' I am persuaded the body of the British people are our friends; but your lying gazettes may soon make them our enemies—and I see clearly that we are on the high road to mutual enmity, hatred, and detestation. A *separation* will of course be inevitable. It is a million of pities so fair a plan, as we have hitherto been engaged in for increasing *strength* and *empire* with PUBLIC FELICITY, should be destroyed by the mangling hands of a few blundering ministers. It will not be destroyed: GOD WILL PROTECT AND PROSPER IT: you will only exclude yourselves from any share of it. We hear that more ships and troops are coming out. We know you may do us a great deal of mischief, but we are determined to bear it patiently; but if you flatter yourselves with beating us into submission, you know neither the people nor the country.

"I am ever your's, most affectionately,

"B. FRANKLIN."

This letter of Doctor Franklin's is the first thing I have seen that utters a whisper about INDEPENDENCE. It was, however, a *prophetical* whisper, and soon found its accomplishment in the source that Franklin predicted—the BARBARITY OF BRITAIN. To see war waged against them by a power whom they had always gloried in as their MOTHER COUNTRY—to see it waged because as the *children of Englishmen*, they had only asked for the *common rights of Englishmen*—to see it waged with a savageness unknown among civilized nations, and all the powers of earth and hell, as it were, stirred up against them—the Indians with their bloody tomahawks and scalping knives—the negroes with their midnight hoes and axes—the merciless flames let loose on their midwinter towns—with prisons, chains, and starvation of their worthiest citizens. "*Such miserable specimens*," as Franklin termed them, "*of the British government*," produced every where in the colonies a disposition to *detest and avoid it as a complication of robbery, murder, famine, fire and pestilence.*

On the 7th of June, resolutions respecting independence, were moved and seconded in Congress. Doctor Franklin threw all the weight of his wisdom and character into the scale in favour of independence.

"INDEPENDENCE," said he, "*will cut the Gordian knot at once, and give us freedom.*

"I. *Freedom from the oppressive kings, and endless wars, and mad politics, and forced religion of an unreasonable and cruel government.*

"II. *Freedom to choose a fair, and cheap, and reasonable government of our own.*

"III. *Freedom to live in friendship with all nations; and*

"IV. *Freedom to trade with all.*"

On the 4th of July, the *Independence* of the United States was declared. Immediately on the finishing of this great work, doctor Franklin, with a committee of the first talents in Congress, prepared a number of very masterly addresses to the courts of Europe, informing what the United States had done; assigning their reasons for so doing; and tendering in the most affectionate terms, the friendship and trade of the young nation. The potentates of Europe were, generally, well pleased to hear that a new star had risen in the west, and talked freely of opening their treasures and presenting their gifts of friendship, &c.

But the European power that seemed most to rejoice in this event was the French. In August, doctor Franklin was appointed by Congress to visit the French court, for the purpose of forming an alliance with that powerful people. It was his friend, Doctor B. Rush, who first announced to him the choice which Congress had made, adding, at the same time, his hearty congratulations on that account.

"Why, doctor," replied he with a smile, "I am now, like an old broom, worn down to the stump in my country's service—near seventy years old. But such as I am, she must, I suppose, have the last of me." Like the brave Dutch republicans, each with his wallet of herrings on his back, when they went forth to negotiate with the proud Dons, so did doctor Franklin set out to court the great French nation, with no provisions for his journey, but a few hogsheads of tobacco. He was received in France, however, with a most hearty welcome, not only as an envoy from a brave people fighting for their rights, but also as the famed American philosopher, who by his *paratonerres* (lightning rods) had disarmed the clouds of their lightnings, and who, it was hoped, would reduce the colossal power of Great Britain.

He had not been long in Paris, before the attention of all the courts of Europe was attached to him, by a publication, wherein he demonstrated, that, *the young, healthy, and sturdy republic of America, with her simple manners, laborious habits, and millions of fresh land and produce, would be a much safer borrower of money, than the old, profligate, and debt-burthened government of Britain.* The Dutch and French courts, in particular, read his arguments with such attention, that they soon began to make him loans. To the French cabinet he pointed out, "THE INEVITABLE DESTRUCTION OF THEIR FLEETS, COLONIES, AND COMMERCE, IN CASE OF A RE-UNION OF BRITAIN AND AMERICA." There wanted but a grain to turn the trembling balance in favour of America.

But it was the will of Heaven to withhold that grain a good long while. And Franklin had the mortification to find, that although the French were an exceedingly polite people; constantly eulogizing GENERAL WASHINGTON and THE BRAVE BOSTONIANS, on every little victory; and also for their tobacco, very thriftily smuggling all the fire arms and ammunition they could into the United States, yet they had no notion of coming out manfully at once upon the British lion, until they should first see the American Eagle lay the monster on his back. Dr. Franklin, of course, was permitted to rest on his oars, at Passy, in the neighbourhood of Paris, His characteristic philanthropy, however, could not allow him to be idle at a court, whose pride and extravagance were so horribly irreconcileable with his ideas of the true use of riches, *i.e.* INDEPENDENCE for ourselves, and BENEFICENCE to others. And he presently came out in the Paris Gazette with the following master piece of WIT and ECONOMICS.

To the Editors of the Paris Journal.

GENTLEMEN,

I was the other evening in a grand company, where the new lamp of Messrs. Quinquet and Lange was introduced, and much admired for its splendour; but a general inquiry was made, whether the oil it consumed, was not in proportion to the light it afforded; in which case there would be no saving in the use of it. No one present could satisfy us on that point; which all agreed ought to be known, it being a very desirable thing to lessen, if possible, the expense of lighting our apartments, when every other article of family expense was so much augmented.

I was pleased to see this general concern for economy; for I love economy exceedingly.

I went home, and to bed, three or four hours after midnight, with my head full of the subject. An accidental sudden noise awaked me about six in the morning, when I was surprised to find my room filled with light; and I imagined, at first, that a number of these lamps had been brought into it; but rubbing my eyes, I perceived the light came in at my windows. I got up, and looked out to see what might be the occasion of it, when I saw the sun just rising above the horizon, whence he poured his rays plentifully into my chamber, my domestic having negligently omitted, the preceding evening, to close the shutters.

I looked at my watch, which goes very well, and found that it was but six o'clock; and still thinking it something extraordinary that the sun should rise so early, I looked into the almanack; where I found it to be the hour given for its rising on that day.

Your readers, who, with me, have never seen any signs of sunshine before noon, and seldom regard the astronomical part of the almanack, will be as much astonished as I was, when they hear of his rising so early; and especially when I assure them *that he gives light as soon as he rises.* I am certain of the fact. *I saw it with my own eyes.* And having repeated this observation the three following mornings, I found always precisely the same result.

Yet so it happens, that when I speak of this discovery to others, I can easily perceive by their countenances, though they forbear expressing it in words, that they do not quite believe me. One, indeed, who is a learned natural philosopher, has assured me that I must certainly be mistaken as to the circumstance of the light coming into my room; for it being well known, as he says, that there could be no light abroad at that hour, it follows that none could enter from without; and that of consequence, my windows being accidentally left open, instead of *letting in the light*, had only served to *let out the darkness.*

This event has given rise, in my mind, to several serious and important reflections. I considered that, if I had not been awakened so early in the morning, I should have slept six hours longer by the light of the sun, and in exchange have lived six hours the following night by candle-light; and the latter being a much more expensive light than the former, my love of economy induced me to muster up what little arithmetic I was master of, and to make some calculations, which I shall give you, after observing, that utility is, in my opinion, the test of value in matters of invention, and that a discovery which can be applied to no use, or is not good for something, is good for nothing.

I took for the basis of my calculation, the supposition that there are 100,000 families in Paris; and that these families consume in the night half a pound of candles, per hour. I think this a moderate allowance, taking one family with another; for though I believe some consume less, I know that many consume a great deal more. Then, estimating seven hours per day, as the medium quantity between the time of the *sun's* rising and *ours*, and there being seven hours, of course, per night, in which we burn candles, the account will stand thus:

In 12 months there are nights 365; hours of each night in which we burn candles 7; multiplication gives for the total number of hours 2555. These multiplied by 100,000, the number of families in Paris, give 255,000,000 hours spent at Paris by candle-light, which, at half a pound of wax and tallow per hour, give 127,750,000 pounds, worth, at 3 livres the pound, 383,250,000 livres; upwards of THIRTY MILLIONS OF DOLLARS!!!

An immense sum! that the city of Paris might save every year, by the economy of using *sunshine* instead of candles.—If it should be said, that the people are very apt to be obstinately attached to old customs, and that it will be difficult to induce them to rise before noon, consequently my discovery can be of little use, I answer, we must not despair. I believe all, who have common sense, as soon as they have learnt, from this paper, that it is daylight when the sun rises, will contrive to rise with him; and to compel the rest, I would propose the following regulations:

First. Let a tax be laid of a louis, (a guinea,) per window, on every window that is provided with shutters to keep out the light of the sun.

Second. Let guards be placed in the shops of the wax and tallow-chandlers; and no family be permitted to be supplied with more than one pound of candles per week.

Third. Let guards be posted, to stop all the coaches, &c. that would pass the streets after sunset, except those of physicians, surgeons, and midwives.

Fourth. Every morning, as soon as the sun rises, let all the bells in the city be set ringing; and if that be not sufficient let cannon be fired in every street, to awake the sluggards effectually, and make them open their eyes to see their true interest.

All the difficulty will be in the first two or three days: after which the reformation will be as natural and easy as the present irregularity. Oblige a man to rise at four in the morning, and, it is more than probable, he shall go willingly to bed at eight in the evening; and having had eight hours sleep, he will rise more willingly at four, in the morning following.

For the great benefit of this discovery, thus freely communicated and bestowed by me, on the good city of Paris, I demand neither place, pension, exclusive privilege, nor any other reward whatever. I expect only to have the *honour* of it. And yet I know there are little envious minds, who will, as usual, deny me this, and say that my invention was known to the ancients. I will not dispute that the ancients knew that the sun would rise at certain hours. They possibly had almanacks that predicted it; but it does not follow, thence, that they knew *that he gave light an soon as he rose. This is what I claim as my discovery.* If the ancients knew it, it must long since have been forgotten; for it certainly was unknown to the moderns, at least to the Parisians; which to prove, I need use but one plain simple argument. They are as well instructed and prudent a people as exist, any where in the world; all professing, like myself, to be lovers of economy; and, from the many heavy taxes required from them by the necessities of the state, have surely reason to be economical. I say it is impossible that so sensible a people, under such circumstances, should have lived so long by the *smoky, unwholesome and enormously expensive light of candles, if they had really known that they might have as much pure light of the sun for nothing.* I am, &c.

An ABONNE.

And now, as Dr. Franklin is permitted to breathe a little from his herculean toils, let us, good reader, breathe a little too, and amuse ourselves with the following anecdotes.

Nothing can better illustrate the spirit, which Dr. Franklin carried with him to the court of Louis XVI., and the spirit he found there.

On Dr. Franklin's arrival at Paris, as plenipotentiary from the United States, during the revolution, the king expressed a wish to see him immediately. As there was no going to the court of France in those days without permission of the wigmaker, a wigmaker of course was sent for. In an instant a richly dressed Monsieur, his arms folded in a prodigious muff of furs, and a long sword by his side, made his appearance. It was the king's WIGMAKER, with his servant in livery, a long sword by *his* side too, and a load of sweet scented band-boxes, full of "*de wig,*" as he said, "*de superb wig for de great docteer Franklin.*" One of the wigs was tried on—a world *too small!* Band-box after band-box was tried; but all with the same ill success! The wigmaker fell into the most violent rage, to the extreme mortification of Dr. Franklin, that a gentleman so bedecked with silks and perfumes, should, notwithstanding, be such a child. Presently, however, as in all the transports of a *grand discovery*, the wigmaker cried out to Dr. Franklin, that he had just found out where the fault lay—"*not in his wig as too small; O no, by gar! his wig no too small; but de docteer's head too big; great deal too big.*" Franklin, smiling, replied, that the fault could hardly lie *there*; for that his head was made of God Almighty himself, who was not subject to err. Upon this the wigmaker took in a little; but still contended that there must be something the matter with Dr. Franklin's head. It was at any rate, he said, *out of the fashion.* He begged Dr. Franklin would only please for remember, *dat his head had not de honeer* to be made in PARREE. No, by gar! for if it had been made in PARREE, it no bin more dan *half such a head.* "*None of the French Noblesse,*" he swore, "*had a head any ting* like his. Not de great duke d'Orleans, nor de grand monarque himself had *half such a head as docteer Franklin.* And *he did not see,*" he said, "*what business any body had wid a head more big dan de head of de grand monarque.*"

Pleased to see the poor wigmaker recover his good humour, Dr. Franklin could not find in his heart to put a check to his childish rant, but related one of his *fine anecdotes*, which struck the wigmaker with such an idea of his wit, that as he retired, which he did, bowing most profoundly, he shrugged his shoulders, and with a look most significantly arch, he said:

"*Ah, docteer Frankline! docteer Frankline!* I no wonder your head too big for my wig. By gar I 'fraid your head be too big for *all de French nationg.*"

THE BLUE YARN STOCKINGS.

When Dr. Franklin was received at the French court as American minister, he felt some scruples of conscience in complying with their *fashions as to dress.* "He hoped," he said to the minister, "that as he was himself a very plain man, and represented a plain republican people, the king would indulge his desire to appear at court in his usual dress. Independent of this, the season of the year, he said, rendered the change from warm yarn stockings to fine silk, somewhat dangerous."

The French minister made him a bow, but said, that THE FASHION was too sacred a thing for him to meddle with, but he would do himself the honour to mention it to his MAJESTY.

The king smiled, and returned word that Dr. Franklin was welcome to appear at court in *any dress he pleased.* In spite of that delicate respect for strangers, for which the French are so remarkable, the courtiers could not help staring, at first, at Dr. Franklin's quaker-like dress, and especially his "BLUE YARN STOCKINGS." But it soon appeared as though he had been introduced upon this splendid theatre only to demonstrate that, great genius, like true beauty, "needs not the foreign aid of ornament." The court were so dazzled with the brilliancy of his mind that they never looked at his stockings. And while many other ministers who figured in all the gaudy fashions of the day are now forgotten, the name of Dr. Franklin is still mentioned in Paris with all the ardour of the most affectionate enthusiasm.

CHAPTER XLII.

Imagination can hardly conceive a succession of pleasures more elegant and refined than those which Dr. Franklin, now on the shady side of threescore and ten, continued daily to enjoy in the vicinity of Paris—his mornings constantly devoted to his beloved studies, and his evenings to the cheerful society of his friends—the greatest monarch of Europe heaping him with honours unasked, and the brightest WITS and BEAUTIES of his court vying with each other in their attentions to him. And thus as the golden hours rolled along, they still found him happy—gratefully contrasting his present glory with his humble origin, and thence breathing nothing but benevolence to man—firmly confiding in the care of Heaven—and fully persuaded that his smiles would yet descend upon his countrymen, now fighting the good fight of liberty and happiness.

While waiting in strong hope of this most desirable of all events, he received, by express, December 1777, the welcome news that the battle had been joined in America, and that God had delivered a noble wing of the British army into the hands of the brave republicans at Saratoga. O ye, who, rejecting the philosophy of all embracing love, know no joys beyond what the miser feels when his own little heap increases, how faintly can you conceive what this great apostle of liberty enjoyed when he found that his countrymen still retained the fire of their gallant fathers, and were resolved to live free or press a glorious grave! He lost no time to improve this splendid victory to the good of his country. In several audiences with the king and his ministers, he clearly demonstrated that France in all her days of ancient danger had never known so dark a cloud impending over her as at this awful crisis. "If Great Britain," said he, "already so powerful were to subdue the revolted colonies and add all North America to her empire, she would in twenty years be strong enough to crush the power of France and not leave her an island or a ship on the ocean." As a sudden flash of lightning from the opening clouds before the burst of thunder and rain, such was the shock produced by this argument on the mind of every thinking man throughout France. The courtiers with all their talents for dissembling could not conceal their hostile feelings from the British minister resident among them. He marked it, not without sentiments of answering hostility, which he could no better conceal, and which, indeed, after the honest bluntness of his national character, he did not care to conceal. The increased attentions paid to Dr. Franklin, and the rejoicings in Paris on account of the American victories, were but illy calculated to soothe his displeasure. Bitter complaints were presently forwarded to his court—angry remonstrances to the French cabinet followed—and in a short time the embers of ancient hate were blown up to flames of fury so diabolical that nothing but war, with all its rivers of human blood could extinguish it. War, of course, was proclaimed—Paris was illuminated—and the thunder of the Royal cannon soon announced to the willing citizens that the die was cast, and that the Grand Monarque was become the Ally of the United States.

"*While there is any thing to be done nothing is done,*" said Cæsar. Franklin thought so too. He had succeeded in his efforts to persuade the warlike French to take part with his oppressed countrymen; but the Spaniards and the Dutch were still neutral. To rouse their hostile feelings against Great Britain, and to make them the hearty partisans of Washington, was his next study. The event quickly showed that he had studied human nature with success. He who had been the playmate of lightnings for the *glory of God*, found no difficulty in stirring up the *wrath of man to praise him*—by chastising the sons of violence. The tall black ships of war were soon seen to rush forth from the ports of Holland and Spain, laden with the implements of death, to arrest the mad ambition of Great Britain, and maintain the balance of power. How dearly ought the American people to prize their liberties, for which such bloody contribution was laid on the human race! Imagination glances with terror on that dismal war whose spread was over half the solid and half the watery globe. Its devouring fires burned from the dark wilds of North America to the distant isles of India; and the blood of its victims was mingled with the brine of every ocean. But, thanks to God, the conflict, though violent, was but short. And much of the honour of bringing it to a close is to be conceded to the instrumentality of Dr. Franklin.

We have seen that in 1763, he was sent (of Heaven no doubt, for it was an act worthy of his all-benevolent character,) a preacher of righteousness, to the proud court of Britain. His luminous preachings, (through the press,) on the injustice and unconstitutionality of the ministerial taxing measures on the colonies, shed such light, that thousands of honest Englishmen set their faces against them, and also against the war to which they saw it was tending. These converts to justice, these doves of peace, were not sufficiently numerous to defeat the war-hawks of their bloody purposes. But when they found that the war into which they had plunged with such confidence, had not, instantly, as they expected, reduced the colonies to slavish submission; but that, instead thereof, one half Europe in favour of America, was in arms against them with a horrible destruction of lives and property which they had not counted on, and of which they saw no end, they seriously deplored their folly in not pursuing the counsel of doctor Franklin. The nation was still, however, dragged on in war, plunging like a stalled animal, deeper and deeper in disaster and distress, until the capture of lord Cornwallis and his army came like a thunder-bolt, inflicting on the war party a death blow, from which they never afterwards recovered.

Dr. Franklin received this most welcome piece of news, the surrender of lord Cornwallis, by express from America. He had scarcely read the letters with the tear of joy swelling in his patriot eye, when Mr. Necker came in. Seeing the transport on his face, he eagerly asked what *good news*. "*Thank God*," replied Franklin, "*the storm is past. The paratonerres of divine justice have drawn off the lightning of British violence, and here, sir, is the rainbow of peace*," holding up the letter. What am I to understand by that, replied Necker. Why, sir, quoth Franklin, my lord Cornwallis and his army are prisoners of war to general Washington. Doctor Franklin's calculation, on the surrender of Cornwallis, *that the storm was past*, was very correct; for, although the thunders did not immediately cease, yet, after that event, they hardly amounted to any thing beyond a harmless rumbling, which presently subsided altogether, leaving a fine bright sky behind them.

CHAPTER XLIII.

The rest of the acts of doctor Franklin while he resided in France, and the many pleasures he enjoyed there, were first, the great pleasure of announcing to the French court, in 1781, as we have seen, the surrender of lord Cornwallis and his army to general Washington. Second, the still greater pleasure of learning in 1782, that the British ministry were strongly inclined to "A PEACE TALK." Third, 1783, the greatest pleasure of all, the pleasure of *burying the tomahawk*, by general peace.

Thus after having lived to see completely verified all his awful predictions to the blind and obstinate British cabinet about the result of this disastrous war; with losses indeed, beyond his prediction—the loss of two thousand ships!—the loss of one hundred thousand lives!—the loss of seven hundred millions of dollars! and a loss still greater than all, the loss of the immense continent of North America, and the monopoly of its incalculable produce and trade, shortly to fly on wings of canvass to all parts of the globe.

Having lived to see happily terminated, the grand struggle for American liberty, which even Englishmen have pronounced "*the last hope and probable refuge of mankind*," and having obtained leave from congress to return, he took a last farewell of his generous Parisian friends, and embarked for his native country.

On the night of the 4th of September, the ship made the light-house at the mouth of the Delaware bay. On coming upon deck next morning, he beheld all in full view and close at hand the lovely shores of America, "*where his fathers had dwelt.*" Who can paint the joy-brightened looks of our veteran patriot, when, after an absence of seven years, he beheld once more that beloved country for whose liberties and morals he had so long contended? Formerly, with an aching heart, he had beheld her as a dear mother, whose fame was tarnished, and her liberties half ravished by foreign lords. But now he greets her as free again, and freed, through heaven's blessing on her *own heroic virtue and valour.* Crowned thus with tenfold glory, he hails her with transport, as the grand nursery of civil and religious freedom, whose fair example of republican wisdom and moderation is, probably, destined of God to recommend the blessings of free government to all mankind.

The next day in the afternoon he arrived at Philadelphia. It is not for me to describe what he felt in sailing along up these lovely shores, while the heaven within diffused a double brightness and beauty over all the fair and magnificent scenes around. Neither is it for me to delineate the numerous demonstrations of public joy, wherewith the citizens of Philadelphia welcomed the man whom they all delighted to honour. Suffice it to say, that he was landed amidst the firing of cannon—that he was crowded with congratulatory addresses—that he was invited to sumptuous banquets, &c. &c. &c. But though it was highly gratifying to others to see transcendent worth so duly noticed, yet to himself, who had been so long familiar with such honours, they appeared but as baubles that had lost their tinsel.

But there were some pledges of respect offered him, which afforded a heartfelt satisfaction; I mean those numbers of pressing invitations to accept the presidencies of sundry noble institutions for public good, as

I. A society for diffusing a knowledge of the best politics for our republic.

II. A society for alleviating the miseries of public prisons.

III. A society for abolishing the slave trade—the relief of free negroes unlawfully held in bondage—and for bettering the condition of the poor blacks.

"It was because," said the trustees, "they well knew he had made it the sole scope of his greatly useful life to promote institutions for the happiness of mankind, that they now solicited the honour and benefit of his special care and guardianship."

Though now almost worn out with the toils of fourscore years, and oftentimes grievously afflicted with his old complaint, the gravel, he yet accepted the proffered appointments with great pleasure, and attended to the duties of them with all the ardour of youth. Thus affording one more proof,

"That, in the present as in all the past

O SAVE MY COUNTRY, HEAVEN! was still his last."

"But though the spirit was willing, the flesh was weak." His strength was so sensibly diminished that it could scarcely second his mind, which seemed as unimpaired as ever.

But there was still one more service that his country looked to him for, before he went to rest; I mean that of aiding her councils in the grand convention that was about to sit in Philadelphia for the purpose of framing the present excellent constitution. He was called to this duty in 1787. The speech which he made in that convention has a high claim to our notice, not only because it was the last speech that Dr. Franklin ever made in public; but because nothing ever yet placed in a fairer light the charm of modesty in a great man; and also the force of temperance, exercise and cheerfulness, which could preserve the intellectual faculties in such vigour, to the astonishing age of EIGHTY-TWO!!

Final Speech of doctor Franklin in the Federal Convention.—
George Washington, President.

MR. PRESIDENT,

I do not entirely approve this constitution at present, but, sir, I am not sure I shall never approve it; for, having lived long, I have experienced many instances of being obliged, by better information, to change opinions which I once thought right. It is, therefore, that the older I grow, the more apt I am to doubt my own judgment, and to pay more respect to the judgment of others. Most men, indeed, as well as most sects of religion, think themselves in possession of *all truth*, and that whenever others differ from them, it is so far error. Steele, a protestant, tells the pope, that "the only difference between our two churches, in their opinion of the certainty of their doctrines, is, the Romish church is *infallible*, and the church of England *never* in the *wrong*."

But though many private persons think almost as highly of their own infallibility, as of that of their sect, few express it so naturally as a certain French lady, who, in a little dispute with her sister, said, "*I don't know how it happens, sister, but I meet with nobody but myself that is always in the right.*" In these sentiments, sir, I agree to this constitution, with all its faults, if they are such; because I think a general government necessary for us, and there is no form of government but what may be a blessing, if well administered; and I believe farther, that this is likely to be well administered for a course of years, and can only end in despotism, as other forms have done before it, when the people shall become so corrupted, as to need despotic government, being incapable of any other. I doubt too, whether any other convention we can obtain, may be able to make a better constitution. For when you assemble a number of men, to have the advantage of their joint wisdom, you assemble with those men, all their prejudices, their passions, their errors of opinion, their local interests, and their selfish views. From such an assembly, can a perfect production be expected? It therefore astonishes me, sir, to find this system approaching so near to perfection as it does; and I think it will confound our enemies, who are waiting with confidence, to hear that our councils are confounded, like those of the builders of Babel, and that our states are on the point of separation, only to meet hereafter for the purpose of cutting each other's throats.

Thus I consent, sir, to this constitution, because I expect no better, and because I am not *sure that this is not the best.* The opinions I have had of its errors, I sacrifice to the public good. I have never whispered a syllable of them abroad. Within these walls they were born, and here they shall die. If every one of us, in returning to our constituents, were to report the objections he has had to it, and endeavour to gain partisans in support of them, we might prevent its being generally received, and thereby lose all the great advantages resulting naturally in our favour among foreign nations, as well as among ourselves, from our real or apparent unanimity. Much of the efficiency of any government, in procuring and securing happiness to the people, depends on the general opinion of the goodness of that government, as well as of the wisdom and integrity of its governors.

I hope, therefore, that for our *own sakes*, as a part of the people, and for the sake of *our posterity*, we shall act heartily and unanimously, in recommending this constitution, wherever our influence may extend, and turn our future thoughts and endeavours to the means of having it well administered.

On the whole, sir, I cannot help expressing a wish, that every member of the convention, who may still have objections, would, with me, on this occasion, doubt a little of his own infallibility, and making manifest our unanimity, put his name to this instrument.

CHAPTER XLIV.

"When ranting round in pleasure's ring,

Religion may be blinded,

Or if she give a random sting,

'Tis oft but little minded.

"But when on life we're tempest driv'n,

A conscience's but a canker;

A correspondence fix'd with heaven,

Is sure a noble anchor."

The time is now at hand that Franklin must die. When that time approaches, or when only the chilling thought of it strikes the heart, how happy is he who in looking on the withered face or snowy locks of a dear friend, can enjoy the exulting hope that he is prepared for the awful change. This leads us to speak of doctor Franklin on a much higher subject than has yet engaged our attention. I mean his religion.

I have met with nothing in the life of any great man in our country about which there has been such universal inquiry, as about the RELIGION OF DR. FRANKLIN.

Some, who in despite of Christ and all his apostles, will "*judge their brother*;" and judge him too by the *letter* which *killeth*, will not allow that Dr. Franklin had any religion at all, because, forsooth, he did not *believe* and "*confess Christ before men*," in the manner they did. But others, construing the Gospel, as Christ himself commands, by "*the spirit*;" which teaches that, "*with the heart man believeth unto salvation, through love and good works*;" and that the right way of "*confessing Christ before men*" is by a *good life*.—These gentlemen tell us, that Dr. Franklin not only had religion, but had it in an eminent degree.

Most people seem inclined to judge of Dr. Franklin by these latter commentators, and wind up with the words of our great moral poet.

"For modes of faith, let graceless zealots fight;

His can't be wrong, whose Life is in the right."

For my part, after all that I have heard on this subject, and I have heard a great deal, I do not know that I have met with any thing that expresses my opinion of Dr. Franklin's religion more happily than the following laconic remark by one of our most distinguished senators, I mean the honourable Rufus King. Knowing that this gentleman was a compatriot of Dr. Franklin during the revolution, and also sat by his side, a member of the grand Convention in 1788, I took the greater pleasure in asking his opinion of that great man in respect of his RELIGION. "Why, sir," replied he, "my opinion of doctor Franklin has always been, that, although he was not, perhaps, quite so orthodox in some of his notions, he was *very much a Christian in his practice.* Nor is it indeed to be wondered at," continued this able critic, "that a man of doctor Franklin's extraordinary sagacity, born and brought up under the light of the Gospel, should have imbibed its spirit, and got his whole soul enriched, and as it were interlarded, with its benevolent affections."

And I have since found from conversation with many of our most enlightened and evangelical divines, that they all agree, with Mr. King, that doctor Franklin's extraordinary benevolence and useful life were imbibed, even *unconsciously*, from the Gospel. For whence but from the luminous and sublime doctrines of that blessed book could he have gained such pure and worthy ideas of God—his glorious unity, and most adorable benevolence: always, himself, loving and doing good to his creatures; and constantly seeking such to worship him? Whence, we ask, could he have got all these exalted truths—truths, so honourable to the Deity—so consolatory to man—so auxiliary of human virtue and happiness—whence could he have got them, but from the light of the Gospel? Certainly, you will not say that he might have got them from the light of nature. For, look around you among all the mighty nations of antiquity. Look among the Egyptians—the Greeks—the Romans, to equal him? Two thousand years have rolled between them and us, and yet the immortal monuments of their arts—their poetry—their painting—their statuary—their architecture—their eloquence—all triumphant over the wreck of time, have come down to our days, boldly challenging the pride of modern genius to produce their parallels. Evidently then, they had among them prodigies of mind equal to our Franklin. And yet how has it yet come to pass, that, with all their astonishing talents, and the light of nature besides, they were so stupidly blind and ignorant of God, while he entertained such exalted ideas of him? That while they, like the modern idolaters of Juggernaut, were disgracing human reason by worshipping not only *four-footed beasts and creeping things*, but even thieves, murderers, &c. *deified*, doctor Franklin was elevating his devotions to the one all-perfect God, MOST GLORIOUS IN ALL MORAL EXCELLENCE.

And how has it come to pass that while *they*, imitating their bloody idols, could take pleasure in *sacrificing their prisoners of war! beholding murderous fights of gladiators!* and even giving up *their own children to be burnt alive!* Franklin, by imitating the moral character of God, attained to all that gentle wisdom and affectionate goodness that we fancy when we think of an angel? To what, I ask, can we ascribe all this, but to the very rational cause assigned by Mr. King, viz. his having been *born and brought up in a land of Gospel light and love?* Indeed, who can read the life of doctor Franklin, attentively, without tracing in it, throughout, that true Christian charity which bound him, as by the heart-strings, to his fellow men—on every occasion going out of self to take an interest in them. "Rejoicing with them, when they acted wisely and attained to honour."—"Weeping with them when they acted foolishly and came to shame." Never meeting with any good fortune, through wise doings of his own, but he made it known to them for their encouragement in similar doings—never falling into misfortunes, by his own folly, but he was sure to publish that too, to deter others from falling into the like sufferings.

Now what was it but this amiable *oneness of heart*, with his fellow men; this *sweet Christian sensibility* to their interests and consequent generous delight in doing them good, that filled his life with such noble charities. "*Where love is*," said the great William Penn, "*there is no labour; or if there be, the labour is sweet.*" And what was it but this, that bore him up so bravely under his many toils and hardships for his selfish brother James?

What made him so liberal of his money and services to the base Collins and Ralph?

What made him so patient and forgiving of the injuries done him by the worthless Keimer and Keith?

What made him so importunate with his young acquaintance in London, to divert them from their brutalizing and fatal intemperance?

What set him so vehemently against pride and extravagance, which besides starving all justice and hospitality among neighbours, tend to make them demons of fraud and cruelty to one another?

What made him, through life, such a powerful orator for industry, frugality, and honesty, which multiplied riches and reciprocal esteem and usefulness among men, and would make them all loving and happy as brothers?

In short, all those labours which doctor Franklin took under the sun—labours so various and unending, for public and private good, such as his fire-engines; his lightning rods; his public libraries; his free schools; his hospitals; his legacies for encouragement of learning, and helping hundreds of indigent young mechanics with money to carry on their trades after his death—whence originated all this, but from that love which is stronger than death, subduing all obstacles, and overleaping the narrow limits of this mortal life?

What but the ingenuity of love, eager to swell the *widow's* mite of charity into the *rich* man's talent could have suggested the following curious method of making a little do a great deal of good?

"Received of Benjamin Franklin, ten guineas, which I hereby promise, soon as I get out of my present embarrassments, to lend to some other honest and industrious man, as near as I can guess, he giving his obligation to act in the same way by the next needy honest man; so that by thus going around it may in time, though a small sum, do much good, unless stopped by a thief.

"JAMES HOPEWELL.

"*Passy, Aug. 10, 1773.*"

What but the noble spirit of that religion whose sole aim is to "*overcome evil with good*" could have dictated the following instructions to Paul Jones, and his squadron, who after scouring the British channel, was about to make a descent on their coasts.

"As many of your officers and people have lately escaped from English prisons, you are to be *particularly attentive* to their conduct towards the prisoners you take, lest resentment of the *more than barbarous* usage which they have received from the English, should occasion a retaliation, and an imitation of what ought rather to be *detested and avoided for the sake of humanity and the honour of our country*.

"B. FRANKLIN.

"*To Commodore P. Jones.*

"April 28, 1779."

What but the spirit of that benevolent religion which is the firm patroness of all discoveries for human benefit, could have dictated the ensuing letter "to the commanders of American ships of war," in favour of captain Cook.

"GENTLEMEN,

"A ship having been fitted out from England, before the commencement of this war, to make discoveries of new countries in unknown seas, under the conduct of that celebrated navigator, captain Cook—an undertaking truly laudable in itself, as the increase of geographical knowledge facilitates the communication between distant nations, and the exchange of useful products and manufactures, and the extension of arts, whereby the common enjoyments of human life are multiplied and augmented, and science of other kinds increased, to the benefit of mankind in general.

"This is, therefore, most earnestly to recommend to every one of you, that in case the said ship, which is now expected to be soon in the European seas, on her return, should happen to fall into your hands, you would not consider her as an enemy, but that you treat the said captain Cook and his people with all civility and kindness, affording them, as common friends to mankind, all the assistance in your power, which they may happen to stand in need of.

"I have the honour to be, &c.

"B. FRANKLIN,

"Minister plenipotentiary from the United States to the court of France.

"*Passy. near Paris, March 10, 1779.*"

The truly christian spirit of doctor Franklin, which dictated this passport for captain Cook, was so highly approved by the British government, that, when Cook's voyages in three splendid quarto volumes were printed, the lords of the admiralty sent doctor Franklin a copy accompanied with the elegant plates, and also a *gold medal* of that illustrious navigator, with a polite letter from lord Howe, informing him that this compliment was made to doctor Franklin with the *king's express approbation.*

What but the religion that brings life and immortality to light "could have sprung those high hopes and rich consolations," which shine in the following letter from doctor Franklin to his niece, on the death of her father, his favourite brother John Franklin.

"DEAR NIECE,

"I condole with you. We have lost a most dear and valuable relation. But it is the will of God that these mortal bodies be laid aside, when the soul is to enter into real life. This is rather an embryo state—a preparation for living. A man is not completely born until he be dead. Why then should we grieve that a new child is born among the immortals—a new member added to their society? We are spirits. That bodies should be lent us, while they can afford us pleasure, assist us in acquiring knowledge, or doing good to our fellow creatures, is a kind and benevolent act of God. When they become unfit for these purposes, and afford us pain instead of pleasure, and answer none of the intentions for which they were given, it is equally kind and benevolent that a way is provided by which we may get rid of them. Death is that way. We ourselves in some cases, prudently choose a partial death. A mangled painful limb, which cannot be restored, we willingly cut off. He who plucks out a tooth parts with it freely, since the pain goes with it; and he who quits the whole body, parts at once with all pains, and possibilities of pains, it was capable of making him suffer.

"Our friend and we were invited abroad on a grand party of pleasure, which is to last for ever. His chair was ready first, and he is gone before us. We could not all conveniently start together; and why should you and I be grieved at this, since we are soon to follow, and know where to find him?

"B. FRANKLIN."

What but that religion which teaches "the price of truth," could have made him so penitent for having said any thing, in his youthful days against revelation? And while the popular infidels of Europe, the Voltaires, and Humes, and Bolingbrokes were so fond of filling the world with their books against Christ, that they might, as one of them said, "*crush the wretch*," what but a hearty esteem of him could have led Franklin to write the following pious reproof of a gentleman, who having written a pamphlet against christianity, sent it to him, requesting his opinion of it.

DR. FRANKLIN'S ANSWER.

"SIR,

"I have read your manuscript with some attention. By the argument it contains against a particular *providence*, though you allow a general *providence*, you strike at the foundation of all religion. For, without the belief of a *providence*, that takes cognizance of, guards, and guides, and may favour particular persons, there is no motive to worship a DEITY, to fear his displeasure, or to pray for his protection. I will not enter into any discussion of your principles, though you seem to desire it. At present I shall only give you my opinion, that though your reasonings are subtile, and may prevail with some readers, you will not succeed so as to change the general sentiments of mankind on that subject; and the consequence of printing this piece will be, a great deal of odium drawn upon yourself, mischief to you, and no benefit to others. He that spits against the wind, spits in his own face. But were you to succeed, do you imagine any good would be done by it? You yourself may find it easy to live a virtuous life, without the assistance afforded by religion; you having a clear perception of the disadvantages of vice, and possessing a strength of resolution sufficient to enable you to resist common temptations. But think how great a portion of mankind consists of weak and ignorant men and women, and of inexperienced inconsiderate youth of both sexes, who have need of the motives of religion to restrain them from vice, to support their virtue, and retain them in the practice of it till it becomes habitual, which is the great points of its security. And, perhaps, you are indebted to her original, that is, to your religious education, for the habits of virtue upon which you now justly value yourself. You might easily display your excellent talents of reasoning upon less hazardous objects, and thereby obtain a rank with our most distinguished authors. For among us it is not necessary, as among the Hottentots, that a youth, to be raised into the company of men, should prove his manhood by beating his mother. I would advise you, therefore, not to attempt *unchaining the tiger*, but to burn this piece before it is seen by any other person—whereby you will save yourself a great deal of mortification from the enemies it may raise against you, and, perhaps a good deal of regret and repentance. If men are so wicked *with* religion, what would they be *without* it? I intend this letter itself as a proof of my friendship, and therefore add no professions to it, but subscribe myself simply yours.

"B. FRANKLIN."

For the following, I owe many thanks to the honourable Mr. Rufus King.

After having answered my question on that subject, as before stated, viz. that he considered Dr. Franklin "*very much a christian in practice*," he added with a fine smile, as if happy that he possessed an anecdote so honourable to the religious character of his illustrious friend, and the friend of mankind—"*now, sir, I'll tell you an anecdote of Dr. Franklin.*" The

CONVENTION of '88, of which Dr. Franklin and myself were members, had been engaged several weeks in framing the present CONSTITUTION, and had done nothing. Dr. Franklin came in one morning, and rising in his place, called the attention of the house.—"We have been here, Mr. Speaker," said he, (George Washington was in the chair,) "a long time, trying to act on this important subject, and have done nothing; and in place of a speedy and successful close of our business, we see nothing but dark clouds of difficulty and embarrassment gathering before us. It in high time for us, Mr. Speaker, to call in the direction of a wisdom above our own.—(The countenance of Washington caught a brightness at these words, as he leaned forward in deepest gaze on Dr. Franklin.) Yes, sir, it is high time for us to call in the direction of a wisdom above our own. Our fathers before us, the wise and good men of ancient times, acted in this way. Aware of the difficulties and perils that attend all human enterprize, they never engaged in any thing of importance without having implored the guidance and blessing of heaven. The scriptures are full of encouragements to such practice. They every where assert a *particular providence* over all his works. They assure us that the very hairs of our head are all numbered; and that not even a sparrow but is continually under the eye of his parental care. This, Mr. Speaker, is the language of the gospel, which I *most implicitly believe*; and which promises the guidance of divine wisdom to *all who ask it.* We have not asked it; and that may be the reason why we have been so long in the dark. I therefore move, Mr. Speaker, that it be made a rule to open the business of this house, every morning, *with prayer.*"

The following also will show Dr. Franklin's firm belief in that very precious article of the religion of Christ—A PARTICULAR PROVIDENCE.

To WILLIAM STRAHAN, Esq. London

France, August 19th, 1784.

DEAR OLD FRIEND,

You "fairly acknowledge that the date war terminated quite contrary to your expectation." Your expectation was ill founded; for you would not believe your old friend, who told you repeatedly, that, by those measures, England would lose her colonies, as Epictetus warned in vain his master, that he would break his leg. You believed rather the tales you heard of our poltroonery, and impotence of body and mind. Don't you remember the story you told me of the Scotch sergeant, who met with a party of forty American soldiers, and, though alone, disarmed them all, and brought them in prisoners! A story almost as improbable as that of the Irishman, who pretended to have alone taken and brought in five of the enemy, by *surrounding* them. And yet, my friend, sensible and judicious as you are, but partaking of the general infatuation, you seem to believe it. The word *general* puts me in mind of a general, your general Clark, who had the folly to say, in my hearing, at sir John Pringle's, that with a thousand British grenadiers, he would undertake to go from one end of America to the other, and geld all the males. It is plain, he took us for a species of animals very little superior to brutes. The parliament, too, believed the stories of another foolish general, I forget his name, that the Yankees never *felt bold.* Yankee was understood to be a sort of Yahoo, and the parliament did not think the petitions of such creatures were fit to be received and read in so wise an assembly. What was the consequence of this monstrous pride and insolence! You first sent small armies to subdue us, believing them more than sufficient, but soon found yourselves obliged to send greater; these, whenever they ventured out of sight of their ships, were either obliged to scamper, or were beaten and taken prisoners. An American planter, who had never seen Europe, was chosen by us to command our troops, and continued during the whole war. This man sent home to you, one after another, five of your best generals, baffled, their heads bare of laurels, disgraced even in the opinion of their employers. Your contempt of our understandings, in comparison with your own, appeared to be not much better founded than that of our courage, if we may judge by this circumstance, that in whatever court of Europe a Yankee negotiator appeared, the wise British minister was routed,—put in a passion,—picked a quarrel with your friends,—and was sent home with a flea in his ear. But after all, my dear friend, do not imagine that I am vain enough to ascribe our success to any superiority in any of those points. I am too well acquainted with all the springs and levers of our machine, not to see that our human means were unequal to our undertaking, and that, if it had not been for the justice of our cause, and the consequent interposition of Providence, in which we had faith, we must have been ruined. If I had ever before been an Atheist, I should now have been convinced of the being and government of a Deity! It is HE who "abases the proud, and exalts the humble." May we never forget his goodness to us, and may our future conduct manifest our gratitude!

B. FRANKLIN.

Now, can any honest man, after this, entertain a doubt that Dr. Franklin was indeed, "*in practice very much a christian.*"

I am aware that some, good men have been offended, and I may add, grieved too, that Dr. Franklin should ever have spoken slightingly of *faith*,

&c. But these gentlemen may rest assured, that Dr. Franklin did this only to keep people from laying such stress on *faith*, &c. as to neglect what is infinitely more important, even LOVE and GOOD WORKS. And in this grand view, do not the holy apostles, and even Christ himself treat these things in the same way? Every where speaking of "*faith* and *baptism* and *long prayers*," when attempted to be put in place of love and good works, as mere "*beggarly elements*," and even "*damning hypocrisies*." However, let honest men read the following letter on the subject, by Dr. Franklin himself. While it serves to remove their doubts and prejudices, it may go to prove that if he had errors in religion, they were not the errors of the heart, nor likely to do any harm in the world; but contrariwise, to make us all much better christians, and happier men, than we are.

The letter is in answer to one from an illustrious foreigner; who, on a trip to Philadelphia, made Dr. Franklin a visit. The doctor, for some malady, advised him to try electricity; and actually gave him several shocks. He had not long been gone, before he wrote Dr. Franklin a most flattering account of the effects of his electricity—begged him to be assured he should never forget such KINDNESS—and concluded with praying that they might both have grace to live a life of FAITH, that if they were never to meet again in this world, they might at last meet in heaven.

DR. FRANKLIN'S ANSWER.

Philadelphia, June 6, 1753.

SIR,

I received your kind letter of the 2d instant, and am glad that you increase in strength; I hope you will continue mending till you recover your former health.

As to the *kindness* you mention, the only thanks I desire is, that you would always be equally ready to serve any other person that may need your assistance, and so let good offices go round, *for* MANKIND ARE *all of a family*.

For my own part, when I am employed in serving others, I do not look upon myself as conferring favours, but as paying debts. In my travels, and since my settlement, I have received much kindness from men, to whom I shall never have any opportunity of making the least direct return—and numberless mercies from God, who is infinitely above being benefitted by our services. The kindness from men, I can, therefore, only return on their fellow men, and I can only show my gratitude for those mercies from God, by a readiness to help his other children, and my brethren. For I do not think that thanks and compliments, though repeated weekly, can discharge our real obligations to each other, and much less those to our Creator. You will see in this, my notion of good works; that I am far from expecting, as you suppose, to *merit heaven* by them. By heaven, we understand a state of happiness; infinite in degree, and eternal in duration. I can do nothing to deserve such REWARDS. He that, for giving a draught of water to a thirsty person, should expect to be paid with a good plantation, would be modest in his demands, compared with those who think they *deserve* heaven for the little good they do on earth. Even the mixed imperfect pleasures we enjoy in this world, are rather from God's goodness, than our merit; how much more such happiness as heaven. For my part, I have not the vanity to think I deserve it, the folly to expect it, nor the ambition to desire it; but content myself in submitting to the will and disposal of that God who made me—who has hitherto preserved and blessed me—and in whose FATHERLY GOODNESS I may well confide, that he will never make me miserable—and that even the afflictions I may at any time suffer shall tend to my benefit.

The faith you mention has, doubtless, its use in the world. I do not desire to see it diminished. But I wish it were more productive of *good works* than I have generally seen it, I mean real good works; works of kindness, charity, mercy, and public spirit; not holiday keeping, sermon reading or hearing, performing church ceremonies, or making long prayers, filled with flatteries and compliments, despised even by wise men, and much less capable of pleasing the Deity. The worship of God is a *duty*; the hearing and reading of sermons *may* be useful; but if men rest in *hearing* and *praying*, as *too many do*, it is as if a tree should value itself on being watered and putting forth leaves, though it never produced any fruit. Your great master thought much less of these outward appearances and professions than many of his modern disciples. He preferred the *doers* of the word to the mere *hearers*; the son that *seemingly* refused to obey his father, and yet *performed* his commands, to him that *professed* his readiness, but *neglected* the work; the heretical but charitable Samaritan, to the uncharitable though orthodox priest and sanctified Levite: and those who gave food to the hungry, drink to the thirsty, raiment to the naked, entertainment to the stranger, and relief to the sick, though they never heard of his name, he declares they shall in the last day be accepted, when those who cry Lord, Lord, who value themselves on their faith, though great enough to perform miracles, but have neglected good works, shall be rejected. He professed he came "*not to call the righteous, but sinners to repentance*," which implied his modest opinion, that there were some in his time so *good*, that they needed not to hear even *him* for improvement; but now-a-days, we have scarce a little parson that does not think it the duty of every man within his reach, to think *exactly* as he does, and that all dissenters offend God. I wish to such more humility, and to you health and happiness, being

Your friend and servant,

B. FRANKLIN.

What but the spirit of immortal love, which, not content with doing much good in life, fondly looks beyond, and feasts on the happiness that others are to derive from us long after we have ceased to live on earth; what, I ask, but that love, could have dictated

DR. FRANKLIN'S WILL.

"When thou makest a feast, call not thy rich neighbours: lest they also bid thee again, and a recompense be made thee.

"But when thou makest a feast, call the poor; and thou shalt be blessed. For they cannot recompense thee, for thou shall be recompensed at the resurrection of the just.

"LUKE, xiv."

Sentiments divinely sublime!—Who, without emotions indescribable, can read them! And yet if they were lost from the Bible, they might be found again in the *Will* of Benjamin Franklin.

While many others "*rise early, and late take rest, and eat the bread of labour and care,*" that they may "*die rich*"—leaving their massy treasures, some scanty legacies excepted, to corrupt a few proud relatives, doctor Franklin acted as though the above text, the *true sublime of wisdom and benevolence*, was before him.

After having *bequeathed* his books, a most voluminous and valuable collection, partly to his family, and partly to the Boston and Philadelphia philosophical societies; and, after having divided a handsome competence among his children, and grand children, he goes on as follows:

"I. Having owed my first instructions in literature to the free grammar schools in Boston, I give one hundred pounds sterling to the free schools in that town, to be laid out in silver medals as honorary rewards for the encouragement of scholarship in those schools.

"II. All the debts to my post-office establishment, which I held many years, I leave to the Philadelphia hospital.

"III. Having always been of opinion, that in democratical governments, there ought to be no offices of *great* profit, I have long determined to give a part of my public salary to public uses; and being chiefly indebted to Massachusetts, my *native* state, and Pennsylvania, my *adopted* state, for lucrative employments, I feel it my duty to remember them; and having from long observation, and my own early experience, discovered that the best objects for assistance are indigent young persons, and the best modes of assistance, a plain education, a good trade, and a little money to set them up; and having been set up in business, while a poor boy, in Philadelphia, by kind loans of money from two friends there, which was the foundation of my fortune and all the usefulness that the world ascribed to me, I feel a wish to be useful, after my death, to others, in the loans of money; I therefore devote, from the savings of my salaries, the following sums, to the following persons and uses:

"1. To the inhabitants of Boston and Philadelphia, one thousand pounds sterling to each city, to be let out by the oldest divines of different churches, on a *five per cent. interest* and good *security*, to indigent young tradesmen, not *bachelors*, (as they have not deserved much from their country and the feebler sex,) but married men."

"2. No borrower to have more than sixty pounds sterling, nor less than fifteen."

"3. And in order to serve as many as possible in their turn, as well as to make the payment of the principal borrowed more easy, each borrower shall be obliged to pay, with the yearly interest, one tenth part of the principal; which sums of principal and interest, so paid, shall be again lent out to fresh borrowers.

"B. FRANKLIN."

In a late Boston paper, the friends of humanity have read with much pleasure that doctor Franklin's legacy to the indigent young married tradesmen of that town, of $4444 44 cents, is now increased to $10,902 28 cents, after having been the means of setting up 206 poor young men, besides 75 others, who are now in the use of the capital.

CHAPTER XLV.

The Death of Doctor Franklin.

One cannot read the biography of this great man without being put in mind of those sweet though simple strains of the bard of Zion.

"Happy the man, whose tender care
Relieves the poor distrest;
When he's with troubles compass'd round,
The Lord shall give him rest."

"If, he in languishing estate,
Oppress'd with sickness, lie,
The Lord shall easy make his bed,
And inward strength supply."

The latter end of doctor Franklin affords glorious proof that nothing so softens the bed of sickness, and brightens the gloom of the grave, as a life spent in works of love to mankind.

See George Washington, who by an active and disinterested benevolence, was called "THE FATHER OF HIS COUNTRY." See Martha Washington, who by domestic virtues, and extensive charities, obtained to herself the high character of "THE MOTHER TO THE POOR."—Both of these found the last bed spread as it were with roses; and the last enemy converted into a friend. Such is the lot of all who love; "not in *word, but in deed and in truth.*"

The friends of doctor Franklin never entered his chamber without being struck with this precious text, *"Mark the perfect man, and behold the upright, for the end of that man is peace."* Though laid on the bed whence he is to rise no more, he shows no sign of dejection or defeat. On the contrary, he appears like an aged warrior reposing himself after glorious victory; while his looks beaming with benevolence, express an air pure and serene as the Heaven to which he is going. Death, which most sick people are so unwilling to mention, was to him a favourite topic, and the sublime conversations of Socrates on that great subject, were heard a second time, from the lips of our American Franklin, pregnant with "*immortality and eternal life.*" No wonder then that with such views doctor Franklin should have been so cheerful on his dying bed; so self-possessed and calm, even under the tortures of the gravel, which was wearing him down to the grave. "*Don't go away,*" said he to the Rev. Dr. Colline, of the Swedes' church, Philadelphia, who, as a friend, was much with him in his last illness, and at sight of his agonies and cold sweats under the fits of the gravel, would take up his hat to retire—"*O no! don't go away,*" he would say, "*don't go away.* These pains will soon be over. They are for my good. And besides, what are the pains of a moment in comparison of the pleasures of eternity."

Blest with an excellent constitution, well nursed by nature's three great physicians, *temperance*, *exercise*, and *cheerfulness*, he was hardly ever sick until after his seventy-sixth year. The gout and gravel then attacked him with great severity. He bore their excruciating tortures as became one who habitually felt that he was as he said, in the hands of an infinitely wise and benevolent being, who did all things right.

His physician, the celebrated Dr. Jones, published the following account of his last illness.

"The stone, had for the last twelve months confined him chiefly to his bed; and during the extreme painful paroxysms, he was obliged to take large doses of laudanum to mitigate his tortures—still in the intervals of pain, he not only amused himself with reading and conversing with his family, and his friends who visited him, but was often employed in doing business of a public as well as private nature, with various persons who waited on him for that purpose, and in every instance displayed, not only that readiness of doing good, which was the distinguishing characteristic of his life, but the fullest possession of his uncommon mental abilities; and not unfrequently indulged himself in those flashes of wit and entertaining anecdotes, which were the delight of all who heard him.

"About sixteen days before his death, he was seized with a pain in his left breast, which increased till it became extremely acute, attended with a cough and laborious breathing. During this state, when the severity of his pains some times drew forth a groan, he would observe, that, *he was afraid he did not bear them as he ought—acknowledged his grateful sense of the many blessings he had received from the Supreme Being, who had raised him from small and low beginnings to such high rank and consideration among men—and made no doubt but his present afflictions were kindly intended to wean him from a world, in which he was no longer fit to act the part assigned him.* In this frame of body and mind he continued till five days before his death, when an imposthumation in his lungs, suddenly burst, and discharged a great quantity of matter, which he continued to throw up while he had strength, but, as that failed, the organs of respiration became gradually oppressed—a calm lethargic state succeeded—and, on the 7th of April, 1790, about eleven o'clock at night he quietly expired, closing a long and useful life of *eighty-four years and three months*."

Come holy calm of the soul! Expressive silence come! and meditating the mighty talents of the dead, and their constant application to the *glory of the giver*, let us ascend with him on the wings of that blessed promise, "*Blessed are the dead who die in the Lord! even so saith the Spirit, for they rest from their labours and their works do follow them.*"

That Franklin is now enjoying that rest which "*remaineth for the people of God*"—and that while many a blood-stained monster who made great noise in the world, is *followed* by the cries of thousands of widows and orphans, Franklin dying in the Lord, and followed by the blessings of thousands, fed, clothed, educated, and enriched by his charities, is in GLORY, may be fairly inferred from the following most valuable anecdote of him.

Naturalists tell us, that so great is the paternal care of God, that every climate affords the food and physic best suited to the necessaries of its population. What gratitude is due to that goodness, which foreseeing the dangers impending over this country from British injustice, sent us two such protectors as Franklin and Washington? The first, (the forerunner of the second,) like the lightning of Heaven, to expose the approaching tempest; and the second, like the rock of the ocean, to meet that tempest in all its fury, and dash it back on its proud assailants? And how astonishing too, and almost unexampled that goodness, which with talents of wisdom and fortitude to establish our republic, combined the cardinal virtues of *justice*, *industry*, and *economy* that alone can render our republic immortal?

Hoping that our *youth* may be persuaded to love and imitate the virtues of the men whose great names they have been accustomed, from the cradle, to lisp with veneration, I have long coveted to set these virtues before them. The grey haired men of other days, have given me their aid. The following I obtained from the Rev. Dr. Helmuth, of the German church, Philadelphia. Hearing that this learned and pious divine possessed a valuable anecdote of doctor Franklin, I immediately waited on him. "Yes, sir," said he, "I have indeed a valuable anecdote of doctor Franklin, which I would tell you with great pleasure; but as I do not speak English very well, I wish you would call on David Ritter, at the sign of the *Golden Lamb*, in Front street; he will tell it to you better. I hastened to Mr Ritter, and told him my errand. He seemed mightily pleased at it, and said, "Yes, I will tell you all I know of it. You must understand then, sir, first of all, that I always had a prodigious opinion of doctor Franklin, as the *usefulest* man we ever had among us, by a long way; and so hearing that he was sick, I thought I would go and see him. As I rapped at the door, who should come and open it but old Sarah Humphries. I was right glad to see her, for I had known her a long time. She was of the people called FRIENDS; and a mighty good sort of body she was too. The great people set a heap of store by her, for she was famous throughout the town for nursing and tending on the sick. Indeed, many of them, I believe, hardly thought they could sicken, and die right if they had not old Sarah Humphries with them. Soon as she saw me, she said, 'Well David, how dost?'"

"'O, much after the old sort, Sarah,' said I; 'but that's neither here nor there; I am come to see doctor Franklin.'

"'Well then,' said she, 'thou art too late, for he is *just dead*!'

"'Alack a day,' said I, 'then a great man is gone.'

"'Yes, indeed,' said she, 'and a *good* one too; for it seemed as though he never thought the day went away as it ought, if he had not done somebody a service. However, David,' said she, 'he is not the worse off for all that now, where he is gone to: but come, as thee came to see Benjamin Franklin, thee shall see him yet.' And so she took me into his room. As we entered, she pointed to him, where he lay on his bed, and said, '*there*, did thee ever see any thing look so natural?'

"And he did look natural indeed. His eyes were close—but that you saw he did not breathe, you would have thought he was in a sweet sleep, he looked so calm and happy. Observing that his face was fixed right towards the chimney, I cast my eyes that way, and behold! just above the mantle-piece was a noble picture! O it was a *noble picture*, sure enough! It was the picture of our Saviour on the cross.

"I could not help calling out, 'Bless us all, Sarah!' said I, 'what's all this?'

"'What dost mean, David,' said she, quite crusty.

"'Why, how came this picture here, Sarah?' said I, 'you know that many people think he was not after this sort.'

"'Yes,' said she, 'I know that too. But thee knows that many who makes a great fuss about religion have very little, while some who say but little about it have a good deal.'

"'That's sometimes the case, I fear, Sarah,' said I.

"'Well, and that was the case,' said she, 'with Benjamin Franklin. But be that as it may, David, since thee asks me about this great picture, I'll tell thee how it came here. Many weeks ago, as he lay, he beckoned me to him, and told me of this picture up stairs, and begged I would bring it to him. I brought it to him. His face brightened up as he looked at it; and he said, '*Aye, Sarah*,' said he, '*there's a picture worth looking at! that's the picture of him who came into the world to teach men to love one another!*' Then after looking wistfully at it for some time, he said, '*Sarah*,' said he, '*set this picture up over the mantlepiece, right before me as I lie; for I like to look at it*,' and when I had fixed it up, he looked at it, and looked at it very much; and indeed, as thee sees, he died with his eyes fixed on it.'"

Happy Franklin! Thus doubly blest! Blest in life, by a diligent co-working with "THE GREAT SHEPHERD," in his precepts of perfect love.—Blest in death, with his closing eyes piously fixed upon him, and meekly bowing to the last summons in joyful hope that through the force of his divine precepts, the "wintry storms" of hate will one day pass away, and one "eternal spring of love and peace encircle all."

Now Franklin in his lifetime had written for himself an *epitaph*, to be put upon his grave, that honest posterity might see that he was no *unbeliever*, as certain enemies had slandered him, but that he *firmly believed "that his Redeemer liveth; and that in the latter day he shall stand upon the earth; and that though worms destroyed his body, yet in his flesh he should see God."*

Footnotes

[1] You never find presbyterians without books.

[2] The gift of William Bingham, Esq.

[3] In India, where out of 140 poor British prisoners shut up in a close small room 120 of them perished in one night.

[4] What physicians call the perspirable matter, is that vapour which passes off from our bodies, from the lungs, and through the pores of the skin. The quantity of this is said to be five-eighths of what we eat.

CPSIA information can be obtained
at www.ICGtesting.com
Printed in the USA
LVHW040957020323
740706LV00007B/740

9 789356 904668